After reading what I have written here so many times (half in disbelief and the other half to stay factual), I realize that the journey is not over, and may be just beginning.

To my parents, who epitomized selflessness and sacrificed so much for all of us. Your gift of emotional strength saved my life.

To my children, family, and friends. Your love, support, and belief in me enabled me to continue to move forward at times when I did not think it was possible.

To the good people of this world who truly live their lives based on the principles of trust, honesty, and compassion. Continue to open your hearts for others in their time of need.

To those who lack the courage and character to practice what they preach. May you one day find it.

Ballast Books, LLC
Washington, DC
www.ballastbooks.com

ISBN 978-1-64307-383-5

Library of Congress Control Number has been applied for

Printed in Canada

Published by Ballast Books
www.ballastbooks.com

For more information, bulk orders, appearances or speaking requests, please
email info@ballastbooks.com

# THE THIRD GIFT

## My Dance With the
## Devil (and Her Mother)

J.D. McCabe with Kenny Intheam

# PROLOGUE

"Wake up! WAKE UP!" the chiseled sheriff's deputy bellowed as he stood by the side of my hospital bed. I faded in and out of sleep as he repeatedly poked me in the chest and tugged on my risk-of-flight gown. In the dimly lit room, as my assigned babysitter looked on, he recited some court orders. I was too mentally, physically, and emotionally exhausted to care or comprehend what he was saying. The only thing I vividly recall from September 16, 2014, at 3:30 a.m. were his words, "You have been involuntarily committed."

# CHAPTER 1
## *Grab a Seat*

Family is not an important thing. It's everything. —*Michael J. Fox*

The weight loss that I initially attributed to my new workout routine hadn't ended. In less than three months, I had lost thirty pounds. Trust me; I wasn't working out that hard (one hour three times a week). I was alarmed, so I started the investigational process to determine what in the world was going on. Then came the dizzy spells, neck stiffness, and pain in both my shoulders. The pain came on *so* quickly. I felt relentlessly pushed to understand what was triggering these physical problems.

But I was more troubled by my wife Erin's constant insinuations—blaming our deteriorating relationship on me. They were blurring my reality, making rational thought more and more challenging. I was starved for clarity every waking moment. Hell, Erin had done an excellent job convincing me that *something* was wrong. Should I get checked?

Erin demanded I schedule an appointment to see a psychiatrist who practiced in the same large group as her psychiatrist. As fate would have it, the first available appointment was three months out. Even though I grabbed the date, the office practically told me I would be better off looking elsewhere. In reality, I was not chomping at the bit to get in there. I only hoped that I was showing Erin a willingness to do my part to fix our relationship.

She continued questioning everything I did and even called the damn office to check and see if I indeed had made an appointment. Wouldn't you know it; they told her I had not. I am still not sure if this was just their way of trying to keep things confidential, but so much for health care privacy laws, right? Knowing damn well that I made the appointment, I was livid.

No surprise—so was Erin.

I'd become sadly familiar with this version of Erin. She verbally stuck fork after fork in me. "You are a liar! You can never be trusted! You did not make an appointment!"

All I could do was sit there, dumbfounded, knowing I'd done what she'd asked, trying to *help* our relationship. I called the office and not-so-nicely let them know the mess they were causing me in my already troubled marriage. They did indeed have an appointment for me but spelled my last name with the wrong first letter.

Now, this sort of thing had happened to me before, but it never caused problems like this. To appease Erin, though, I canceled that appointment and obtained a referral from our family practitioner for another psychiatrist. September 9, two days before our twenty-first wedding anniversary, would be my initial meeting. Believe me, I never imagined myself doing this, ever. But by the grace of God, I was ready and felt it could be an excellent thing if I embraced it.

Depression or any mental illness was nonexistent in my personal health history, and there was no family history from either parent. In spite of all that, I was losing my sense of self, and the grown-up in me knew that *something* needed to change. Gone was my knowledge of who I was as a husband, and, if that weren't enough, I was questioning my abilities as a father. I allowed myself to be judged and defined by my wife and my mother-in-law, Doris.

Erin was with me for this initial appointment, and she pledged to be there to help me get through whatever was going on. I can't imagine the thrill she must have been experiencing, as things were unfolding the way she imagined. In a matter of one thirty-minute visit, after both Erin and I completed a bipolar II questionnaire, I was diagnosed with bipolar II! For my entire life, more than four decades, I had enjoyed the love of my immediate and extended families, a modestly successful career, and darn good health. All this changed in a blink of an eye. Erin hid her pleasure with the diagnosis with a show of support. At the time, I was thinking of the bigger picture and still believed, for the most part, that *I* had done *something* wrong and needed to do all I could to save my marriage and protect our family.

September 11, our twenty-first wedding anniversary, came and went without any acknowledgement from either of us. The eleventh was a Thursday, and the coming weekend promised fantastic weather. Despite the warmth outside and the clear Wilmington, North Carolina, skies, I was feeling anything but warm on the inside, and Lord knows, not a single thing was clear.

Except for random petty, useless arguments, we pretty much did our own thing leading into the weekend. As usual, I got real busy doing yard work, washing windows, scrubbing floors, and just keeping myself occupied. The music on my iPod was becoming my new best friend. I found empathetic peace in music and its expression of others' pain and triumph. Songs that I'd listened to my entire life were beginning to take on new meanings. I found solace knowing my new friend could reignite my inner pilot light even if only for a few minutes. Early Saturday afternoon, I encouraged Erin to go to dinner with the mom of one of our daughter's friends. I was exhausted by the constant tension and figured it would be good for *both* of us to have some alone time. It was so damn nice outside, I wanted to relax with a couple of beers in peace.

Erin left for dinner at about 5 p.m. and came bouncing back through the door around 9 p.m. In that time, I drank three or four beers. The second she walked in, she was like a damned K9 unit, sniffing for a beer on my breath, and oh, was it ever game on.

After my diagnosis four days earlier, my psychiatrist had advised me not to drink because it could make my condition worse. Erin seized on this like a king-sized crocodile snatching a baby calf enjoying a cool creek-side sip. I didn't stand a chance. I hadn't helped my cause, but damn it, *how much could one man take?* I *was* trying. I did want it to get better, but I also knew damn well I didn't just up and become bipolar over the last year without a little bit of abuse from somewhere, if that is even possible. Her inquisition further belittled and completely shredded whatever dignity I had left. "Our anniversary weekend too, Danny," I remember her saying.

She showered and yet again locked herself in the guest room. I decided to go for a walk around our neighborhood. I returned home, showered, and made the grave mistake of trying to engage Erin in conversation. I unlocked the guest room door, remained outside the room, and began to ask Erin for clarity on whatever stupid issue we argued about that day. She sat up in bed and could've burned a hole through me had she stared a second longer. I received no response other than a look of darkness on her vacant face.

As I locked the door from the inside and shut it, I muttered, "Perhaps I won't be here in the morning, and your problems will be solved."

Not ten seconds later, as I padded down the hallway in my underwear, I realized what I had done. I turned around and headed back to Erin's room, but instead of clarifying that I didn't mean how it sounded, I stood outside the door and said, "Perhaps the good Lord will take me tonight and your problems will be solved." I headed up to our son's bedroom, and since he was away at school, I lay down. I had no plans to sleep. I needed a moment to lie down and attempt to make sense of what was going on.

Twenty minutes later, I heard a big "thud" downstairs, followed by the sound of our garage door. I got up and trudged down the stairs, still only in my underwear, and headed toward the garage. I was emotionless. I opened the door that led to the garage but remained on the top step. Erin's car window was down halfway, and I simply asked, "Where are you going?" The response I received was Doris's shrill voice, yelling, "Get out of there! Get out of there!" Yep, Erin had her on speaker.

Erin raced out of the garage, and I dreaded what was coming next.

I immediately called my brother Al and his wife, Jane.

We had spoken for well over an hour when the doorbell rang. The Wilmington PD was on my front porch in a situation I had only seen before on TV. I told Al and Jane that I would call them back, not 100 percent sure if I would be able to. Were the police here to lock me up? I was honest with the officer and told him about my bipolar diagnosis just days earlier and the four beers I drank throughout the afternoon. I expressed my concern about Erin, her fibromyalgia and my belief that it might be causing her paranoia. I was very calm, and he walked off the porch. Just minutes later, but what felt like hours, I headed to the backyard as I called Al and Jane back. Looking over our privacy fence, I saw a police cruiser parked on the side of the street next to Erin's car. Erin had returned to the scene. As I described this to Al, he pleaded with me to stay in the house and not go anywhere near, to keep both my calm and my distance. He said it several times, but of course, I told them I would call them back, and I headed out front and walked to the corner of our street. As downright pissed as I was, I stood from a distance and angrily yelled, "Thanks, Erin! After twenty-one years of marriage, this is what I get?"

I could see the officer display a more defensive posture as I walked back toward the house. I called Al and Jane back almost immediately and told them what had happened. Al quietly asked me why I hadn't listened to him. Honestly, I had no answer.

Erin did not come home that night.

I barely slept, and in the morning, I felt like I *had to* make the three-and-a-half-hour drive to Charlotte to see our son, Billy. My daughter, Katie, already seemed lost to me, and I wanted our son to hear directly from me what was going on. Before leaving, I made sure to feed the dogs. I knew Erin would eventually ask me to do it anyway, and as expected, I received her text not long after. Nothing but a sterile, "Feed the dogs." Thankfully, Katie had spent the night with girlfriends. This was becoming commonplace, as she did not want to be around the house on weekends. None of us could blame her. Not wanting her to wonder where Dad was, I texted that I was helping a friend move.

Yes, I lied, but I did not want her or Erin to know where I was. I sensed I was one move away from Erin turning our son against me, and I couldn't risk the chance of our time together being interrupted.

When I arrived in Charlotte that morning, Billy and I took a long walk around his apartment complex. At this point, I didn't care what he had heard. I laid it all out for him: the good, the bad, and everything in between. We discussed Erin's allegations of infidelity and drug abuse. I assured him that I loved his mother and that none of this was real. I pleaded with him to believe in me.

I can't put into words the pain and agony I felt to have to have this conversation with one of our children.

It needed to happen.

Back from Charlotte that afternoon, I walked into the house to find Erin and Katie huddled up on the kitchen floor, almost as if Erin was there to protect Katie from big, bad Dad. Within moments, I learned that Katie now knew that her mom had called the cops on me the night before, and of course, Katie was very upset. I hurt, not for myself but for Katie. Seeing her parents go down like this was crushing her. I hurt, knowing she'd done nothing to cause this. The constant fighting, coupled with everything that her mother—somebody she is supposed to trust unconditionally—was telling her. Word quickly spread to Katie's friends and their parents. Erin was making sure to extend her groundwork to paint me as the monster way beyond our family boundaries. Erin was going for blood now, any way she could. Erin asked me if I had talked to Billy, and I lied and said no.

Barely a few minutes passed before I confessed that I'd gone to see him.

Erin exploded, muttering, "You are a pathological liar, and we need to separate," right in front of our daughter.

At that point, I agreed. My head was spinning.

I headed over to our local YMCA, hoping to blow off some steam. The entire workout, all I could think about was how wholly chaotic and disgusting this bullshit was. I had done nothing wrong! I hadn't cheated on Erin. I wasn't doing drugs. I *knew* all of these things.

I returned home, and the "girls" were bathing the dogs in our shower. Another blow to the ego, as it seemed that they were happy that Dad was finally going to get his shit together and move out.

My mind was racing so much that I had to call Al. He was emphatic that I needed to calm my ass down, saying, "Danny, in the last week, you have been diagnosed as bipolar and had the cops called on you. You need to be cool." Learning from my mistake just a few days before, I took his advice and kept my cool. My calm demeanor would be just another example for Erin of my "volatile" moods and my "erratic, all-over-the-place temperament."

That evening, I sat upstairs in my office, running through my entire life and marriage and broke down. I sobbed uncontrollably like a lost little boy, alone with nowhere to turn. I sat there thinking that *I* did this, that *I* was to blame.

Erin and I talked briefly that night, and I reaffirmed to her that I was willing to separate if there was a chance that we could at least reconcile. In typical Erin fashion, my question was met with silence.

Monday morning, September 15, I had my second psychiatric appointment. I looked like an absolute mess; she looked like an angel, probably thinking my bags would soon be packed. I told my psychiatrist about the cops' Saturday night visit and that Erin and I would be separating. I was open and honest with him about going to see Billy in Charlotte and the fact that I had four beers on Saturday night. I told him that I lied to Erin and Katie about going to Charlotte but that in a matter of a few minutes I had come clean with them. I told him *everything,* and it was as if, all of a sudden, I *did* need a psychiatrist. He reminded me again that he had strongly suggested that I not drink, given my condition, and he then wrote me an order to have a drug test. He wanted to rule out drugs as the cause of my mood issue. He ordered a look-back test, where they take the hair from several locations of your body and test the DNA for possible drug use in the last three months. I was not at all worried, as I knew I was completely clean, yet for some reason, I was still visibly shaken and anxious at the prospect of the test. My body had always manifested stress and anxiety in strange ways, and this was no different. I called Al at work, as I needed to talk about all that was going on. He said, "I feel you shaking through the phone."

Fifteen minutes after the drug test I was able to collect myself emotionally to lead a call for work lasting almost two hours. I still have no explanation for the timing other than God's goodwill to provide me with the distraction.

That afternoon, I also had a follow-up appointment with our family practitioner to address my continuing weight loss and blood-work issues. With all that had gone on in the last several days, I almost forgot about all of the other things that life was hurling at me. Erin was out running errands, but I called her anyway. Once again, through my tears, I asked her about the possibility of working this out. No answer other than her "gracious" agreement to go with me to my doctor's appointment that afternoon.

I sat on the edge of the exam table staring down at the floor, feeling hollowed out. The doctor arrived, but we did not end up addressing my weight or enzyme issues. Within a matter of minutes, Erin was volunteering her concerns about the events that had unfolded over the weekend: the cops, my drinking, my Saturday yard work, and our pending separation. The doctor asked how I felt about all this. As I lowered my eyes to the floor, I said, "If I lose my family, I am not sure what I will do."

I looked up, and with his back to me as he typed on his computer, he stated quite nonchalantly, "This sounds like bipolar, and if you don't go to Holy Hell I will have you involuntarily committed." Of course, Holy Hell was not the actual name of the psychiatric facility. But I would come to think of it that way.

He left the room and returned with a small, white piece of paper describing my intentions of possibly harming myself.

Erin and I exited the office and in the parking lot with her hands above her head and palms together in the form of thanks to God, she proclaimed, "Thank God we finally have the answer." As I sat in our parked car, I was thinking, "How in the hell did my life come to this?" Erin reached over to me. "It's okay, Danny. I will be here for you, and we will work through this together. We don't have to call it a mental illness or bipolar, we can call it a watermelon." (No joke, that's what she said . . . a watermelon.)

To Holy Hell we went.

Arriving after a 25-minute drive, I approached the front desk with my little white piece of paper. As I handed it to the staffer behind the glass, he looked at me and said soberly,

"It is about an eight- to ten-hour wait . . . Grab a seat."

I looked around to see a lobby jammed full of folks with whom I didn't belong. It was nothing personal. These people were genuine human beings with mental illnesses who needed help. In a way, I felt as if I being there was merely wasting a spot for somebody more deserving. I looked at Erin and said, "I am not staying here."

Knowing the doctor's orders, though, I was well aware that I had no choice but to do something. Given my line of work, I knew of the hospitals in the area that had inpatient psychiatric units, so we headed to another facility. On our way there, I called the family practitioner to inform him of our plans, as *I absolutely did not want the cops taking me.* We arrived at the hospital and entered through the Emergency Department. Once again, like an embarrassed grade-schooler handing his detention slip to the principal, I offered them my little piece of paper.

This time, I was immediately escorted to an exam room.

I was not by myself, but by God, I'd never felt more alone.

# CHAPTER 2
## *The First 17*

True love means that you care more about someone else's happiness than your own. No matter how much pain it may bring you. —*Author unknown*

I met Erin in the spring of 1991 while playing on a slow pitch softball team in Pittsburgh, Pennsylvania. It wasn't a competitive softball league. Back then, like many people our age, I was looking to get some exercise, have some fun, get together with the boys, and drink a few beers. Our bigger-than-life pitcher (seriously, the dude was huge!) would bring his suds out to the mound. Sporting a tank top, cigarette dangling, he certainly broadened the meaning of *pitcher*, stashing his beer supply just behind the rubber within easy reach between pitches. Now, I was a decent ballplayer, but on that particular April day in '91, it became about anything but me channeling my inner Nomar Garciaparra. Standing at shortstop, still buzzing from our pregame suds, I looked up into the stands, and there she was: the most gorgeous woman I had ever seen. Blonde hair, blue eyes, her lean, athletically toned body clad in green-and-navy-checked shorts. After the game, everyone gathered in the bar to have a few rounds.

Admittedly, I was never much for small talk with the ladies and was even less of a flirt, so the task of chatting up Erin was intimidating. Something was different with her, though. She was fiery—I liked that. I ended up getting her phone number that night. I also learned that she had been previously married for a short period. She wed at the age of twenty-two to a man ten years her senior who brought his eleven-year-old daughter to the union. It did cause me pause, and perhaps it was the reason that I did not initially call Erin.

Three months passed, and I had not given Erin another thought. As fate would have it, I ran into her in June at a tavern in Pittsburgh, Pennsylvania. She looked pretty as ever, maybe even more so, and of course, I tried the old "I've meant to call you" line. (Did I mention my lack of smoothness?) Her response reminded me of why I was so attracted to her in the first place. "I haven't been sitting by the phone waiting." BAM!

We hung out for a little while, had a few drinks, and talked. I began to learn more details about her first husband. She told me she had married Derek looking for a father figure. Allegedly, he was controlling, abusive, and very jealous. One of the first things she mentioned about him was his behavior at her bachelorette party. "He dragged me off the dance floor. The cops were called." I also learned that her now ex-husband had moved in with her father, Martin, in Florida for a little over a year. This seemed strange to me.

Of course, I asked Erin why her dad would do this to her and was told that he took in her ex-husband because he was attracted to him. Subsequently, I found out Martin was gay and then, naturally, this made more sense. Yes, you read that correctly. Her now admittedly gay father opened his home to *her* ex-husband, Derek, because he essentially was hoping something would come of it. Erin was healing from an abusive marriage and estranged from her father; I felt bad for her.

The evening ended abruptly when a man approached Erin and greeted her by her former married name. Erin, madder than hell, quickly made her way to the front door, swung it open, and headed for the parking lot. I followed her out to make sure she was all right.

We were intimate that night in my strawberry-red Mercury Topaz, my first company car. It turned out to be quite roomy.

By July, we'd started casually dating, and my first phone call to Erin was to her grandmother's house in Ohio. Erin was born in Ohio and moved to Pittsburgh, Pennsylvania, when she was six years old; her mom, Doris, had met a man who would later become Erin's stepdad. Her grandmother answered the phone, and I asked to speak with Erin. Her grandmother, also quite the fiery Polish woman, asked me, "And this is regarding?" All I wanted to do was talk to her granddaughter, to hear her voice. I said, "This is Danny, and Erin asked me to call her at this number." Erin was very close to her grandmother. I admired that, and this relationship was part of my attraction to Erin.

Before Erin, I had never been in love. I was young, until now focused on only my interests and, like many young men my age, finally starting to get a real taste of what the rest of my life might bring. Frankly, at the time I met Erin, I wasn't looking for anything serious. Isn't that how life often goes? Maybe that was a good thing, or perhaps I should have run away as fast and as far as my legs would take me.

I was twenty-six years old and beginning my professional career. I played sports, coached my younger brother's basketball team, worked full time, and traveled extensively for work. Erin was transitioning as well. She was "healing" from her abusive marriage and planned to start school full time in the fall of 1991. She was entering an intense two-year program in the healthcare field. Because of that, she needed to complete some prerequisites over the summer. By coincidence, one of those courses was algebra, and I was good at math. We would meet out at Keystone Lake for some tutoring; I quickly realized my reasons for doing so had little to do with variables or coefficients. The lake was so peaceful, and we loved going there as we started getting to know each other. It was where we shared our first meaningful kiss, knee deep in the water enhanced by a stunning sunset.

As previously mentioned, we were only casually dating; Erin was also seeing two other people. By the end of the summer of 1991, Erin decided that she wanted to date only me. I was ecstatic! I knew I was developing feelings for her unlike any I had felt before. Erin would later tell me that one of the other guys she was dating (while she was dating me) ended up in a psychiatric facility after she broke up with him. The first time I held her hand, I swear I felt a spark. It was a sensation you are supposed to feel. You know, that one they tell you about when you're a kid. That spark that ignites a fire in your heart. It was something I had never experienced before. Was it the beginning of love?

Or, was it evol, a backward kind of love?

Early on in our time together, I was not always the most courteous or respectful to Erin. I would show up late for dates, and at times I would treat her as if she was just one of the boys. On occasion, I would drink too much (have I mentioned my younger self partied hard with the boys?). One particular instance, I had been drinking heavily, and we got into an argument. Keep in mind, this was before cell phones, texts, Instagram, and all the other social media mess, so I had to go old school and call her house. The only problem? It was two in the morning, and I woke her parents. I called them the next day and apologized to her mom and stepdad, promising them it would never happen again.

It never happened again. I am not a perfect man by any means. However, just as my father taught me, I accepted accountability for my wrongdoing like a mature adult is supposed to do. I quickly realized that I needed to make some adjustments and that I needed to change some of my selfish ways. She was worth it, and I was beginning to fall in love with her. I have learned a lot throughout my journey; one lesson is that the goal of any relationship should be to make each other better. Successes, failures, mistakes, and experiences: they are all a part of the journey of togetherness. It was not just about me anymore. It was about us.

In the fall of 1991, Erin began her intense two-year program. She was dedicated to her studies, and I was six months into my new job in pharmaceutical sales. My first job out of college was merely that, a j-o-b. I was fortunate enough to find a career and not a "job" in the pharmaceutical industry. I've been grateful for the last twenty-seven years to wake up and enjoy going to work every morning. A majority of folks cannot say that, and I know how lucky I am.

As time moved forward, any question marks about my relationship with Erin were turning into exclamation marks. I was no longer asking myself, I was telling myself: I was definitely in love with Erin. She was excelling in school, and my new job was going very well. I was fortunate to have an excellent boss, Freddie C., who was an outstanding salesperson, and he showed me the ropes. Life was good. We had talked about marriage, and I was ready to commit. My sister-in-law Jane had worked in the jewelry business and maintained some contacts at a custom jeweler in Pittsburgh. Erin's father was not in her life at this time, so I decided to meet with her mother, Doris, at her place of employment to ask for her daughter's hand in marriage. I was nervous as all get out. Doris was delighted when I told her I wanted to marry Erin, and many years later, she would remind me that on that day she told me her daughter was "complex and complicated."

In spite of lacking a romantic flare, I came up with a decent plan for the proposal. I had planned to ask Erin during an evening ride on the incline on Pittsburgh's Mt. Washington. Instead, we were engaged on October 22, 1992, in the living room of my little house. Erin was at my house that evening neck deep in her studies. She was upset about a physics test a few days earlier. She was convinced that she had done poorly on the exam, so I decided that I would cheer her up by asking her to marry me. What a tradeoff that was, I might say. As she sat on our blue-and-white-striped couch, I popped the question.

She said yes, and we then journeyed to both of our parents' homes to share the good news.

Erin not only got an A on that exam, she graduated from the program with honors in May of 1993. She was a late bloomer as far as school conventionality was concerned but was bright and worked her tail off to complete the curriculum. I was so proud of her. Our hard work and subsequently our lives, together, were converging as seamlessly as nature's seasonal transitions.

September 1993, we were married at the beautiful Heinz Memorial Chapel in Pittsburgh, Pennsylvania. The wedding was very small, and I was more than okay with that. Erin had been married before, and I did not want a big wedding, so it only made sense to keep it intimate.

The reception followed and, like the wedding, we had no more than 80 to 90 people attending, just our families and close friends. Afterwards, we headed to Hawaii for our honeymoon. We were excited about spending ten days in Maui.

When we were out to dinner one evening, a server at the bar happened to be in my line of sight. Erin accused me of "checking out her ass." Well, she was in my line of sight, and I did look, but I certainly wasn't ogling her. This little incident would be thrown in my face over and over again twenty years later. As I think about the incident now, it reminds me of Will Ferrell in the movie *Old School*. He and his wife are in counseling for their marriage, his wife brings up the fact that he checked out the server's ass at the Olive Garden, and his response was, "She was wearing a thong."

I did not stare long enough to determine what kind of undergarment the server wore, but I've been doing my best to find some humor in all of this.

As the honeymoon ended, our life began!

Before entering into parenthood, we honed our skills with a chocolate lab puppy, Terris, the first of many dogs that we would welcome into our home. I always loved watching Erin with animals. She had a gift and was terrific with them, another one of her many attributes that enabled me to fall more deeply in love with her. Her compassion with animals was admirable. She loved all kinds of animals; from rescuing wounded birds to moving turtles off the road, it was one of those qualities about real love that you only feel and see in those few people you give your entire heart and world to. Your parents, your wife, and your children, that type of love.

On January 17, 1995, the first of my three gifts from Erin arrived. After seventeen long hours of labor, our son was born in Pittsburgh, Pennsylvania. We brought William home, put him in his little swing, and looked at each other wondering what we were supposed to do next. Every diaper noise we heard, he was changed. Thankfully, we quickly moved beyond that. Before the kids arrived, Erin only worked part-time. I was okay with that in the general sense of supporting whatever she felt in her heart to make her happy. She was great with our son and that, to me, meant more than anything did. Early on, William, whom we call Billy, was a difficult baby. He was often colicky and did not sleep much. I had many late nights driving him around the block trying to get him to relax and even used to put him in his carrier on top of a running dryer to get him to calm down. Much like his mom and dad changing his diaper at the slightest sound or smell, he thankfully outgrew that stage. He has turned into an incredible twenty-four-year-old young man. He is brilliant and compassionate, and I could not be prouder to call him my son. He inherited his mom's love of animals.

My sales career had been progressing very well, and in March of 1996, I accepted a promotion to a district sales manager role in Louisville, Kentucky. I did not make the decision unilaterally, but in my discussion with Erin, she was supportive of the move, and that meant a lot to me. Unlike Erin, I came from a large family. To be from two different types of family settings but to still have the cohesion we did felt so welcoming.

After we moved to Kentucky, she would later comment to me, "Had we stayed in Pittsburgh we would have ended up divorced."

We loved settling into Louisville, easily expanding our network of friends. We wanted more children but were having some difficulty in conceiving again, so we put that on hold. Erin decided that she wanted to go back to school and get her bachelor's degree. Billy was probably less than two years old when she went back to school. I was traveling quite a bit but flexed my schedule as much as I could to support Erin's desire to further her education. We had a lot going on, but again, it wasn't anything more to me than what a normal young family would encounter as they figure out how to navigate their lives together.

Life was very good!

In approximately December of 1997, it got even better. Erin was pregnant with the second gift. She graduated from the University of Louisville in August of 1998 when she was eight months pregnant with Katie. She graduated magna cum laude, and I could not have been prouder of her. She successfully balanced her time as a wife, mother to our young son, and excelled as a student.

September 21, 1998, Katie arrived. With a headful of jet-black hair, she was and still is as beautiful as any gift I could ever have hoped for. Unlike her brother, she was a contented baby. She slept well and was naturally very happy. However, as most parents know, girls can be a handful as they enter their teen years. She is off to college now, and in spite of all she has had to endure throughout three years of her high school, she graduated with honors from a challenging school. That makes the father in me glow with the very brightest proud lights. She has turned into an outstanding, mature, and intelligent young woman.

We lived in Louisville for five years and thoroughly enjoyed all that the birthplace of one Mr. Cassius Clay had to offer. Erin decided to follow her passion for animals and began building a pet-sitting business. The pet-sitting business was something she could do with the kids, and I was right there by her side helping her build it. We started with flyers, riding around many neighborhoods stuffing the flyers into mailboxes, and had a good time doing it. She was great at the job and built a very successful business.

As 2001 approached, Billy was almost six years old, and Katie was two-and-a-half. My employer of nearly ten years began to experience some challenges. I was concerned about the longevity of the organization and accepted a position with another pharma company.

As much as we loved Kentucky, we decided to make a move to Wilmington, North Carolina, in April of 2001. The new role required much less travel, allowing me to be around much more often for our very young children.

It took us about nine months to settle into North Carolina. We missed

Kentucky, but Carolina quickly became home. I was very appreciative of Erin's selflessness during yet another relocation. It was a beautiful move for our family.

We began to settle into our new life. Our subdivision was full of young families and plenty of kids for our kids to play with, reminiscent of Louisville. The community was fun, with plenty of parties and celebrations, especially around Halloween, Thanksgiving, Christmas, and Mardi Gras. We had some great neighbors from Louisiana who threw a killer Fat Tuesday party the likes of which any Cajun would be proud. With my assistance, Erin began to build another successful pet-sitting business. She was exceptionally busy around the holidays, and I did what I could to help out with some of her clients. I don't quite have the gift she had. Many dogs sensed my fear and would not let allow me to enter their homes without them growling and wetting all over the floor. However, I did what I could.

Now, on the career front, I was struggling somewhat as an individual contributor compared to being the "boss" in my previous role. I began to second-guess the move. I attended a conference in New Orleans in December of 2001 and enjoyed an excess of what Bourbon Street had to offer. I got caught up in several of Pat O'Brien's infamous "hurricanes." It was a late night, but nothing inappropriate happened. I did not speak to Erin until 11 a.m. the next day, despite her having tried to reach me many times. I lied to her and told her I had food poisoning. I wish I'd just been honest. I fully understood what she was thinking. Husband is out late, randomly, until 4 a.m. and doesn't speak to you until lunchtime? I certainly get it. Later that day, I came clean and told her the truth.

I will never understand what may have triggered all that would occur with Erin's health issues, but they started around this time, in late 2001 and early 2002. Before that, she was a very healthy individual and rarely saw a doctor.

In late 2001, almost out of nowhere, we ended up at an esteemed academic medical center where Erin was evaluated for the possibility of an autoimmune disorder or fibromyalgia. As I sat in the exam room with her, the doctor said with zero bedside manner, "It's all in your head. You are a type A personality, and this is all stress related. You do not have an auto-immune disorder or fibromyalgia." These comments were made without any discussion about her test results. His abrasive and abrupt demeanor left both Erin and me dumbfounded. She would seek a second opinion and would inform me that she indeed has fibromyalgia. "This is what is causing the tingling sensation in my skin and nerve pain."

Our kids were aware of their grandfather, Erin's biological father, and they knew that their mom had not talked to her father in almost ten years. Erin's brother had no relationship with their father either, and this cemented what I had been told by Erin about her dad. He wasn't discussed much, but I accepted her word that he was a deadbeat dad. He provided very little finan-cial support during her childhood and he took in her ex-husband. With a smile on her face, Erin would relay to me that she expressed her displeasure with her father in the form of nasty letters faxed to his place of employment.

It was June of 2002, and Billy, seven years old at the time, told Erin, "Mom, why don't you just call your dad?" The sweet innocence of a child can do magical things to a parent. Erin heeded his advice. She phoned her father and left him a message. It was a gorgeous North Carolina Saturday afternoon, and Erin and I had taken the kids to the pool. We returned home, and there was a message on our answering machine from her dad. I can still picture it, and I can hear her father's voice coming through the machine. "Erin, it's your father." I got emotional, and Erin broke down as well. I was thrilled that they were reconnecting, but the added jazz that the inspiration came from our son was a prideful feeling that I will never forget. I was so proud of Erin for being the bigger person and accepting her father back into her life.

I was so happy for her. Erin's father, Martin made a trip to our home in North Carolina, and their relationship was renewed. We made several trips to his home in the Florida area. It was great to see our kids have a relationship with their grandfather.

God puts people into or back into your life for a reason. Erin's rela-

tionship with her father was going well. I recall asking Erin if her dad
ever apologized or provided any explanation to her for the things he had
allegedly done. Erin told me, "We do not bring up the past and have never
discussed it. I am very happy to have Dad back in my life even if our relationship is superficial." She idolized her father. Prior to her first marriage
falling apart, their relationship was very good. In her teens, she would visit
him in Chicago and Florida quite often. Her best friend since eighth grade,
Krystal, often joined her on these trips.

In December of 2007, a few days after Christmas, we received a panicked call from Erin's father's life partner, Brad. Erin's dad had had a massive
heart attack and was on a ventilator. He never recovered, and Erin had to
make the difficult decision to remove her father from life support. He passed
away on New Year's Eve 2007.

It is with all of the might that God has put inside of me that I believe
this event was a tipping point for Erin. Guilt is a very toxic emotion, and
perhaps Erin was regretting the ten years of her father's life that she had
lost. In February of 2010, her father's life partner, Brad, also passed away at
a relatively young age. We attended the funeral in Florida, and both of our
children were courageous enough to speak about their grandpa in front of
the attendees. He was a kind man who possessed a great sense of humor.
Billy was fifteen at the time, and Katie was a little over eleven years old.
Without question, this was devastating to Erin. Again, she was very close to
both her dad and Brad most of her life, except for the ten years she had lost.

At this point, Erin and I were nearly seventeen years into a stable and
happy marriage. Marital discord and fighting were essentially nonexistent.

For seventeen years, she was a dedicated mother and a good wife, supporting me on the home front so that I could focus on my career. I looked
for ways to let her know how appreciative I was of her, and more times than
not, she reciprocated. I assisted with her business and helped to carry the
load at home, raising our children and maintaining a strong sense of faith
and family. We were all that I ever dreamed we would be together.

"Dad, you and Mom were like teenagers in love. What happened?" Katie once inquired.

So, what did happen?

In roughly August of 2010, Erin began to accuse me of cheating . . . boldly, blatantly, and unexpectedly. I was faithful to Erin, and up until that point, I believed that she was to me. What could have provoked her?

This would be the first on a laundry list of baseless accusations that ultimately led to my undoing.

As fall came and the leaves on the trees seemed to be changing as rapidly as our relationship, I tried my best to keep my name clear of such inconceivable rumors. I desperately tried to keep my head straight for the sake of my professional career and life as a father. I could not fathom that my wife, the woman that I created my two beautiful children with, would ever try to ruin my name.

The holidays came, and the holidays went, altered somehow by the change of feeling between Erin and me. Was it still, somehow, bad blood from some of my earlier mistakes? Or was Erin finally beginning to show who she really was? Was she uncovering all the red flags that I missed for years?

# CHAPTER 3
## *Miracle Worker*

*The only time you suffer is when you believe a thought that argues with reality.*
*—Byron Katie*

The last vacation that Erin and I took alone was in May of 2010 to Sarasota, Florida. The team I managed at the time had achieved an incentive trip, a long weekend at the Ritz Carlton. By chance, we shared the hotel that weekend with the Jimmy V Foundation. Tons of sports notables were there: Dick Vitale, John Saunders, Chris Berman, you name it. It was a middle-aged man's dream: a beautiful woman by my side, a gorgeous beach vacation and, of course, sports celebrities. Erin was kind enough to get my too-cool-for-school self a Roy Williams autograph as he sat poolside with his wife. You know how the story goes, no manly-man can swallow his pride enough to ask another dude for his signature, but you know darn well we will graciously accept when someone asks for us. Regardless, we had a great weekend. Most importantly, these days Erin seemed to be a picture of health.

That August, I made a move to another organization. Our son would be heading into his sophomore year in high school, our daughter had started middle school, and as we approached our seventeenth wedding anniversary,

I believed things were right in our marriage. I do think Erin was still emotionally hurting during this time, and rightfully so. Her pain was exponential from losing her father a few years back coupled with the loss of Brad.

It was April of 2011, and I was working in Charlotte for my new role. I called Erin at a lunch break, and she alerted me that she was just out driving around when she suddenly began experiencing a rapid heart rate and numbness on the left side of her body. She headed to our family practitioner's office. My immediate thought was "It's her *damn fibromyalgia*."

She had been doing so well. I left Charlotte immediately and headed back to Wilmington. By the time I got there, Erin had been taken by ambulance to the hospital. I raced over, found her room and, as I walked in, my heart sank. I lost it. I started welling up; I could not believe the state she was in. I'm no doctor, but I was confident that she must have had a stroke. The left side of her face was drooping; she had weakness on the entire left side of her body, and she was cognitively impaired. What had happened to my dear Erin?

Before I could even make sense of all that was going on, the Occupational Therapy and Physical Therapy folks were working with her. She looked lost. She could not perform simple mental tasks. She could not add numbers. She couldn't count by three. It was gut wrenching, and it got worse as images of our kids flashed before my eyes. While there was a history of cardiac issues on both sides of Erin's family, she was only 43 years old! Something wasn't right.

Following a four-day hospital stay, the ultimate finding was that she did not have a stroke. What? What else could it possibly have been? The doctors ultimately classified it as a cerebral vascular accident of unknown origin. Erin regained her strength through physical therapy and within a few short weeks was back to "normal." While things still did not completely add up in my head, I was just happy she was okay. I was never once inclined to believe that Erin had lied or covered things up. I genuinely had no reason to. It was the first in a series of cardiac issues Erin would experience.

Later that spring, Erin began to see a specialist that she referred to as her "miracle worker." She discovered this physician through some folks at a small shop in downtown Wilmington that she frequented. This miracle worker used to be in a significant practice but now was out on his own. That, in and of itself, could've been a red flag to many in the medical field. Couple that with the fact that he did not accept insurance (cash only) but would allegedly file the claims—this guy was an absolute ticking time bomb. I went with Erin twice and thought nothing of paying $250 in cash each time. I wanted her to get the care she needed to figure out what was going on, and his waiting room overflowed, so how bad could it be?

He was the most inappropriate physician I have ever come across! He would try to find common ground with me by talking about lap dances and women with big breasts. Then he would go on to give Erin a cursory (a.k.a. bullshit) exam and send her off with several prescriptions.

Erin had another stroke-like event just a few months later in November, and again I ended up with her in the ER. She experienced identical symptoms to those she had in April, and sure enough, her miracle worker insisted and insisted that he speak to the folks in this emergency room. He specifically requested to speak to the attending physician, not a fellow or resident or nurse, and he wanted to fill the attending physician in on what was going on with Erin. At the time, I was so worried about Erin's declining health and perplexed as to what was going on that I failed to look any further into anything. Erin had been stable for so long. What was it that seemed to be steadily taking my wife away from me?

I had no rational answers.

After recovering from this latest episode, Erin began to volunteer in a program for terminally ill cancer patients. I was so proud of the love, compassion, and resiliency that Erin was showing to our kids, now in some of the most critical growing years of their lives. I bragged to anybody who wanted to listen about what she was doing. I could never have done this type of work and told her many times how proud of her I was. At the time, I believed Erin's end-of-life experience with her father was her motivation. The story just seemed to fit so well.

*My poor, poor Erin.*

Soon Erin was a very busy volunteer for this program, eventually taking on a coordinator role. Erin and I attended a few fundraisers, and even donated some money. It is a very worthy pursuit. Erin's shifts often occurred at night and would last all night long. To this day, I think of the many times Erin would come to me at 8:00 p.m. on any given night and say, "I have someone dying, and no other volunteers have responded. Do you mind if I go?"

"Of course not," I would tell her.

I had no problem with this, and I even offered to drop her off and pick her up, as I was concerned about her safety in a parking deck late at night.

"I will just call security to escort me," Erin always reassured me. I lost count of how many times she would come home at 6 a.m. or later the following morning.

Erin would eventually burn out from this program, and at the time, I fully understood why. She was volunteering quite a bit and her unpredictable hospital visits and long hours were not something that any person could endure long-term . . . let alone somebody with the ongoing stress, anxiety, and health issues that Erin was supposedly having.

Erin transitioned into a pet therapy program at this same institution, again as a volunteer. She was a perfect fit, and this was right up her alley from her days caring for so many sick and wounded animals. It was also at this time that Erin began to express an interest in looking for work. We certainly could have used the extra money, but there was no pressure from me. I just wanted Erin to be happy and healthy, and at this point, I supported everything that could contribute to the "happy" and focused every ounce of available effort to pursue the "healthy."

Erin led me to believe that all her volunteering could potentially turn into a paid part-time position. I was not pressuring her to work, but I was excited about it, believing she was so well suited for the pet therapy opportunity. Based on my suggestion, Erin met with a career counselor. She had two degrees but had not been in the workforce for some time, and we both agreed that, hell, maybe it would be good for her to take a career assessment to re-evaluate her strengths, weaknesses, and areas of interest.

Unfortunately, we found the employment version of the miracle worker. We got hosed.

Erin's very first meeting with the career counselor, she was charged $3,000.00. Yes, three *thousand*, not hundred. I was *not* happy about this, but, given that the suggestion had come from me, I kept a level head about it. She had an assessment done, and he did help redo her resume, but beyond that, there was not much else. "Three thousand dollars for that?" I said to myself. I called and gave him a piece of my mind, and I was, by some small miracle, able to get just about half of it back. I was not upset with Erin; I felt that she had been taken advantage of.

I began noticing declines in Erin's cognitive ability and her capacity to complete simple tasks quickly. I was growing concerned about the impact of both strokes and her continuing cardiac issues. She went through every heart test possible, and all they were able to find was that she was having a hard time maintaining volume, whatever that meant. I also began observing memory loss that Erin had never shown signs of before. I get the realities of life and the fact that, as is the case with anybody, we *were* getting a little older, but it was hard to fathom how quickly she had declined. She was becoming forgetful with her business, occasionally calling me for directions home from the institution that she had been volunteering at for several *years*. There were two instances when she forgot to pet-sit for a client, and the dogs were alone for twenty-four hours with no means of getting outside. She was normally very meticulous, especially with her business. Was it the strokes, her disease, a combination of the two, or something else?

To this point, I never once asked Erin to let me see any of her growing number of medical records. As preposterous as it sounds, I blindly and unconditionally took my spouse's word for gospel. To add fuel to the fire, our health care system's lack of alignment with electronic health records enabled Erin to bounce from institution to institution and specialist to specialist, self-reporting all of her issues to prescribers, healthcare professionals . . . and her husband!

In addition to her unexplained cardiac, cognitive, and memory issues, Erin began to have challenges with constipation later that year. She would also experience mouth sores, patchy hair loss and pain during our intimate times. Her health's downward spiral made for an incredibly sad and endless cascade of doctor visits that provided few answers or explanations.

Erin's miracle worker, to his credit, ended up doing Erin some good. He assisted her in getting her into a top-ranked health system for a thorough and proper evaluation. I was elated. I hoped and prayed somebody could *finally* find some answers to all her issues.

Erin made her initial visit in April of 2013 by herself. I stayed behind to take care of Katie who was now in the eighth grade. (By then, Billy was a high school senior.) One hope for her visit was that somebody would fully evaluate all of the medications that she was taking to determine if any might be contributing to her issues. Again, still no doctor, but it only made sense to me that all of these different medications, tests, and treatments had to be having some psychological and physiological effect on her.

Erin made a return trip to this facility just a few months later in July. Again, I did not go with her. I came to realize over time that Erin *enjoyed* these trips. She had every specialist at her disposal. They repeatedly examined her from head to toe but made no medication adjustments and offered no new insight.

According to Erin.

The only verbal insight I received from Erin was a confirmation of her small fiber neuropathy. I was so disappointed for her. We both deserved some answers.

She continued to see multiple specialists locally when she returned from the Clinic (the name I'll use to refer to that establishment). She began to have difficulty swallowing, and her bowels were becoming increasingly worse. Fibromyalgia be damned, I was beginning to suspect there were far worse, underlying problems, but it was so hard to put my finger on *anything* yet. These specialists never found anything structurally wrong with her heart, her esophagus, or her bowels to explain her symptoms. All of the money on these specialists resulted in no answers. All of the over-the-counter meds turned into what now seems like so much time, money, and effort simply wasted.

The frequency with which Doris visited us in North Carolina during this period increased, and one evening, as we stood in our kitchen, she whispered to me, "Does she want something to be wrong with her?" Erin overheard this and was not happy with her mom's question.

Interestingly enough, Erin rarely saw her rheumatologist, the primary doctor who treated her fibromyalgia. In fact, in the past six years, she had seen her only *once*. I, as we know by this point, was thinking all of these issues were due to her illness.

I thought that Erin's no longer being on estrogen following her stroke-like event in 2011 caused the painful intercourse she experienced in 2012 and 2013. Erin would often comment, "My OB/GYN said my lining is so thin from the lack of estrogen and that causes the discomfort when we are 'together.'"

As the days in 2013 came and went, Erin's appearance consumed her. Erin's hair loss earlier in the year was especially devastating. She ended up getting hair extensions. The extensions lasted maybe six months before she took them out and moved on to dyeing her hair red. These hair extensions cost $2,000, but I supported every effort she made to feel better about herself. She began using $200 face creams, $100 neck creams, push-up bras, $300 haircuts, and lip injections. The injections did not go well. She experienced an allergic reaction that made her lips blow up like Will Smith's character in the movie *Hitch*.

Remember, Erin was reared to be all about family, trust, honesty, and transparency.

Despite sudden hyper-focus on appearance and her emotional passions, her allegations about *my* infidelity and lack of trust intensified.

It began to be all about the phones with Erin. For the longest time, my company phone was direct-billed to my employer. I never received a bill like most folks. Their generosity allowed me to add family members, enabling me to take advantage of their volume discount. Billy was on my plan, but up until August of 2014, Erin and Katie had a separate phone plan. I did not object to this nor, frankly, did I care. I do not mean "care" as in callous. I just genuinely never even thought twice about the fact that it could be or would become an issue. Billy had a few girlfriends throughout his high school years, and when breakups occurred, Erin occasionally checked his phone records to see if he was contacting an ex. Once, through AT&T, she was able to access our records. She questioned one particular number that our son had called, and she dialed it. It was Billy's best friend, TJ, from grade school who had moved out West. Erin then pivoted to asking me questions about my calls, and so it started. I had *nothing* to hide, not a damn thing.

As things continued to heat up, Erin made comments like, "My girlfriend said that every time she sees you that you are on the phone." It was my job, and I was on the phone a lot. I developed some sneaky instincts because of the constant questioning in an attempt to avoid her inquisition. For example, I closed my computer lid as Erin entered my office. Now I see how suspicious this action looked. I was growing so tired of answering questions about whom I had been e-mailing or calling. Erin rarely asked to see what I was writing, but kept a remarkable track of my behaviors.

It was on April 1, 2013, that Erin began seeing a psychiatric nurse practitioner. She claimed this was necessary because, "I am struggling with the loss of my father and Brad." No more than two visits in with the therapist, the focus became about the lack of trust in our marriage. "We have not had it since day one, and trust is the foundation of marriage," Erin reported to me following one of her appointments. She would endlessly hammer me with this. The never-ending scrutiny, the verbal and emotional abuse, became overwhelming. As was often the case with my job, I worked from home when I was not traveling. Erin frequently entered my office demanding to see my phone and my e-mails. "My therapist said that I have a right to have access to your phone and e-mails. She thinks that you are cheating on me." Quite pissed, I slammed my hand on my desk. Erin interpreted this as being defensive and secretive.

"I have nothing to hide," I said. "Why does your therapist think that I am cheating on you?"

"I told her about my need to get cootie tested and about my green discharge down there."

So I gave her constant access to my work and personal e-mail, and my phone. I never asked her to extend me the same courtesy.

I offered to accompany Erin to her therapist, but Erin did not oblige. Instead, she informed me that the nurse practitioner was no longer practicing, primarily to stay home with her kids. Erin saw her only five times, and she stopped doing so at the end of July 2013. What was the real reason for the seemingly abrupt end to visits with this therapist?

June of 2013 brought us significant milestones that every family should cherish. Billy graduated from high school, and Katie graduated from grade school . . . both with high honors. I was saddened to think about our first child transitioning off to college. To this point, I was very close with both of our kids and was thankful for the decision I made to change employers in 2010. My parents were both in excellent health, and they made the trip to North Carolina to share in our son's graduation. Erin's mom, Doris, also made the trip. Our son would be heading off to study engineering in the fall. We were extremely proud of both of our kids. However, as I reflect on these milestones, I literally shake my head. I had no clue what was going on in our marriage.

Billy, diagnosed with attention deficit disorder at the end of fourth grade, began taking Adderall as fifth grade commenced. These meds work well if you have a legitimate deficit. If you don't, they can be very harmful. He lost a significant amount of weight but flourished educationally. He stopped taking these meds toward the end of his sophomore year in high school as he started working out. The appetite suppressant effect was not conducive to building muscle. Our family practitioner provided the management and medication oversight for Billy's condition. He had been our family doc since the kids were young. We trusted him. As our son started college, he struggled. The transition from high school, coupled with his engineering curriculum, was daunting. On a fall break in 2013, we made him an appointment to see our family practitioner as even Billy was contemplating needing Adderall again to help him focus. Erin took our son to this appointment. They did not see our usual family practitioner but another doc who was new to the practice. Rightfully so, she refused to prescribe Adderall to our son without him consulting a psychiatrist. To say that Erin was pissed when she came home would be an understatement. I believe that I called our family doctor, and he wrote Billy one additional Adderall scrip.

Over Christmas break, a psychiatrist saw Billy for the possibility of renewing his Adderall prescription. She too did the right thing and wrote one last order. This psychiatrist was in an extensive practice with a psychiatrist Erin began seeing. Our son took the meds sparingly, and I am incredibly proud to say that he finished both semesters of his first year on the Dean's List. That would be his final prescription for Adderall.

# CHAPTER 4
## *Just Another Day at the Beach*

You don't choose your family. They are God's gift to you as you are to them.

—*Desmond Tutu*

Spring in North Carolina can be quite alluring. The trees leaf out, the days get warmer, and each spring brings assurance that kids will soon be out of school.

My forty-ninth birthday was quickly approaching. Given the fact that I had not done so in years, I decided it would be a good time in my life to start working out again. Billy, who had become a gym rat at the end of his sophomore year in high school and was quickly approaching wow-you-got-so-big size, was my inspiration. After I spent some time with him at the local YMCA, he put together a simple one-hour workout for me. Not only do I still carry the card on which he wrote that workout (I laminated it), I still pretty much follow the routine almost four years later.

It was around this time that I made a soda drinker's worst mistake: switching from Coke to Diet Coke. I recall this day vividly as it was "leg day," when I hosted a bachelor party for my friend who was about to remarry. We went to dinner, saw a comedy show, and hit a few bars in downtown

Wilmington. I know, I know; it was crazy town. What do you expect from a couple of mid-40s dads? I was home by midnight and had been checking in regularly with Erin, as she was not a big fan of me having, and particularly hosting, this get-together.

It was in early April of 2014 that my friend got married. "Big G" and his new wife, "little g," got married on a picture-perfect day on the beach. With the bright sun and sparkling ocean as a backdrop, love was in the air. I felt honored to be the best man. The bride's parents were gracious enough to provide the wedding party accommodations in a beautiful oceanfront beach house. Erin and Katie were also part of the ceremonies, and it was a fantastic day.

We left the wedding reception a little early and went back to the beach house. Erin, as we had become accustomed to her doing, went to bed about 9:00 p.m. Katie and I (along with several other folks from the wedding) stayed up to watch the UConn Huskies win the NCAA Men's Basketball Championship. Taking us back to our time in Louisville where we gained so many friendships rooting for the Cards, the night got even sweeter watching Kentucky lose!

As the game ended and my daughter snuggled with me on the couch, I can remember a few of the other guests remarking, "I hope our daughter is that way at her age." She was almost 16, and all those years, I had felt so much love from her. I was always her Daddy, and she was absolutely my little girl.

That night was the last time I'd hear my sweet Katie call me Daddy for close to two years.

A few short days later, Erin again accused me of infidelity—this time, "ogling" other women at the wedding. I was not "ogling" any other women. However, this time, her accusation was more vicious, and accusations like them became more frequent. They were starting to tear us apart.

In May of 2014, the sweet, sweet journey of couple's therapy began. As this was my first time having any experience with any therapist, I tried to keep an open mind. Our counselor was about as good as you would expect to find through an employee assistance program. I will say, though, I did learn a few things. Most significant was to be more open to sharing my feelings. Something we often tell our kids but forget ourselves, especially as we get older: If something is bothering you, discuss it. In the past, if I had an issue with Erin, I would only say something like, "I'm good," and I would let things fester or blow away. The therapist's guidance was to express my feelings in the form of, "This is how I feel," not "This is how you make me feel." Again, it might seem trivial, but it had some impact on me, and I was willing to do whatever I could to get our marriage back on track.

As we were going through therapy, I continued to work out. Early May, I began to see some results from my time in the gym. I noticed some weight coming off. When I started working out, I was about 225 pounds on a six-foot frame. Following my son's advice, I had started taking pure whey protein following my exercises. My initial thought was that working out three days week and switching to a diet soda was paying some dividends.

Erin's stance with this therapist was, if anything, consistent. Her story was that we never had trust in our marriage and that I was a convincing liar. It was in these sessions that I started to see her developing an actual story around my "moods" and my "anger issues." It was through this therapist that, for the first time, Erin started to use my daughter against me. It was one thing for Erin to sit there and claim distrust between us over the years, but to hear her say that my daughter didn't trust me was impossible to comprehend. I didn't know if it was true. I certainly didn't think it was, and I knew I had never given my daughter a reason to distrust me, but it was still heartbreaking—downright shattering to the love I had in me as a father. I was losing a grasp on what was going on, and as I've mentioned before, it even began to affect my mind, making me question not only who I was, but more importantly, who the hell was I married to? What was the person that I had known and loved for so long, becoming?

About a week before vacation with Erin's family, I was traveling for business in San Antonio with both male and female colleagues. It was during this time in Texas that Erin began to question me about my relationship with one of my female coworkers, Mila. During one of our conversations she remarked, "An emotional connection with someone else is also cheating." I had known Mila for almost ten years at this point, and we had worked at two different companies together and reported to the same boss within both companies. While you could (and should) indeed call her a friend just like any others that I'd worked with for so long, our relationship was strictly professional. Our roles were very similar, we worked closely on many projects, and I might add that Erin was very well aware of her. We'd exchanged family Christmas cards with Mila for almost a decade. However, like so many other things that seemed normal through the first seventeen years of my marriage, this too took a hell-bound turn, and I was left searching for answers as to why this was all happening. The home that I'd lived in for so many years was slowly starting to burn down around me, and I had no idea where the fire was coming from or how to put it out.

Despite our marital challenges, we still headed on vacation with the kids, Erin's mother, brother, and his family to Topsail Island in North Carolina. My uneasy gut had me not necessarily looking forward to it, but I think I was longing for some sense of normalcy. For Erin, it was just another chance to add hot water to an already boiling pot. We had been to Topsail a few times already and always immensely enjoyed ourselves.

Erin's mom was very gracious to pay for the entire beach house for the week. We didn't take many vacations, but when we did, it was never without her. She was always welcome. I used to admire her relationship with Erin. They were extremely close, almost inseparable, and this trip to the beach was no different.

We were there for a week, and it was one of the longest weeks in my life. I should have trusted my gut.

We arrived on a Saturday, and once we unloaded the cars, I went to the grocery store to get some essentials. Erin knew where I was going and asked me to pick up a few things for her, but when I returned forty-five minutes later, I faced questions from not only Erin but also Katie this time as to where I had been and why I had been gone so long. Erin called me "sneaky" and a "liar" . . . all this in front of her family. On this vacation, every morning, I would wake up to the familiar beach sounds: seagulls, waves crashing, kids playing and, at least this particular week, Erin saying, "If you are not happy in the marriage, then get out."

I did nothing to provoke this. Not a thing, besides a completely necessary forty-five-minute haul to the grocery store. My "moods" quickly became less than jolly. I had had enough of the accusations. However, I was determined to try to make the best of this vacation.

"Someone is lighting you up," she would remark when texts or e-mails hit my phone. Of course, as I explained to Erin hundreds of times, I received personal and work e-mails in addition to text messages. My phone never required a passcode to get in; never did I feel the need to put my phone face down, and never once was I not completely honest if she asked who it was. She could have just swiped the screen and looked all she wanted. I had always managed my e-mail accounts and text messages tightly, deleting any unnecessary information. I was not fond of clutter, and Erin had known that for years. Erin would try to turn this fact into something that it wasn't. I wasn't sneaky or deceptive, but she would continue to build a wall, stacking brick after brick between us.

Both literally and emotionally, I felt stranded on an island.

To say that Erin dismissed me would be an understatement. She refused to be bothered to take a twenty-minute ride with our son and his friend to get some ocean fishing rods for the week. I asked her three times, only to later receive counsel from her mom that it is about communication in a marriage, and, "If you wanted her to go with you, you should have stated that it was important to you."

"Okay, Doris. Got it."

As the week rolled on, I took one of the last couple days to head down to the beach by myself in part for the obvious . . . it's the beach for goodness sake! But frankly, I needed to get away from the house to breathe. As I let the calm of the water and the soothing sounds of the beach smother me, reality returned. I, unfortunately, needed to get back to the house.

So, I headed in for a drink. Ultimately a drink more bitter than I could have ever imagined.

I will never forget walking in the sliding glass door, the details of the room and the sun bouncing off the long granite countertops where Erin and Doris greeted me.

I didn't have a chance to say hello before Doris chimed in. "If you put your hands on my daughter, I will kill you. You have something deeper going on, Dan. Perhaps you are addicted to porn, or addicted to drugs. Maybe it was something that happened in your childhood. I don't know. You need to dig deep, Dan." I was clearly lacking context. I was blindsided. This death threat and the words emanating from Doris's mouth were news to me. I had known her for twenty-three years and never had a cross word with her. The cause(s) of my alleged aberrant behaviors were mine to discover through soul searching.

I was shocked. Purely, utterly shocked. It is so clear to me now that Erin had been working her mother for some time and filling her head with all sorts of nonsense about my sexual interests, anger, and moods.

I was near speechless. The only thing that logically came to my mind after a long pause was, "What have I ever done to lead you to believe that I would hurt your daughter?" She waited for a few seconds, looked down at the floor, and then remarked: "You shook the dishwasher rack and broke it."

It was such a stupid response that I almost chuckled. "What are you talking about?" I asked her. "As has been commonplace lately, your daughter and I have been arguing quite a bit. In the heat of one of our discussions, as I was unloading the dishwasher, I grabbed the rack and shook it. I did not break it."

It was this threat coupled with all of the comments from Erin over the past several months about me being emotionally confusing and moody that caused me to begin to think that maybe I did have a mood issue. Later that day, Erin and I took a walk on the beach. I'll never forget hearing her say, "I am so sorry that you had to hear that from my mother." I believed that Erin was genuine as she communicated with me.

I had finally started to confirm that something was seriously wrong, either on my end or hers, rather than my innate speculation and wishful dismissal of what should have been obvious. Something was going on, but I was far from putting my finger on it, and it was driving me insane. I became moody after feeling dismissed, threatened, and verbally assaulted by Erin every morning. Instead of feeling great about the nearly thirty pounds I'd lost in a couple of months, I was shunning myself left and right, hearing Doris blurt comments like, "Why don't you get a pair of shorts that fit you?" I began to shut down emotionally and did more and more things to keep myself busy. I always liked to keep busy, but this week remembered *never* wanting to settle down—so much so, I was driving myself to the point of exhaustion. Doris did not hesitate to comment on this as well during our beach trip. "All I know," she said, "is that Dan gets real busy when he is upset."

Nevertheless, I continued doing my part to help all week. Erin's brother and I were grilling one evening, and I felt compelled to have a conversation about Erin and me. I was honestly never close with him, and sadly, his "little sis" was not either. I assured him that I had not been with any woman other than his sister and had been nothing but appropriate with women. I told him that I was never destructive and never came close to putting a hand on Erin in a violent manner. I made it clear that I loved his sister very much. Of course, I did understand that this was all "he said, she said," but I also knew how completely innocent I was of the accusations against me. Naturally, man-to-man, he would believe me. Right?

Without hesitation, he looked at me quite sternly and remarked, "Are you sure?" Was he aware of Doris's verbal assaults toward me? If so, why did he not seize the opportunity to address Erin's fear of me?

With all that was going on during this trip and all that had occurred going back months, I was becoming very concerned about our future. Where were my life and my marriage going? My family was everything to me, and I did not want to see it fall apart.

Shocker, I did not sleep well on this trip. After tossing and turning one evening, I took a walk on the beach at 4 a.m., and as you can imagine, that did not end well. I returned to the house around 6 a.m. as the sun was coming up. Erin was up by then and, yes, she launched into an interrogation.

Erin's issues with paranoia were beginning to dawn on me. It was at the end of one day on the beach that Erin's sister-in-law, Denise, was going to the store when I whispered in her ear to get me a pack of cigarettes. Everybody pretty well knew that I still smoked, but it was never something I wanted to shout aloud or boast in front of the kids. A short while later, I walked into our bedroom to find Erin in the bathroom, pissed as can be. "What were you and Denise talking about?" she asked. I told her exactly what we discussed, but she did not accept that. I told her to ask Denise, but she said she could not trust me. I was a pathological liar. I was trying to hide things from her.

I had heard it all.

As our time at Topsail ended, it was only fitting that on the last day I had an encounter with what I believed to be a shark shortly before leaving the beach for the last time. I know it almost seems too perfect for the story to be true, but I swear it to this day as I dipped my entire body beneath the water, I felt something brush against my legs a few dozen feet out from the shore. When I came up, I immediately looked and saw the shadow of a body under water and the pointed fin above slowly, eerily swimming away. I had swum with dolphins before; this was no dolphin. I ran out of the water for the last time.

That encounter became a metaphor I now tie to that entire week. I was bathing in the purity of the ocean blue unaware of the shark that had been preying on me long before I saw it coming. The bitch of it all? The shark swam away, but Erin continued to stalk her prey day after day after day.

# CHAPTER 5
## *Dog Days of Summer*

Suspicion always haunts the guilty mind. —*William Shakespeare*

As my story goes, I regrettably continued to let everything eat at me, and I ended up doing a few things that only hurt my cause.

A few weeks preceding the July 4th holiday and our last marriage counseling meeting, I made a move that I still can't explain. I was coming home from a long day of seeing customers and saw Erin at a gas station about a mile from our home—the very gas station where I typically stopped to have a cigarette before heading home for the night. It may sound strange, especially considering that my family knew I smoked, but it was just my routine. I was on the phone with a female colleague, and I panicked. Slamming on the brakes, I made a crazy U-turn to avoid pulling into the gas station. I could not stand the thought of my wife badgering me about who was on the phone with me. I knew it would not be, "Hi, honey, how are you?" or "How was your day?" I knew she saw me as I drove away, and I instantly thought, "What in the hell have you just done?"

I felt we had been making progress recently and knew that this was going to set us back. There was no thought before making the turn, just reaction. I should have just pulled in and said hello. After my idiotic Joie Chitwood move, I was home in five minutes and called Erin as soon as I walked in the door. I apologized profusely and was very clear on how I would feel if she'd done something like this to me. I did understand how that probably looked, but I was paranoid. Her constant distrust set me off— every accusation, every pointed finger had me so on edge and confused that I forgot how to act normally.

At the time, Erin seemed to accept my apology. However, when she returned that night around 8:30 p.m., she was as irate as I had ever seen her. She had *allegedly* been attending a volunteer meeting that evening. I distinctly recall her screaming, "Do you think I am a fucking idiot? Who is she?"

Of course, I told her there was nobody. She wasn't going to come any-where near accepting this for an excuse. I even shared with her the follow-up e-mail that I sent to this female colleague as a result of our conversation, but Erin began demanding her phone number and wanted me to text her. I refused to do either. Not because I was hiding anything, but because, I did not know this female colleague well and was not comfortable dragging strangers into our marital situation.

No surprise, Erin brought up the U-turn during our next therapy session. She had come prepared to use it against me; she had even drawn a diagram to make sure she accurately communicated what happened.

Then a small miracle occurred. The therapist cut Erin off and said, "If you can't trust your husband, it is time to separate." It wasn't miraculous because I wanted to separate; instead, it was the first time in what felt like a lifetime that somebody even remotely took my side.

End of session, end of that therapist. Erin wasn't having a bit of anybody that didn't want to feed into her fabrications or agenda, so she stormed out and walked way in front of me as she rapidly moved toward our car. "I bet you are flying high on cloud nine," Erin spat at me as I got in.

"Okay, Erin," was all I could reply.

When we returned from the therapist, Erin said she was leaving. I said that I would go as planned to Pittsburgh. I had previously discussed making a trip there for July 4th weekend to see my parents and extended family since Dad's health was getting worse. I admittedly had not discussed these plans with Katie. I quickly packed a bag and headed toward our daughter's room to tell her where I was going. I walked into a sight that would pierce any father's heart: I could not get near her. Erin was sitting on her bed holding her close as our daughter was crying hysterically. I knew what was going on. Erin had gone in and, instead of telling her the truth about what the therapist said, she spun the entire thing on "Dad's mood swings" and proceeded to emphasize that "when he gets upset he leaves." I got down the road about five to ten minutes and called Katie to explain where I was going.

Erin and I decided it would be best if we did not talk to each other for a while.

As with any significant life event, this was neither trivial nor stress-free. Regardless of all that was going on and irrespective of how disgusted I was, Erin was still my wife and the mother of my children. Our mutual silence lasted maybe two days before I texted Erin merely to let her know I was thinking about her. Our exchanges were civil as I recall us even exchanging the "L-word" a few times. After many long late-night talks sitting outside my parents' home, we decided that I should return home.

Before leaving the steel city, I visited Doris. We had a friendly conversation, and I assured her, as I had so many times before, that I loved her daughter, and this was just a rough patch that all marriages encounter and have to work through. Of course, we had to revisit the concepts of truth, honesty, communication, and transparency in our marriage. We even had some laughs about Erin and her constant investigations of me that turned up nothing, joking that one day she would make an excellent private investigator.

My mom was beginning to suspect that something was going on in my marriage. My father more than likely had no comprehension of any turn of events. Sadly, if he did, the effects of his progressing dementia prevented him from communicating that he was aware. Regardless, nobody else in my large family knew what was happening, and I hoped to keep it that way for as long as I could.

Just like the dog days of summer, things on the home front remained unpleasant and heated. While Erin and I managed rare moments of symmetry in communicating, the all-over-the-place nature of our dialogue was driving me up the wall. My job was going well in spite of my personal goings on, but I grew to dread weekends at home because I could not avoid the drama. We would argue about the most trivial things and, although I did my best to de-escalate, we would end up with more and more distance between us.

By late July, we were coming off yet another hellacious weekend. As usual, I kept myself busy with yard work, washing windows, cleaning floors, anything I could to keep my mind and body distracted until sweet, sweet Monday arrived, and I could escape to my job.

One of the anythings was alcohol.

Drinking is not a proper way to cope with strife . . . I know that. You know that. We all know that. As usual, Erin was out and about, and I filled my day doing chores while listening to my iPod's jammy jams. I drank maybe four or five beers throughout the day and had a few shots of vodka. At one point that day, Katie told me I needed my eyebrows trimmed. She was right. Groucho would have been jealous! I was laughing at myself wondering how I'd let them get out of control, but I knew this was a chance for me to at least spend some time with her. Therefore, I asked her to do it, and she obliged.

What a mistake.

She smelled the alcohol on my breath and asked if I had been drinking, and I said no. I lied to her. I lied to my daughter, to her face, out of fear of reprisal for the way I was using alcohol to cope with the stressors of my situation.

Katie attended a cheer clinic later that day, and I was home alone on the back porch drinking a few more beers, keeping to myself. I was not sure where Erin was, and frankly, I didn't bother to care. A short time later she arrived and immediately started to poke the bear. She stormed at me as if she were on some manhunt, asking me how many beers I'd had and why I had been drinking so much. I sarcastically remarked, "I bought eighteen and may drink them all." I wanted nothing to do with her.

Disgusted, Erin sprinted back inside, took a shower, and locked herself in Grandma Doris's room. Katie returned home not long after and she too locked herself in her room. She then began blasting me with text messages as I minded my own business on the back porch. I found the key to Katie's bedroom door, and I entered her room. I stood by her bed and told her she needed to stop and that this was no way for somebody to treat his or her father. I did not lay a hand on her. I did not even yell at her. I did not go near Erin. I showered and went to bed.

To this day it breaks my heart into a million pieces to know that I frightened Katie and would later learn via text messages that she thought I was going to kill her that night. Erin did a number on her, preying on her anxiety and playing her to the point that she grew to fear me—her father, her flesh and blood, the man who was supposed to be her ultimate protector. It wasn't how I imagined fatherhood growing up; not a thing in the world could have prepared me for that.

Our daughter and I were so close up until this. Those times too, were quickly fading away.

I later learned from her that when she arrived home that evening from her cheer clinic, her mom informed her, "Dad is drunk, and it is not safe. Get into your bedroom and lock the door."

Mom was weaponizing our daughter.

August arrived. It, like every passing month these days, was just that, the arrival of another month during which my life would never be the same. My weight continued its decline. My appetite was okay, but there were some nights, especially on weekends, that I had difficulty sleeping. Erin had been keeping herself busy working on a beautiful letter that she had planned to send to her step-nephew, a convicted felon in jail for multiple crimes. Initially, I supported this idea and was proud of the compassion Erin showed. It took her a long time to put this letter together, but I did start to notice that she, too, was unable to process things as sharply as she used to. I thought it was her fibromyalgia and tried to engage her about it, but it was another "dismiss Danny" Saturday in our home. I was not in the best of moods, so I didn't fight it. She was bouncing around the house, gleaming so proud that she finished her letter. She asked me, nicely for a change, if I wanted to read it. I said, without even thinking, "No, I'm good."

I felt like a convicted felon in my own home, nothing short of the worst person alive. A letter full of compassion and support for an *actual* convicted felon was the last thing I wanted to read. It is not as if I was not proud of her reaching out to him or that I wasn't sympathetic for him. I was. However, when does a man draw the line in his own home on continuing to be trampled?

"No, I'm good" was another gas station moment, another emotional, innate reaction—purely thoughtless.

Around 11:30 p.m. on Thursday, September 4, 2014, Erin approached me for the first time about consulting an attorney to see what her options were.

I remember the details like it happened yesterday. I was standing by the stove, as Erin leaned up against the kitchen counter. With no exaggeration or disrespect do I tell you that she had the shittiest grin on her face when she broke the news. "I have an appointment with an attorney tomorrow to see what my options are." It reminded me exactly of the same shitty smile she would make when she would share with me the fact that she sent nasty letters to her dad's place of employment while estranged from him. She held that shitty grin as she continued, "You turned white when I told you."

I'm sure I did. I knew things were wrong, but I still did not want to see this coming.

I retreated to my office upstairs and spent two hours pouring out my heart and my soul to Erin in a letter. Up until this point, I had embarked on a journey to "own" that I had done this to our marriage. I believed that my lies about drinking too much at a business function thirteen years ago and my deception with hiding cigarettes from Erin and our kids in 2010 did this. Erin and Doris had been beating into me that trust is the foundation of a marriage. I believed that I was the reason for the lack of trust in our marriage. I had heard, "All it takes is one lie, Danny" one too many times from her.

Sleeping that night was not an option as I was wide-awake from Erin's revelation. At 4 a.m., I knocked on Erin's bedroom door, *our* bedroom door, and informed her that I was going to get a pack of cigarettes. There is an all-night convenience store close to our home, and I returned not more than fifteen minutes later. Erin was up and waiting for me.

"Are you doing drugs? Are you doing cocaine or crack?" she asked.

She had not a care in the world about my emotional state. I didn't know what to say. On top of accusing me of infidelity and lying, Erin was now cold-heartedly accusing me of hard drug use.

Erin went and had her consultation with what would be her first of many attorneys. I didn't inquire too much about it, but Erin said, "I hope it is all right with you that my initial four-hour session cost 'us' $600.00."

Erin and I were "together" that night, September 5, 2014.

However, our lives, our family, and our love were falling apart.

By day, she was consulting an attorney, and by night, we were intimate. Emotionally bewildering. This confusion was beginning to cloud my ordinarily sound judgment.

# CHAPTER 6
## *5 to 10*

One thing you can't hide—is when you are crippled inside. —*John Lennon*

September 15, 2014: I looked up as, with his back to me, the doctor typed on his computer, and then stated quite nonchalantly, "This sounds like bipolar, and if you don't go to Holy Hell, I will have you involuntarily committed."

*"Presenting Problem: The patient is a 49-year-old C male who presented to the ER with concerns about his mood. The patient indicated that he was recently diagnosed with bipolar disorder by a psychiatrist. The patient notes his mood lability has been increasing significantly, particularly toward anger outbursts. The patient presents calm and cooperative. He describes how when he becomes agitated, he gets into what he describes as a very elevated mood. The patient reported that he is a social drinker and that he has started to drink more often over the last few months. The patient further notes that his relationship with his wife has gotten increasingly worse over the last four years, to the point that his wife contacted an attorney. The patient also acknowledged that if he lost his family that he is not sure what he would do. The patient has not identified a plan for suicide. As such*

*identifying his mood lability, and stressors identified, the patient is recommended for involuntary commitment to an appropriate accepting psychiatric facility to ensure his safety and stability."*

I remember how unnerved I felt in the psychiatric emergency room. I was exhausted, mentally and physically. It had been a long three days . . . Hell, it had been a long six years, enduring meritless accusations. No wonder I felt lost and at my breaking point.

Sleep had been rare and my appetite nonexistent during my stay. I passed the time by making small talk with my babysitter or by staring at the ceiling, failing to grasp the depths of my emptiness. *What the hell have I done to my family, Erin and my two beautiful kids?* I asked myself. *How did I let it get this far? Were there warning signs that this was coming?* I wasn't allowed to even walk down the hall by myself or use the bathroom in my room without supervision. It was a fucking nightmare.

Erin and Katie visited the first evening. It was great to see Katie; and in wanting to feel some sense of "home," I'd even say Erin was a welcome sight. Even so, I was guilt-ridden and did not want our daughter to see me like this. I had not spoken to our son since my visit with him in Charlotte on the fourteenth. I ached to know what might be going through his mind as events continued to unfold. I relentlessly wondered that about both kids.

With every visit, Erin kept busy working the nurses and lighting up the phones, letting anyone she could reach know about my admission and diagnosis. In her mind, she was a saint for finally getting me the help I needed. It was becoming more and more apparent that I was the one portrayed as a villain tearing my family apart. Erin's countless calls to my sister-in-law Jane, Doris, Billy, and Katie were rendering an image of me that would alarm anyone. I have faith in saying this not only because of the calls that occurred but also because of the following:

*"Wife reports patient has been depressed and cleaning and manic, changed personality to telling more falsehoods, has labile moods, a new habit of excess alcohol, and she fears for self and patient."*

Through all the chaos leading up to my commitment, I had not only kept my full-time job, but I also kept my employer and colleagues unaware of my marital struggles. Unavoidably, there was a growing concern among my colleagues because of my dramatic weight loss. Somehow, I needed to get word that I would be out at least a few days. The hospital had taken my phone, and the only colleague's number I knew off the top of my head was Mila's, so I gave it to Erin. At this point, Mila and I still worked at the same company. I was hoping she could get my new boss's cell number to me. Given Erin's accusations of infidelity with Mila, I didn't consider at the time what an absolute act of innocence this was. Why in the hell would I have given Erin, my wife, Mila's number if any accusation was even remotely true?

Erin reached out to Mila via text and was able to message my boss later that week. Admittedly, I felt a little uneasy telling my employer I was locked up in a psychiatric unit. To her credit, Erin's creative talent helped to again skirt reality by saying that I was being evaluated for a neurological condition potentially caused by Lyme's disease . . . nice!

In case I have forgotten to mention this before, this particular hospital is an acute care facility that also houses an inpatient psychiatric unit. As strange as it may sound, I had hoped to be admitted to that unit. I dreaded being transferred elsewhere, because the "elsewhere" would likely be a dedicated psych hospital. Staying in a "regular" hospital seemed more acceptable to me, even if it was a secured behavioral health unit. If I could stay here, one of the psychiatrists on staff could care for me. Every time I asked to be seen (and I asked a lot), I was assured that I would be. It never happened. Hospitalists were the only physicians that came to my bedside, and those visits were cursory and brief. The only behavioral health evaluation occurred during my intake in the ER.

At 3 p.m. on Wednesday the seventeenth, the Wilmington PD arrived in my room, startling me just as the sheriff's deputy had a few days prior. While that deputy had quickly let me know the reason for his early wake-up visit, I had no idea why this new officer was in my room. As I would later find out, Erin knew the entire time and did not tell me. She should have been on her way to pick Katie up from school. Instead, she was at the hospital, outside of my room. I also assumed if I were going to be transferred anywhere, Erin would be taking me. WRONG! The officer soberly said, "I am here to transport you to Holy Hell (fictitious name for the psychiatric hospital); they have a bed for you."

My anxiety shot through the roof. I was now heading to the place that I had desperately hoped to avoid. Since I had no clue about North Carolina statutes as they relate to involuntary commitment, I felt forced to comply.

Soon enough, I would become very well educated about both these statutes, exposing me to just how broken the system is.

They did not put me in handcuffs; both the officer I had met earlier and a second officer who had arrived on the scene escorted me out of the back entrance of the hospital. At the very least, the rock star treatment was a kick, sneaking out of a back exit to avoid the paparazzi. Kidding, of course; I felt more like a convicted felon. I took my place in the back seat of the police car, and off we went to Holy Hell. Before we arrived, the officer kindly pulled over to allow me a cigarette. As you can imagine, these moments were a blur. I lost track of time, not even vaguely aware of when my intake was finally completed.

They took everything: shoelaces, phone, belt, necklace, anything they deemed a potential risk. I was wearing size 38 waist jeans and, given my weight loss, I needed that belt. Embarrassing plastic cable ties replaced it. I had to cable-tie the belt loops in my jeans to keep them partially up. Not only did I *feel* like a convicted felon, but I was starting to look like one too.

Erin met me at Holy Hell and was by my side as they began the intake process. There was no goodbye hug as they escorted me to my unit. As I looked over my shoulder to watch her walking away, an overwhelming wave of sympathy for her and all that I was putting her through washed over me. I can clearly paint the picture of how dark, dull, and hopelessly broken I felt.

The bed in my new unit was a small mattress on plywood outfitted with one thin sheet and a threadbare blanket. I imagined this must be what a prison cell resembles. Given that I arrived with only the clothes on my back, I had no clean clothes to wear. My roommate was asleep; I should be so lucky. It was hard enough for me to get past sleeping in the same room as another psychiatric patient, awake or not. It was even more difficult when every ten to fifteen minutes someone opened the door, shining a flashlight in to make sure that you are still alive and haven't somehow hung yourself with the paper-thin sheets and blankets.

My first day began bright and early at 5:30 for breakfast roll call. But I could not join my new friends for breakfast. This required having a doctor's order, so I was served my meals that day in the unit. Only the finest institutional cuisine on brown plastic trays with, you guessed it, plasticware as utensils. I did all I could to keep it together. I knew that having a bad attitude about anything would not make my stay any better. I started to orient myself to my surroundings and the folks that were on my unit. I also made an effort to schedule an appointment with my assigned social worker to discuss what it would take *to get me the hell out of there.* There were about twenty-five people on my unit, two of which had the same first name as me. Another silly fact that would later become important. My task was merely to be a good patient, attend the scheduled sessions, and cooperate with all staff requests. I didn't know the requirements to be discharged but wanted to do whatever I could within my limited power. The more significant issue, though, was that I still did not fully comprehend what involuntary commitment meant.

After breakfast, we gathered in a little meeting room for what I learned was a daily session led by a mental health technician. We filled out a self-evaluation form to verbally state our goals for the day. The self-evaluation centered on the following two questions:

Do you want to hurt yourself?

Do you want to hurt someone else?

You would think that the social workers trained in mental health would lead these sessions. But the mental health technicians led the majority, if not all, of our "therapy" sessions. As of this writing, in North Carolina and many other states, there are no certification requirements for them. Only a handful of states, including Kansas, Colorado, Arkansas, and California, require psychiatric technicians to pass the certification exam administered by the American Association of Psychiatric Technicians. In North Carolina, a high school diploma or equivalent was all you needed for employment as a mental health technician. While I gladly give these people their due for working hard and making something of their lives, I felt that if this was all going to go down, I at least wanted the best and most professional help I could get to help our family and me.

Following our brief session in the meeting room, everybody lined up for his or her morning meds. No exaggeration and so sad to me, this was the highlight of the day for many. I was not on any morning meds at this point. Thankfully, all I had been taking was 25 milligrams of Lamictal to help with my moods and anxiety. Following the medication session, they checked our weight and blood pressure, and any other vitals deemed necessary for each client. There was no cable service for the two black-and-white TVs that had to have dated back to the early '90s. The "regulars" controlled the TV. There was indeed a pecking order in place here. *Dorothy, I am not in Kansas anymore . . .*

When you have about twenty-five people living in such close quarters in a ward that is continuously on lockdown, it is nearly impossible to find any substantial alone time to decompress. I was scared and mentally exhausted from all that had transpired over the last week. A week of course, as you could imagine, that felt like an eternity. Being the newbie on the unit did nothing but heighten my anxiety.

A few of us ate our meals in the unit and the rest in the cafeteria, though most didn't want to venture that way, as a gentleman had gotten into a fight there the previous night. I decided he was going to be my new friend for the next several days, as I did not want to piss him off. We also happened to share the same first name. It only made sense, right? There were three

Daniels in the unit, so the nice paper signs outside our doors distinguished between us by adding the first initial of our last names.

Once lunch was over, I began to clear my head a little and started to assess all of the people I would be living with for God only knew how long. There were the regulars, or the Holy Hell frequent flyers, who had legitimate mental health issues. They all knew each other and would rotate in and out of Happy Town on a regular basis. There were alcoholics and drug addicts that either voluntarily admitted themselves or were involuntarily committed due to statements made while impaired about wanting to kill themselves. Of course, there were folks that had legitimately *tried* to end their lives. Then there was me. I felt I belonged nowhere.

To this day, I wonder about a lot of them and pray they are on a better path. It was a heartbreaking experience. In a way, I am thankful for this piece of my story because it opened my eyes to things I had never seen. Many of my fellow patients were as young as Billy, with so much life ahead of them.

Late Thursday afternoon, I received a message that Erin had dropped off some new clothes for me and that my two brothers, Anthony and Al, would be coming to town. It was nice to receive those messages because having family and clean clothes reminded me that I still had a life outside these walls. I had almost forgotten that. I was on day four between two different facilities and had developed tunnel vision. I did not get to see Erin, though I was trusting that I could soon. A few others in my unit had visitors that were able to make special arrangements to see them, so I was holding onto the hope that I could too.

I followed up that afternoon with my assigned social worker to see if she had received my request for an appointment. I tapped her on the shoulder as she stood at the nurse's station, though no nurses were in view. Bristling, she asked me what I wanted. I quickly played that off and introduced myself. I told her that I would like to meet with her and that I had filled out a request.

She asked, "What would you like to meet with me to discuss?"

I simply stated very honestly that I would like to discuss the process for discharge.

"Have you been involuntarily committed?" she asked.

I responded that yes, I had been.

"Then it is up to your physician, and there is no reason for us to meet."

Those forty-five seconds would be the only time I would get with my assigned social worker during my six-day stay.

The dinner bell rang at four o'clock. Again, I ate in the unit, as I had not yet received my hall pass to the cafeteria. Following the meal, I had my first appointment with my inpatient psychiatrist, sometime between five and six o'clock, a staggering sixty-six hours since *any* certified mental health professional laid their eyes on me. I wish I'd been more familiar with mental health law at the time, since per North Carolina law, patients involuntarily committed are to be reassessed within twenty-four hours. I could only imagine how this broken system had affected many patients in the past.

My inpatient psychiatrist had a bustling private practice in addition to his duties at Holy Hell. It came as no surprise that my time with him was *no more* than five to ten minutes. We discussed my marital issues and the lack of trust, my past lies about cigarettes, and drinking too much at a business function years ago. He seemed to be more interested in my line of work, as he was a spokesperson for a product that I once sold for a former company. He mentioned the need to have someone assess the situation at home, since Erin had reported that she and our daughter were afraid of me at times. But as God is my witness, there is no way he spent enough time with me to genuinely gain any appreciable context. In mere minutes, he was able to determine that I was experiencing severe anxiety or panic and that major depression was present. He also found that suicidal ideas and intent were present but that I "convincingly denied suicidal plans" per notes that were pulled directly from my medical record. He never discussed his assessment of me during our brief interactions.

All of this in less than ten minutes.

If I had major depression, why was I not started on an antidepressant? Why wouldn't he have spent more time with me? Why wouldn't I have shown any signs of this until now? These were all questions that soon ran through my head. In the most typical fashion, the only change he made was to add more medications. "All you are on is 25 milligrams of Lamictal? That is a very low dose. I am going to start you on an antipsychotic as well."

Besides, without any further time of day given to me, he recommended that my social worker assess the situation on the home front with Erin due to the allegations that she and Katie were fearful of me.

Day turned to night, and the little suitcase that Erin had brought me earlier that day arrived in my room. They had held it up until this point so someone could inspect the contents. My contents, my belongings, *my* life.

Inside the bag, I found not only my clothes but pictures of the kids when they were younger and a picture of Erin and me. She'd also included a prayer book that her grandmother had given her years earlier, along with the most beautiful letter she had ever written to me. I sat in my room staring at the pictures and read her message repeatedly. Staring my children in the eyes through images and only hearing my wife's voice through her writing left me unimaginably hurt and tormented. I can't say I bawled because nearly all emotion had left me at this point, but the tears I had left streamed down my face onto the sleeves of my oversized shirt.

Unfortunately, the letter is long gone, so I am unable to share it word for word, but the gist of it was how much she loved me. One part I do specifically remember read, "I don't ever want to see you as emotionally lost as you were those three days in the hospital." She then went on to tell me that a song that used to remind her of her mother now reminded her of me. She closed the letter by stating in all caps, "I LOVE YOU DANIEL"

She gave me a little sense of hope that everything was going to be all right. How could we not be? She still loved me, right?

That evening, I got to know my first roommate a little bit. He was twenty-eight and had a three-year-old daughter. I shared the pictures of Erin and our kids as we briefly discussed how we ended up in here together. He had made multiple attempts to take his own life over the years, and in his most recent effort, he had tried to kill himself with an overdose of cough syrup. Again referencing the eye-opening portion of the journey, I did not think that was possible but if you drink enough, it's possible that it could kill you. He educated me about the hallucinogenic properties cough syrup can have and the five bottles he consumed. Although he didn't feel ready to go home, he was scheduled to be discharged the following day. Like so many other patients I came to know, he did not feel that he'd gotten the help he needed. It was all about managing the medications without any regard paid to actual therapy. One of the last things we talked about was the fact that his wife had recently reached her breaking point with him; she took their daughter and moved away. It made me sick to my stomach, as my worst nightmare seemed to be playing out right in front of me. However, at this point, I was thankful that my wife was willing to stand by me as we worked through this "watermelon."

Friday morning arrived after another sleep-deprived night, even though I'd taken an antipsychotic supposedly loaded with sedative properties. My hall pass to go to the cafeteria arrived. Given what felt like mental solitary confinement over the last few days, it was nice to be able to get off the unit and go for a little walk as I was entering day five of being locked up. Like schoolchildren, we walked single file, but once we arrived in the cafeteria, we had to wait for the other group from another unit to leave. The food was awful, but as my father would always tell us, "I am eating for the hunger that will come." After twenty minutes to eat, it was back upstairs for the same old routine of "Do you want to kill yourself? Do you want to hurt anyone?" I made several futile attempts to connect my social worker with Erin to see what was going on and how things were at home. I also called Erin a few times to have her try and connect with my social worker before my Friday night visit with my psychiatrist.

The brightest news was that Anthony and Al were supposed to be coming later on in the day. Anthony's wife, Jackie, was the former assistant director of mental health for a state in the northeast, and she had prepared Anthony with the questions he needed to ask. Al, Anthony, Jackie, and Jane had some real concerns about what was going on with Erin and me in Wilmington. They wanted answers and wanted them fast. Friday was not a typical day for visitors, but that did not deter my family. They made arrangements to meet with my assigned social worker at one o'clock—the same social worker that had utterly dismissed me and left me hanging on more than one occasion. Phone records validate that Al and Anthony had multiple communications with Erin during this time and kept her informed of their plans. They invited her to be a part of their meeting with the social worker as they figured she would have some valuable input.

Erin had some "errands to run."

These errands, I later discovered through checking our marital accounts, included shopping at Victoria's Secret and Urban Outfitter, opening up a new bank account and grabbing copies of police reports. Even now, I wonder how things would have been in reversed roles, Erin was locked up, Doris and Erin's "Big Bro" came to town, and I declined their invite to attend the same type of meeting.

The purpose of the meeting with the social worker was primarily to determine why I was involuntarily committed and to uncover any potential steps to expedite my discharge. Get me back home, back to my real life. Anthony had prepared questions on his iPad, providing a convenient way to record the conversation with Ms. Dismissive. North Carolina is a single-consent state, so they did not need her permission to record the conversation. She was very clear that I must have had a plan to commit suicide; otherwise, there was no other reason I would have been involuntarily committed. I had *never* had an actual plan, as stated in *both* my hospital and Holy Hell records.

I visited with Al and Anthony that afternoon essentially free from any supervision. I could tell by the looks on their faces that they were not only concerned for their brother's health and marriage but were pissed at how the system was handling this. They were not missing what I would continue to overlook for a long time: Erin had put me in there!

During my second session with the inpatient psychiatrist, he was in a great mood, and we even laughed about a few things. We briefly revisited the accusations of infidelity that Erin had been hammering me with for the last six years and he closed the session by stating, "You have an elephant shitting in the corner of your marriage. If you have not been caught with your pants down, then why do you continue to tolerate this?"

It was the smartest thing he had yet to say to me! Why *did* I continue to tolerate all of this nonsense? I still don't have a rational answer to that question just as I don't have a clue as to why he, once again, felt the need to ramp up my medications after that meeting that seemed to go so well. It continued to feel like a lose/lose situation for me.

The fear I experienced following my admission amplified times one hundred on Friday evening when a new patient arrived from another unit because he had gotten into a fight. We now had *two* combative patients on our unit. I thought of him as Vanilla Ice because he wore a ball cap tilted to the side, identical to the real-life version, and would bounce around on his toes throughout the whole unit singing rap songs all day long—my gosh, was it horrible. He was one of the regulars I referred to earlier. He was so stinkin' proud of the cell phone he smuggled in by modifying his sneakers. He had cut out the foam underneath the insert and placed it in there. He had hidden the phone and a few half-smoked cigars. My immediate thought was that if he had gotten this shit in here, there was a decent chance that he could have smuggled in a small knife or some other type of instrument that could be harmful. Wax a chump like a candle indeed.

In addition to that, Friday is when the sexual harassment began. A more substantial version of what looked like Jordan Peele from the *Key and Peele* series began his overtures while sitting on the nasty couch in the common area.

"Hey, Danny, why don't you come over and cuddle with me?"

"Jordan" was a regular. He had recently returned after another failed attempt to take his own life—two short weeks after his last discharge.

This very same day my new roommate arrived. He was a homeless man I'd encountered about a year before. I had taken Katie to cheer practice one Saturday, and as I often did while she was practicing, ran a few errands. While pumping gas, I glanced in the direction of the homeless fellow standing outside, and he said hello quite angrily with his middle finger.

Fortunately for me, even though he'd been assigned as my roommate, he decided not to sleep in the room. Instead, he slept in the small common area behind the couch. Yes, not *on* the sofa, but *behind* it. However, he did make his way to my room around 3 a.m. to urinate on the floor beside my bed—that night and every damn night thereafter.

The Lord was indeed testing my patience.

The rooster crowed at 5:30 a.m. Saturday morning. As I stepped out of bed, I was happy to realize I'd avoided the "golden shower" puddle, although I was exhausted, as usual, from lack of consistent sleep. To make matters even more stressful, as we lined up for breakfast a few guys taunted my new roommate.

Standing in the middle of the common area, they pointed at him behind the couch. "Get this motherfucker a shower! He smells like ass and ketchup!"

Yes, "ass and ketchup," a combo I never quite thought I'd hear together. To make matters worse, that night we discovered that our unit was crawling with bedbugs. I don't think we ever found the underlying cause of it, but most of the other occupants, myself included, concluded that they came from a young man we called "James" after James Franco. No kidding, we had some Hollywood look-a-like conspiracy going on. Not to worry, though, we had the oh-so-gracious Erin handle the situation by calling the North Carolina Department of Health and Human Services.

Al and Anthony were still in town, and I was delighted I'd get to see them again during visitation. Erin was coming in as well to meet with the weekend social work staff and me to talk about what was going on. I was excited to be able to see her, since I had not seen her since my arrival. I was looking forward to holding her hand, to looking her in the eye with all the love that I thought we still shared.

Before visitation, the social worker Erin and I would meet with later that day attempted to lead a session on conflict resolution. It was the first time in a long time that I laughed aloud, and it sure felt right. The situation, of course, was not funny, but the irony brought me great enjoyment.

Three minutes into the session, our friend Vanilla Ice and another individual got into it in a nearby common area. At first, it was a verbal exchange across the room with f-bombs flying left and right, but before one could sing "Ice, Ice, Baby," they collided in the middle of the room with fists of fury. Although a team of technicians quickly broke it up, I found it alarming that there were no security personnel in the facility. My alarm didn't prevent me from seeing the humor, though.

To get to our meeting, Erin had to walk through the unit. She got a glimpse of where I was living and met a couple of my new friends. As it had been with me, it was an eye-opener for her. As we walked through the unit, she whispered to me, "We have to get you out of here!"

*No kidding*, I thought.

Our meeting with the social worker was successful. He was going to speak with the psychiatrist working the weekend shift to see what he could do to get me discharged. Katie's sixteenth birthday was on Sunday, and I was praying with all of my strength that I could get home by then. There is no way I could miss that, especially not because I was in a damn psychiatric hospital.

Following our meeting, Erin and I joined Al and Anthony for visitation hours. My ample gray stubble was in full effect, making me look like shit. I couldn't have cared less; it was just a blessing to be with my brothers and to hold Erin's hand across the table. I was confident things were going to be okay if I could get out.

But I did not go home on Saturday, and I ended up missing my daughter's sixteenth birthday.

I spoke to the weekend psychiatrist and asked him what had happened. He told me he'd spoken to my attending physician about my inappropriate admission, but the doctor said he wanted to see me on Monday.

I was devastated. However, as I would come to discover, Erin was practically giddy.

To make my day complete, the Department of Health and Human Services showed up in full force to fumigate the bedbugs, resulting in our move to the little gymnasium where we spent five hours bunking with the unit staff. I tried to pass the time by shooting a few buckets with a half-inflated basketball but gave up on that in a hurry before they attempted to go full nursing home on us: Bingo for everybody! That ended as quickly as it started due to another disagreement, this time between two females. My new admirer continued his sexual innuendos, letting me know what he wanted to do to me with his fingers.

"Hey, Danny, if I can bring you pleasure with one finger, imagine what I can do to you with five!" (I have cleaned up the version of what he actually said to me.)

"You don't even know how to respond to that do you, Danny?" he added.

"You are right. I don't!" *How many more days are they going to keep me here?*

Sunday night bedtime arrived after missing Katie's sixteenth birthday. My mind was obsessed with what my kids were thinking. I missed not seeing and talking to them. The increased dose of my antipsychotic began taking effect, and I was just flat-out tired. I couldn't take any more of pacing the halls, looking out windows, trying to imagine walking freely down the street, so I worked as hard as I could to fall asleep.

About 9 p.m., one of my unit mates knocked on my door to let me know that my wife was on the phone.

For about two seconds, I considered telling him that I did not want to talk to her. But I relented and got out of bed to take her call on the pay phone, yes, the pay phone. I said hello.

Erin chuckled. "I don't know when you are getting out of there!"

I almost hung up on her. "I have been locked up in a psychiatric hospital for seven days," I said, "and you are laughing in my face."

"It is just my anxiety, Danny," she shot back.

Our conversation was short-lived, and there was zero mention of Katie's birthday. It was what seemed typical these days, brief civility followed by bickering. I regretted not calling Katie earlier in the day, but I could not stomach the thought of talking to her through Holy Hell's pay phone while she was celebrating another year of life without me. Not believing my conversation with Erin, I returned to my room. As it turned out, that was just another rehearsal for Erin . . . there would be many more.

Nearly asleep, I awoke to someone playing the piano and singing. I thought I was dreaming, but once again got out of bed to see what was going on. There was a "gently used" upright piano in the common area, and my *roommate* was playing it and singing like a songbird! Like an ab-so-lute songbird. He was outstanding, but even though I applauded him and praised his performance, he delivered his usual encore later that evening with a steady stream of piss whizzing by my head. The staff had yet to address it.

Upon awaking Monday, my first thought was how much I looked forward to my evening appointment with my psychiatrist. At breakfast, I had a brief, hopeful moment that I was getting out when a staff member approached me offering me a packet of information on outpatient services. "You qualify for our outpatient program once you are discharged," the staffer said, but I now know that was just another way of saying, "You have insurance, and we would like some more of that money, please."

Today was pet peeve day. This "therapy" session intended to address our pet peeves, and I had never laughed so hard in my life. We all wrote our pet peeves on slips of paper and placed them in a plastic bowl, which we passed around the room. As the bowl traveled from person to person, you reached in to grab a slip to read. A handful of regulars refused to participate and simply passed the bowl along. When it stopped on a rather mousy young woman, the fun started. She pulled out the slip of paper and began reading, "My pet peeve is people that smack their lips when they are eating food"—she briefly paused and looked around the room— "like they are sucking a cock." The focus of the game was for us to guess who may have written the pet peeve and not a single person got that one right. It turned out to be the quietest person on the unit. That's what made it so damn funny.

I had gotten to know him a little bit. He had voluntarily checked himself in after he tried to take his own life. He was leaving the next day, though, still suicidal. My conversation with him was typical. I remember him very, very clearly saying to me, "I'm not sure why I checked myself in here. I haven't received any help at all."

I was growing impatient trying to get out of there to get back to my life and my kids and my home. I wanted to shower without the fear of sexual assault. I'd had enough of my new best friend Daniel's plans for when he got out. "The FBI is going to take me to Arby's, and *then* I am going to Myrtle Beach to get high and get my guns." I'd had enough of someone abruptly cutting off our conversation to smash their head on the nearest wall until it bled. My heart was breaking for the young suicidal kids, enrolled in college and concerned about missing exams. I'd had enough of the regulars abusing the young women sexually and verbally. I wanted my life back. I wanted nothing more than to return to the first seventeen years that Erin and I had had together with our beautiful children.

Monday evening finally arrived and my psychiatrist, then of all times, was not so friendly anymore. He was pissed that he received a call over the weekend inquiring about my discharge.

"I told you that I would meet with you on Monday to discuss your discharge. I know the traits of the people in your line of work. You are all manipulators and spinners. You're salespeople." Down the road, I would hear this line repeatedly from Erin verbally and Doris (via text). To be blunt, I probably should have stood up for myself at that moment, but recognized he controlled my future. I don't recall much of our five-minute meeting beyond the only thing I needed and wanted to hear:

"There will be documents for you to sign tomorrow morning, and they are legally binding." I did not give a shit as to what that meant.

I was finally going home.

Though I signed the discharge papers at 8:09 a.m. the following morning, I would not be "paroled" until after 2 p.m. I sat in the common area with my bedbug-infested clothes packed in the little suitcase Erin had brought me. I did not go to breakfast or lunch, and I sat about as close as I possibly could to the door in my unit. I called Erin multiple times to keep her updated on when she could pick me up.

The social workers completed the necessary mounds of paperwork, and I was free to walk out of the unit. Before leaving, the lovely woman at the desk on the ward remarked to me, "I don't want to see you back here. *She loves you.*"

If I could track her down, I would ask how in the heck she defines love.

I made my way to the lobby and there she was. Maybe it was my med cocktail kicking in, but though she looked exhausted, she was as beautiful as the first time that I saw her. I was still carrying the guilt of all that I had put her, Billy, and Katie through.

Nine days.

I spent nine days in psychiatric lockup in what felt like the most extended, most depressing 216 hours of my life.

But I didn't care. I was finally going home.

I will be forever grateful to Al and Anthony for interrupting their lives and making the trip to Wilmington, despite my insisting that they need not come. I shouldn't have worried. They later let me know they were able to turn it into a bit of a boys' trip. I was glad that they could unwind a little. A local watering hole was on the receiving end of an "Irish Goodbye." They left the establishment without paying and inquired with each other on the way out the door as to who paid the bill. Neither one did!

# CHAPTER 7
## *Welcome Home*

Sometimes God calms the storm, and sometimes he lets
the storm rage, and He calms you. —*Nicky Gumbel*

Stepping out of Holy Hell's front door a little after 2 p.m., I looked up
to the beautiful blue sky and thanked the Lord for providing me with the
strength to get through the last nine days. I had a newfound appreciation for
the sun's warmth on my skin and the wind in my face. I cherished the ability
to walk freely to my own car. What I really looked forward to was taking
a real shower without the fear of assault. I was confident I was on the right
side of rock bottom, and that my marriage and our family unit would be
okay. Sadly, the Man above had other plans, and my storm would not only
continue raging, but its intensity would increase dramatically.

Erin wasted no time tearing into me. We weren't even out of the
parking lot.

"Why did you lie to the discharge nurse about having a follow-up appointment with your psychiatrist?" she snapped. "Why did you tell her that
I made an appointment for you?"

"My head's a little messed up right now," I said, my senses humming with the medication cocktail and the brightness of the day. "I don't recall if I told her that you made an appointment or not. Can you cut me a little slack on this one?" I pleaded. "I just wanted to get out of there and was not focused on what was or was not said!"

Arriving home was very emotional for me, my mind immersed in a fog of grateful disbelief. Before walking through the front door, I threw out the clothes, sneakers, and even the suitcase I had at Holy Hell. It wouldn't have mattered if the clothes still fit; I was more concerned about bringing bedbugs into our home.

In my absence, Katie had turned sixteen and earned her learner's permit (moments I missed that eat at me to this day). Since she was not driving solo yet, Erin still had to pick her up from school. I could not wait to get rid of my itchy gray beard, so I went straight to the bathroom for a much-anticipated shave and a shower. I could barely look at myself in the mirror. I was thin, looked old, and could not wrap my head around all that had just happened. "But I am home now, and all is going to get better," I kept telling myself.

I sat in the shower as the hot water washed over me. It was so beautiful to have a bar of soap and shampoo that did not come out of a little plastic packet. There were many days in Holy Hell that I mistakenly washed my hair with toothpaste and brushed my teeth with soap, since the packets they provided in our plastic pail all looked the same. The simple things that I used to take for granted now meant so much!

It was a long drive to Katie's school, so Erin and Katie had not yet arrived home. I headed upstairs to my office to begin the daunting task of clearing out my work e-mail. At this point, I had been away from work for seven business days, and I dreaded turning on the computer. As it booted up, I glanced to my right and noticed something sitting on my fax machine. What do you know? It was a copy of the Wilmington police report from their September 13 visit to our home. The fax arrived on September 19, the day that Erin was too busy to join Al and Anthony during their visit to Holy Hell. I was not upset but thought it was insensitive of Erin to leave this on my fax machine. It came in on the nineteenth, so why was it still sitting there on September 23? I hope you are starting to appreciate Erin's knack for emotional torment. She inherited this skill from her mother, Doris. I called Erin and very calmly asked her about the police report.

"Oh, I am sorry," she said. "You told me you were going to get a copy of this report, so I decided that I should probably get a copy too."

Sitting downstairs when Katie arrived home from school, I greeted her in the hallway with a hug. I could sense from the look on her face that she was leery of me. I don't blame her, as I am sure she did not know what to make of the events of the past week. I imagine Mom had filled her head with all sorts of God-knows-what about me. It was great to sleep that night in my bed, a real bed. That is until the nightmares and night sweats woke me up.

September 24, 2014, was my first full day of freedom from Holy Hell. I had a follow-up appointment with my psychiatrist, and Erin was compassionate enough to join me. We discussed the events that had unfolded the prior week but did not address the phone call that Erin had made to his office on September 13, the night she called the cops on me. The results from my look-back drug test performed on September 15 were not back yet. Erin inquired with my doc about my lies.

"Are Danny's lies part of having bipolar?" she asked.

"No, they are unrelated," my doc responded.

At this point, I was not aware of the contents of the letter that Erin had written to my psychiatrist and my family practitioner on Sunday, September 14, the day after she called the cops on me.

My first full day home after the worst nine days of my life and my wife was barely around. I was anxious and afraid to be alone. I would later hear about the multiple times that I called her that day. Her solution for my anxiety was to take clonazepam (a "downer") that I had been prescribed to help me sleep. I used this medication sparingly. Later that evening, we walked our dogs around the neighborhood, and although not a very long walk, I had to sit down halfway into it. I felt like I was walking in cement.

The increased dose of my antipsychotic was kicking in.

I decided that night that I was going to step myself off this poison. Erin and my psychiatrist were supportive of this decision. Besides, I never accepted my bipolar diagnosis. Especially after living with folks with real mental issues for nine days. However, I was willing to explore the possibility that I might have a mood issue resulting from what was occurring with me physically. I was ready to do whatever I could for the sake of my family and my marriage.

(Oh, by the way, on this very day, I supposedly signed a form giving Erin power of attorney over my IRA. I did not remember doing this! IRAs and our future retirement were not top of mind for me while in Holy Hell. Who was the manipulator and spinner?)

The subtle accusations that began less than five minutes after my Holy Hell discharge increased dramatically just two days after my homecoming. I discussed with Erin my desire to contact an attorney because I felt like my civil rights were violated by not being re-evaluated after twenty-four hours following my involuntary commitment. After all, it was the law in North Carolina. She suggested that I contact her cousin Ricky's wife, an attorney in Ohio. I asked her why she did not reach out to her for divorce advice. "I needed someone in North Carolina," she replied.

"I do as well," I countered. As I was not fond of everybody knowing our business, I then asked her how often she is talking to him or her.

"I have talked and texted with them." She then asked me, and I kid you not, "How did you know that I was talking to my cousin Rick?"

I snorted, "BECAUSE, you just told me that you were talking and texting with them!"

Erin got irate and accused me of going into her phone records and reviewing the numbers she was calling and texting. I was the primary account holder for our family plan, and I certainly could have done this, but I did not. Boy, the list of things I wish I had done sooner.

This little argument would carry over into the next day. Our son arrived home early in the afternoon from college so we could all go watch Katie cheer at her football game. Erin had gone into our phone account, started scrutinizing certain numbers, especially how often I had talked to Mila. She also asked about a few other numbers. I assured her that there was absolutely nothing going on with Mila. She let it go, and as she was getting into the shower, she remarked, "I just want to get along."

A few hours went by, and she was back at it with the phone number interrogations. As I was pulling out of the driveway, with Billy in the back seat, she leaned over to me. "I just did that this afternoon to piss you off!"

I emotionally shut down and ignored her the rest of the evening at Katie's football game. *I just got out of a psychiatric facility,* I thought, *and you are doing things to piss me off?*

We returned home from the game. I walked into our bathroom, and Erin said as she sat on the throne, "What did I do now?"

"Are you fucking serious?" I responded.

September 29, 2014, six days post–Holy Hell, I met with an attorney. I needed to reassess my perception of the right side of rock bottom!

I took an additional eight days off work in an attempt to collect myself and get my mind right. I planned to return to work Monday, October 6, and Erin was doing all she could to ensure that my mind wasn't right. She kept count of my pills, calling me with accusations of medication noncompliance. She would either text or call Big Bro to report the same. I counted my pills; I was taking them every day.

I was confident that my civil rights had been violated, so I requested copies of my medical records from both the first hospital (where I spent my first three days) and from Holy Hell. Immediately upon receipt of the documents, Erin and I thoroughly reviewed them. You know, openness and transparency! We highlighted multiple inaccuracies in both sets of records. One collection of documents stated that my mother had bipolar! Where did they get this misinformation? Erin? It also reported that I was drinking a half a pint a day. I rarely drink hard liquor. Another part of the record stated that I was not drinking every day and therefore did not need the alcohol withdrawal protocol. So which is it? Regardless, though, without a doubt, by far the most incredible inaccuracy was as follows, courtesy of my Holy Hell records which took my storm to a Cat 5:

"The following information was provided by Daniel and accompanying documentation. The patient describes alcohol abuse. Despite self-knowledge of psychological or physical problems, he has continued abusing drugs. The substance has been taken by mouth. This substance has been abused for months. The course of Daniel's use has been episodic with periods of partial or full remission and relapse."

Three paragraphs above that statement, the same medical record stated, "Daniel denies illicit drug use." No shit! "At this point, Daniel has had two comprehensive drug tests, and he is awaiting the results of a 'look-back' DNA drug test."

The results were in for the first two tests, and Danny Boy tested negative for everything!

Saturday, October 4, another beautiful fall day in North Carolina, and Big G was on his way to the house. I'd been the best man in his wedding just six months prior. Big G used to work for me, and we remained friends and have become even closer over the last few years. He was coming over to do some repairs around the house because Erin and I had decided to put it on the market. We had four dogs in the home including two with ravenous appetites, a little Pomeranian named Teddy and a Sheltie named Sadie. Teddy was a connoisseur of the woodwork, and Sadie's palette leaned toward munching on our blinds. Big G is very skilled and had all the right tools to make the necessary repairs. Erin left early that morning to run some errands. Big G arrived at 9:00 a.m., about the time the phone rang.

I answered the phone to Erin yelling at the top of her lungs, "You are a pathological liar, a slimeball, a sleazebag, and we're done!"

I began to shake. "What the hell are you talking about?"

"You modified your medical records from Holy Hell and removed the phrase 'in pill form,'" said Erin.

I ran upstairs to my office, pulled out my records to review them, knowing that I had changed nothing. When I asked Erin how I modified them, her response was, "You scanned them into your computer and changed them."

*We reviewed these records twice together, and she steals a copy to harass me about something that isn't true?* I hung up with her and came downstairs still trembling.

One look and sweet Big G asked, "Is there something we need to talk about?"

It was at this point that Big G and little g found their way into our marital mess. I completely opened up to him about everything, including my nine days in Holy Hell. It was not an easy thing to do with a former employee, but I trusted Big G. I called Doris to express my concern to her regarding her daughter's state of mind. (Big mistake. It would be the last time that I would initiate any phone communication with Doris.)

"Your daughter is losing her mind," I told her. "She is accusing me of modifying my medical records and doing drugs, when I have had two thorough drug tests that were both negative."

Doris's response? "No comment! You two need to separate."

Erin did not come home that day until I texted her that Big G had finished his work. I was no help to him and will be forever grateful to Big G and little g for more than home repair.

I spent the night at a hotel, and it was later that evening that I received a text from Erin. "If you share your medical records from Holy Hell with anyone else, I will have you thrown in jail."

I was not sure of her thought process here. They were my medical records, and I could share them with whoever I wanted.

I returned to the house at six o'clock on Sunday morning, took a shower, and went to church. I went alone. Erin informed me that she'd slept that night with my dresser in front of the bedroom door in case I came home. Was her fear real or part of the story she was building? At this point, I had no clue. All of this occurred less than two weeks after my discharge from Holy Hell.

Monday, October 6, I was back at work. I would be in Charlotte later that day for business, but first had an early-morning appointment with my psychiatrist. Before leaving the house, I submitted another medical record request form to Holy Hell so that Erin could receive a sealed copy proving that I had changed nothing. Request denied! During my appointment with my psychiatrist, I explained what had transpired over the weekend, and I asked him to request a copy of the records so that he could review with Erin. He agreed to do this but failed to mention to me the following letter that he received from Erin that morning. I only became aware of this document further down the road. The letter read as follows:

10/6/2014

Good morning Dr. [psychiatrist],

This is Erin [married name], Dan's wife. My husband has an appointment today at 8:30 and I just want to make sure he gets the right treatment based on what he is telling you because I do indeed want him to get better. This short note is not to accomplish anything else. PLEASE keep this confidential between us. I do remember discussing on our first visit when I was present that you gather information from other sources for helping with a diagnosis for Dan. We just started seeing another marriage counselor last week, and if you need additional information, his number is 555–5555.

I just want to tell you that what we are hearing from Dan at home is that you may not think Dan has bipolar disorder. I don't know what he is telling you about the home conditions. However, the reality is my daughter is afraid and feels unsafe at home due to his anger/rage episodes. Her friends aren't able to come over because of a couple of events. I pride myself on not "bad-mouthing" my husband to my children. They will tell you that, in fact, I tell them the opposite. I tell them not to be rude or inconsiderate to him; he is still your father who loves you very much. She is at a point where she has witnessed too many episodes of anger, and is ready to start a life without him living with us. In one night, in a matter of a couple hours, he can be calm, kind, and civil. He will leave and come back irate, talking and not making much sense. He leaves again for a couple of hours and comes back rational. This is in front of my daughter which is really confusing her and scaring her.

I don't want him to tell you his moods have been better. They haven't. He is denying he has any bipolar type of disorder. I don't know if you read the Holy Hell aftercare treatment plan, but it also stated he needs to see a psychiatrist, psychotherapist (which he said he didn't have to until I found his discharge papers) and marriage counseling. He is opening my mail (found a checking account I opened because of my lawyer's advice), found my daughter's and my pre-packed bags in the car just in case he had another anger episode. Went through my phone, found my private Yahoo account for my lawyer's correspondence.

There are many other situations I can discuss. However, I am writing this letter to you to read BEFORE his appointment today at 8:30 to help him, not hurt him. He may deny moods and say things are going good. However, they are not. We are on the verge of separation due to his CONTINUING lying, anger, and last but most importantly denying he has a mood disorder.

Erin [married name]"

The only accurate statements above are that I did open her mail on one occasion, and I did "find" both her and Katie's pre-packed bags in the trunk of her car. I opened her mail after the arrival of three separate envelopes from the same bank. I was pissed that she did not share that with me. What happened to openness and transparency? I cared not at all that she opened her account, but the reasoning was not logical. She had full access to our marital account, her credit card, and a checking account for her business. Perhaps she wanted me to notice those in the mail. She opened the accounts when I was locked up. I unintentionally found her and Katie's pre-packed bags after using Erin's car to grocery shop. I placed the groceries in the trunk. I did not remove the bags but did ask why she had them in her car.

"Just in case you had another anger episode. The last time I had to run out of the house in my slippers," she quipped.

Over the next several weeks, I would spend many nights on the road on my hands and knees, my head buried in a Marriott bed, praying to God to help me keep it together. I want to be clear that I was not suicidal; I was struggling with all that had happened. The "love letter" I received from Erin while I was in Holy Hell was a distant memory, and I just did not understand what was now occurring. My thoughts turned to Billy, Katie, and the responsibilities that I had for them. I had a lot to live for but prayed for God's assurance that I would get through this. Billy had continued to stand by me, but I had all but lost Katie. She was still at home and had been played and manipulated by Erin for the last six months. I thought about my parents, Al, Jane, and my other brothers and sisters and their respective families. At this point, though, only Al, Jane, Anthony, and Jackie knew what was going on. They honored my request to keep the details of my situation between us for the time being. They personify what it means to exude character.

Erin was busy working my sister-in-law and little g (Big G's wife). At lunch with little g, she shared the whole drama, including her issues "down there"—green discharge and all.

Looking back, I am not sure how I kept my sanity. I had once been certain Erin's fibromyalgia, and her past stroke-like events were causing her some significant paranoia and cognitive impairment.

Accusations of transferring money to Al from our marital account began. Many nights as I lay in bed, she would shine a flashlight in my eyes and tell me I looked stoned. Perhaps she wanted me to reminisce about my nights in Holy Hell. I started removing myself from any situation where we argued. As you can imagine, this resulted in us rarely seeing each other in our own home.

One particularly entertaining jab happened after I was gone twenty or twenty-five minutes. Upon my return, Erin blurted, "You look stoned! Your eyes are squinty like Ernie or Bert from Sesame Street. Whichever one has the squinty eyes." I'd gotten to the point that my only reaction was to shake my head and laugh. I did not get angry or overreact. "Ernie or Bert?" You can't make this stuff up!

Erin's infidelity accusations were taking a back seat to drug allegations. She disregarded my clean medical records from Holy Hell, focusing more on my continued weight loss. I can only imagine the conversations between Doris and Erin regarding my medical records. The results finally came back from the look-back test and, of course, I was negative yet again.

My private psychiatrist also spoke at length with my inpatient psychiatrist at Holy Hell regarding the drug abuse remarks in the medical record. His comment to my outpatient doc was, "He was not admitted for a drug issue, and there is nothing in his discharge summary about it either so just disregard it." He was willing to meet with Erin about the record and her allegations that I modified my medical records, yet she never accepted the offer.

"I called the nursing director at Holy Hell, and she said that if that statement is in your medical records, it must be true," stated Erin. I would never receive an apology from Erin whenever I would address her allegations with factual proof. It exhausted me, countering all her lies and paranoid behavior.

Welcome home, Danny!

On the job front, things continued to go well. By the grace of God, I was able to keep it together, in spite of Erin's continued attempts to derail me. In mid-October, I was in Marietta, Georgia, conducting training for about 150 people. About an hour before my presentation began, I got a call from Erin that I should expect an e-mail from her attorney regarding separation and mediation. I had no idea that this was coming, as we never discussed it.

We had a long conversation later that night and decided we would continue to work on our marriage. Another confusing dose of "I hate you, don't leave me."

There was growing concern about my health among my work colleagues as they were aware that I had been in the hospital for nine days in September. I informed a few folks about some of my blood work issues. I purchased a few books on bipolar disorder, and I read them cover to cover. The more educated I became, the more I realized that I did not have bipolar, and my outpatient psychiatrist began to backpedal on his diagnosis. "I believe you have a unique form of bipolar with irritability and agitation." Why ever would I have a reason to be irritated and agitated? LOL!

I applied for a promotion to a new position and began preparing for those interviews. About the only thing I looked forward to in November *were* the interviews. Doris was coming to town for Thanksgiving, and I had no idea what to expect. I had not talked to her in months and was not sure what her approach with me would be after all the September drama. It was also in November that I took out a $4,000 loan from my 401K to begin to pay down Erin's mounting charges from her first attorney. I asked my lawyer to return my retainer fee and used that money to pay Erin's credit card bills. I had only one live meeting with my attorney and exchanged a few e-mails, so my expenses had not been that great. Yet! Erin never requested her retainer fee back, but then again, there was probably not much left, as her e-mail traffic to her attorneys rivaled Trump's tweeting frequency. I never pressed Erin but did inquire, very nicely, if she was going to request the remaining funds back and Erin chided, "I am going to keep it with her in case you have another episode."

Doris arrived in town and naturally stayed in our home. Over the course of twenty-one years, she was welcomed into our house many times, and many happy memories followed. This time, not so much. Brevity keeps me from including them all, but I hope you enjoy some of my faves.

Not-so-happy memory #1: As we sat around our kitchen table, Doris reached her hand across it, put it on top of mine, and asked, in front of her grandchildren, "How are your pills working for you, Danny?" Nice.

Not-so-happy memory #2: Erin would occasionally remark to me that she was feeling like my time in Holy Hell was her fault. Her "struggle" with these emotions was a topic of discussion in therapy with Doris present. Upon their return home, Doris's demeanor would be entirely different.

Our conversation in the laundry room, more like a lecture, began. "Danny, the way you are feeling emotionally and mentally has nothing to do with your family. You have a problem, and you need to get educated about it and own it."

At least it was not another death threat, but this time I did respond. "I have read two books about bipolar, and the more I read, the more I question the diagnosis. It is unheard of for somebody over the age of forty to be diagnosed with bipolar without any history of problems with depression or mania."

She did not like that response. "See what I mean? You are questioning it. You need to own it!"

Geez.

Not-so-happy memory #3: During another chat, I reminded her of something Katie had said to me: "Dad, you and Mom used to be like teenagers in love." Doris's saccharine response was, "The keyword is *used to be.*" *Thanks, Mom.*

Not-so-happy memory #4: Innuendos were flying the entire visit about my drug use as Doris and Erin compared pictures of me on their phones from last year's Thanksgiving and the present one. They did this as they sat in the back seat of the car with Katie. Yes, I had lost about forty pounds at this point, with no explanation.

Not-so-happy memory #5: Thanksgiving dinner was awkward. Katie would later refer to it as us being a fake family. As it turns out, she was right. Erin no longer wanted anything to do with our family unit. She wanted me out and fueled that same sentiment with our daughter.

It was that Thanksgiving that Erin was going to be the strong and independent Erin again. I usually do the mashed potatoes, and they always get raves, but this year Erin wanted to do the potatoes. No problem. Mash the potatoes.

We had a few guests over, and Doris had to mock me in front of the guests in our home. She smarmily made fun of my dishwasher and me. "Nobody gets near Danny's dishwasher."

I attempted to address these comments with Doris as she stood on the other side of the counter rubbing her hands across the granite, a weird habit she had. I attempted to explain to her that as a young child my father had a particular way that he liked the dishwasher organized. We had a huge family, and he liked to maximize every inch of space in the dishwasher. As kids, we had weekly chores. In a large family, everybody pulls their weight.

Doris cut me off. "No need to explain. You like to be in control. I recognize how difficult it was for you to let Erin mash the potatoes tonight."

I called Holy Hell to see if they had any rooms for the night! Just kidding, of course!

Thanks for the (not so happy) memories.

Moving on! Early December of 2014, I had a follow-up appointment with my family practitioner regarding the ongoing weight issues and continued abnormal blood work. They checked me for all sorts of things, including hepatitis B and hepatitis C, in an attempt to figure out why my white blood cell (WBC) count continued increasing and my weight continued to drop. Alarmingly, a couple of my liver enzymes as well as my creatine phosphokinase (CPK) were way off. Elevations of CPK are common following a heart attack, any traumatic muscle injury, or a brain injury. I would also learn that it is a marker for a muscle-wasting disease. Nevertheless, I was hoping that they would find out what was going on, as my concern was consuming me.

I electronically received the results of the multitude of tests within a few days. I was shocked to see that they had done an HIV test. I was not concerned, as I had not been with anybody but Erin in the last twenty-four years. My results for HIV and hepatitis C and B were all negative. The other enzymes were still way off, and I would have those retested in a few weeks.

Erin was well aware of the appointment, and she arrived home minutes after I had reviewed my results. I pulled up my electronic records and discussed the results with her. She went ballistic.

"Why did they test you for HIV? After twenty-two years of marriage, you are being tested for AIDS?"

Never mind the fact that I tested negative—her only concern was that the test occurred. I'd not been made aware that they were testing me for HIV, and in North Carolina, and probably every other state, either written or verbal consent is required. I did not know this, but Erin educated me after she made a few phone calls. She was adamant that I lied about not providing consent. I did not care, nor was I concerned about having HIV.

Immediately, I sent an e-mail to my family practitioner to get clarity on his rationale and the reason for the lack of consent. He responded, "I apologize for the miscommunication. As per our telephone conversation, my intention for checking HepB/C and HIV was simply to rule out other causes of mildly chronically elevated liver enzymes and weight loss. Take care."

It did not satisfy Erin, as she deemed the communication "too gray." Erin would shortly be off to her OB/GYN to be tested. I had no problem with this. She supposedly tested negative, but she never shared her actual documented results with me. Her "sharing" with me was verbal only.

"I will need to get retested in six months," she told me, "as it is a policy for my OB/GYN." My family practitioner stated that all I needed was one test, unless I was concerned about exposure. I came very close to calling her OB/GYN to clear my name and to let him know that I had not been cheating on my wife. I had his number all cued up on my phone but never made the call. I informed Erin of this fact, and she went off.

"Don't you *dare* call my doctor! That would be a HIPAA violation, and he thinks the whole situation is so sad. You have bipolar, and I have had to get cooties tested in the past."

While attending an upcoming conference in California in mid-December, I would have my third and final interview for the promotion. It was a very competitive process, and I felt blessed and privileged to have made it to the final round. Erin was well aware of this and knew the specific time that I would be interviewing. She called me thirty minutes before my interview, as I was making my final prep, to inform me that "separation may benefit us both." Perhaps this was advice from Doris after the whole HIV situation.

Once again, God blessed me with the strength to hold it together, and the interview went very well. I received the promotion and a new position!

December 30, just a few more days before we could put this year in the rearview mirror. Billy was still home on Christmas break during his soph- omore year in college, and he graciously agreed to take Katie skiing with him and his then-girlfriend. They were going to make a day trip to Boone, North Carolina. As Erin sat in the bathtub, she surprisingly asked me if I wanted to "have a night." That is how she often referred to our being "to- gether." I was surprised because it was just thirteen days earlier that she was so concerned about the whole HIV situation. It was emotionally confusing to me, but it had been over four months since we were intimate with each other, so I thought, *What the hell. Why not?* We enjoyed a few beers, as it was okay with her for Danny to drink when he was not drinking "out of anger."

Our time together progressed and quickly became the angriest and most aggressive sex that, hopefully, I will ever experience. The anger and aggression were entirely on Erin's part, and she was very descriptive with what she wanted to do to me. Suffice it to say she made no bones about wanting to be the aggressor. I did not object, and she essentially assaulted me. It *had* been a while, and, in the excitement of the moment, it was a crazy but quick session, if you know what I mean. Erin flew out of bed, mocked my performance, and began berating me. I apologized for my performance but said it was terrific. I did ask her why she was so aggressive and why she seemed so angry. "I am angry at you because you think you are holier than thou now that you are seeing a psychiatrist. I have been seeing a psychiatrist since I was six years old." I remained extremely calm and did not overreact as I was learning a little something from my psychiatrist.

"I am just trying to see your perspective in this whole mess, Erin!" I said. I let it go after that and made my way into the bathroom. As I passed the bathroom mirror, I noticed blood running down the left side of my face. I am not sure what she used to cut me. Perhaps it was a wedding ring or an earring. She was that aggressive.

We did not make love that night. I believe it was Erin's first attempt at making evol.

# CHAPTER 8
## *God, Your Husband, Your Family*

Love and honesty are the things that make a good wife and mother.
—*Jada Pinkett Smith*

As the calendar flipped to the new year, I was hoping for new beginnings for Erin and me. I prayed for it! Professionally, I welcomed the challenges my new position would pose. The year included my own health scare, additional medical issues for Erin and, if it was even fathomable, greater emotional turmoil and confusion in our marriage. My relationship with Katie would only get worse, and I would feel like a guest in my own home.

At the start of the year, I was due to be in Chicago for my company's annual meeting. However, I received a call from my family practitioner that my latest blood work results were not good and that I needed to see an oncologist immediately. There was an alarming elevation in my white blood cell count. Erin was there by my side, not so much to support her husband but to take advantage of an opportunity to inform my oncologist of my bipolar diagnosis. As the doc reviewed my medication list, I mentioned my 100-milligram daily Lamictal dose for mood and anxiety. Erin quickly elaborated, "He has bipolar II."

Billy celebrated his twentieth birthday in January, so Erin and I made a trip to Charlotte to take him, his girlfriend, and some of his roommates out to a lunch celebration. On the three-and-a-half-hour ride, Erin virtually ignored me. Her face rarely left her phone, as she was wholly absorbed in LinkedIn and texting (probably with Doris, but God only knows who else).

We arrived at Billy's apartment, kicking off our stay with his friends opening gifts and getting caught up. As we sat around their kitchen table, Erin used the opportunity to preach to the young men, passionately expounding, "Trust is the foundation of any relationship and marriage." As many times as I had heard this lecture in the past several years, I was beyond tired of it. I contributed a bit of my own fatherly wisdom: "Forgiveness is also essential in a relationship and marriage." It was my sentiment that Erin's forgiveness was lacking for my lies regarding drinking too much in New Orleans and my deception with smoking.

Late January, I was working in our corporate office and got caught in a nor'easter reminiscent of my childhood in Pittsburgh. Following an early dinner with my new boss, I returned to the hotel at about 7:30. He was staying in the room right next door, so before calling Erin, I turned on the TV. Upon answering the phone, she inquired about the noise. I told her it was the TV and explained that I had it on because I was not sure how our conversation might go. I did not want my new boss to hear us arguing.

I turned the TV down, and Erin quickly said, "It is quiet now, you must have stepped away."

"I did not step away; I turned the TV down."

We talked briefly, and afterward, I called Katie on her cell phone to say goodnight. I hung up with Katie and the phone in my room rang.

It was Erin, checking up on me. "It is okay if you want to be down in the bar having a beer, Danny."

Resigned, I replied, "I know it is okay, but it is the Springhill Suites and they don't have a bar. I have been in my room, and if I tell you I am in my room, I would like for you to believe me."

Her lack of trust and constant questioning were frustrating; her mental badgering was exhausting. I still grimace as I relive all of her passive aggressiveness. It once made me tremble. She was indeed trying to drive me insane. You nailed it, Dr. Psychiatrist! I *was* irritated and agitated!

Erin had suffered from chronic constipation for the last four or five years. After seeing many specialists, the consensus was that surgery to remove almost her entire large bowel seemed to be the best option. I was supportive of this decision. I wanted her to find some relief from the pain that typically accompanied eating a meal. The specialists described her large bowel as "dead," but they could never figure out why. There was no structural reason for this and, as usual, I would attribute this to small fiber neuropathy from her fibromyalgia. As always, I was right by her side every possible second during this significant procedure. It was a lengthy surgery, but I had Doris's icy text messages to keep me company throughout. It was on the exact day of her operation when a financial planner Erin had met at a program for abused women began to investigate me via LinkedIn. I found his timing to be quite interesting. Erin effectively took on the role of the abused wife, portraying herself as an abused, terrified woman married to a crazy man. She was adept at tugging the heartstrings of anybody or any support group that would listen.

I said nothing to Erin about the financial planner. She experienced some unexpected bleeding complications post-surgery, and I was extremely concerned. I did not leave her room, spending the next forty-eight hours cleaning blood out of her backside and sleeping in a hospital chair. Erin also had me bring her pillbox from home, as "the hospital is not giving me all of my medications on time." One of the nurses remarked to Erin, "You have a good one here. He is a good boy. Most husbands would not be this attentive." There was no response from Erin.

Erin's disposition was entirely different at home than it was during her hospitalization.

A particularly frightening moment occurred as I was bringing her pain medications, something to drink, and a snack. As I entered our bedroom, she sat straight up in bed, screaming at the top of her lungs, "Our daughter is afraid."

Now when I say "the top of her lungs," I mean our neighbors *had* to have heard her! I remained calm and tried to ask why our daughter was afraid. I received no rational explanation of what I would have done to make Katie fearful while Mom was in the hospital. Even in her post-surgery state, Mom stayed in character, continuing to alienate my daughter from me.

Three days later, Erin alleged that I had requested documentation from our insurance company for Erin to sign releasing her private health information.

I spent an inordinate amount of time painstakingly working with our insurance company to prove that I did not request those forms. They provided e-mails and a written letter to validate that I had not asked for those documents. No apology from Erin, only, "I have all the proof that I need that you requested those documents. You make me sick!"

Why was she so concerned about me having access to her medical records?

I grabbed my computer, left the house, and began documenting all that I had endured, finally taking Al's and Jane's advice to create a paper trail to protect myself. I sat in a movie theater parking lot during an ice storm for three-and-a-half hours, only to return home to, "You smell like a brewery. Did you have a few drinks?"

"I had a bottle of water and a coke," was all I said to Erin.

Overall, I'd say psychotherapy wasn't my psychiatrist's strength. One bit of counseling I embraced was to lower my expectations for my relationship with Erin. I began starting to, as he put it, "drop the rope." He encouraged me to do my best to avoid responding to every accusation and not overreact. He acknowledged that she might have paranoia issues but had no explanation for it, save her fibromyalgia or her previous stroke-like events. I was a good patient through February and for most of March.

Nevertheless, the verbal onslaught continued. One evening, Erin theorized that perhaps my drinking and anger resulted from my relationship "going south."

"You mean *our* relationship?" I asked.

"No, *your* affair!" she spat.

So now, we were back to my infidelities. I tried to laugh it off.

Another zinger I could only chuckle at was her observation, "You have calmed down since your release from Holy Hell because you have stopped doing drugs." These pearls seemed to coincide with her bath time.

On another occasion, we had sat together and watched a movie called *The Judge,* starring Robert Duvall and Robert Downey, Jr. Downey Jr.'s character and his dad were estranged for years, and this movie struck a chord in me. I wistfully remarked that we had wasted enough time and that we needed to move forward in repairing our once-happy marriage. Erin acknowledged my proposal, which provided me with some sense of peace.

After the movie, as I was washing my hair in the shower with my back turned to her, she pounded on the glass door, and yelled, "Look at me. I don't care anymore, but you need to fix your relationship with our daughter!"

The next day, I asked what had prompted her angry outburst, and Erin replied, "Something must have happened to cause that."

What did? Rinse, lather, repeat!

As if things weren't going badly enough, Doris was coming to town to celebrate Erin's forty-seventh birthday. I was the lucky bastard who had to pick her up at the airport—solo! I did not know what to expect based on the frigid text messages I received from her during Erin's surgery, but I set out to try to do my best. It turned out to be a surprisingly reasonable visit and, for the most part, it seemed like old times. Doris and I went shopping together for Erin's birthday and had a few laughs. Doris purchased Erin some luggage, and as we were leaving Kohl's Department Store, I suggested I carry the luggage, so the wheels did not get dirty.

Oh, the look I got! I swear I saw thought bubbles coming from her noggin, forming a cloud that read, "There he is, controlling things again." Damn, sucked in by a few pleasant moments!

March 2, 2015

Dear Danny,

I just want to thank you for making my birthday very special sincerely. From shopping with my mother, getting my favorite cupcakes (one which I ate last night), all of my presents and a lovely dinner. Just know these are genuinely appreciated and are not taken for granted. Having the family together and having a bit of normalcy in our lives was quite refreshing.

I know I haven't been able to let you into my life again emotionally, and I am sorry for that. I truly am, not only for your sake, for mine as well. The fact that at age forty-seven I have begun to doubt what true, stable, honest love is, and wonder does it even exist. This is a defense mechanism I've unfortunately learned throughout my whole life. When you said, "I wish you loved me like you love your mother," I can see why you feel that way. First, a mother's love and a husband's love are really two separate identities that in my opinion can never be put side by side. When I was a little a girl, I used to dream of someday having a man love me in a way that I've never experienced, only in my thoughts and prayers. My mother gave many gifts in life; the most important treasure I received from her and my grandmother was a feeling I was always unconditionally LOVED. The love between our family was demonstrated day in and day out, good times and very awful times. I knew I could fall to my knees and I would be lifted back up because I trusted and believed I would land on my two feet. I had this feeling because I never doubted their words or actions, so I knew even if I fell again, I trusted them enough to give it another shot to land on my feet.

Due to what I have said above, I can see how you feel that way. Can you see how I got here? I feel this is where we as a couple should be. We knelt down together twenty-one years ago at that altar and made commitments and promises to one another in front of the Lord. Dan, you are a good man. You have worked very hard throughout life to provide and support our family. I am extremely proud of you and of all your accomplishments in life. That's something I've NEVER taken for granted. I know you truly love our children and only want what is best for them and their future. You've definitely been there for me during good times and during not so good times. I have and wanted to be there for you as well. You are a giving man, and if I ask you to help me with something, I know you will be there. I know you love me and always have. I am here for a reason, and that is because I still love you and I know you are trying to bring me back emotionally. I want to say, "If I fall on my knees, I know without a doubt I trust Dan to be there when I land on my two feet because I have absolutely no reason to doubt otherwise. I feel that way because I trust him, I truly trust him." I don't know if you can relate to this analogy, but this is the best one I could come up with.

Is this something that can ever change? I don't know. I look forward to seeing what our therapist has to say. Just remember that I do love you, and I pray every night that the Lord will somehow intervene. One thing I will ask you, if you fell to your knees, (not counting pre-separation plans), would you trust me, hands down, no doubts that I would be there when you landed?

Sincerely,

Me

Bedtime, exactly ten days after I received Erin's beautiful e-mail, she hurls this at me, "I know how important sex is to guys. If you want somebody else just let me know." I asked her where this came from and her response was, "I was just making conversation. Good night!"

The Ides of March rolls on! My oncologist, family practitioner, and psychiatrist agreed to take me off my 100 milligram Lamictal regimen to see if it was contributing to my continued abnormal blood work. This seemed to give Erin incentive to turn up the heat. Our exchanges were already simmering, but why not throw gas on the fire?

It became all about the phone again with people "lighting me up," my phone constantly "dinging." She even checked the manual for my Ford Escape, looking at its tank capacity, since according to her, I was buying "an awful lot of gas." It was a company car, and I drove it a lot. In her mind, you see, I was buying drugs at gas stations and meeting folks there to "hook up."

We did not have a full day in March without some bullshit. There were many sleepless nights. When my tossing and turning wouldn't stop, I'd head upstairs to Billy's room, as he was now living in Charlotte full time. One morning I awoke to a couple texts from Erin.

"Well back to old times! I guess we may have to get used to this. Enjoy your space. We will talk tomorrow about the inevitable."

The second text at 12:26 a.m.: "Amazing you went upstairs because you couldn't sleep but you seem to be out like a light in no time!" "Dropping the rope" would have been smart, but I addressed these texts later the next day.

Ironically, I found out that she could not sleep either and had made her way to the guest room. I jokingly said I should have sent *her* a text.

She said, "I would have texted you back the middle finger." Then it became all about me being off my pills. "Your demeanor is different now that you are off your medication," she reminded me for the millionth time. When I was taking Lamictal, I had been taking 100 milligrams per day. Unbeknownst to me . . . Erin was on 500 milligrams daily! "Now that you are off your pills, you could lose your job," Erin advised. She was implying that my bipolar could act up.

In March of 2015, spring arrived early in North Carolina, so Erin and I decided to do some yard work together. It was a beautiful Saturday, and I cherished the opportunity to spend some "normal" time with her. Okay, I was a glutton for punishment.

"I am afraid to do yard work with you," she said, "as I don't want you getting angry if I don't do it right." She cut one side of the yard and switched to trimming bushes. "You gave me the hardest hill to do."

As she trimmed the bushes, she cut the electrical cord and was visibly upset that I would get angry.

"I have cut four or five cords myself," I reassured her, laughing. "It's no big deal."

By the end of March, separation was once again an option precipitated by four events.

The first occurred on March 27. Working from home that day, I informed Erin that I was going to get my car serviced and inspected. I kissed her forehead and told her I was leaving. I'd been gone about ninety minutes when Erin called to ask where I was. She *knew* where I was. As I talked to her on the way home, Erin wanted to know why my car was so noisy. She thought I had my window down. I said both of my windows were up and suggested the noise came from the rain, my tires, and the road.

She ignored my suggestion, saying, "It is all right if your window is down. I know you smoke in your car."

I got frustrated. "If I say my windows are not down, I would expect you to believe me."

The second event occurred that evening. Katie was out for the night at a girlfriend's, so Erin and I decided to go out for a few drinks. Not a good idea!

"This is like the most awkward first date I have ever had," Erin said.

I tried to keep things light by talking about the kids and what a good job we had done with them at this point. Erin quickly pivoted off that to walk down the road again of my fabrications, her lack of trust, and my "ogling" of other women.

"All the guys keep looking over here. You're being too loud and they recognize we are fighting. They are probably thinking, that poor woman," said Erin. I was not loud at all. We left after about an hour and again made our way to separate rooms.

The third event occurred the next day. After another night of churning emotions, I awoke about 8:15 a.m. I planned to do some yard work, but before I ventured outside, I went into Katie's room where Erin had spent the night. She was awake. I told her that I loved her and in spite of the rocky night before, I still hoped to see a movie with her later that evening.

She said she loved me too as she lay in Katie's bed, working her phone. After finishing the grass, I came inside to tell her I was going to Lowe's to get a new weedwacker. I was having trouble getting the old one started and thought it had seen better days.

As Erin lay in Katie's bed, she sneered, "And get some more money too!"

I said, "What do you mean?"

She responded, "You know what I mean."

She had been going through our bank transactions on her phone looking at ATM cash withdrawals. After six months of dealing with accusations post my Holy Hell release, I could not "drop the rope." Sorry, Doc! I lost it.

I slapped the shit out of Katie's dresser and called Erin "a fucking paranoid bitch." Stupid, stupid, stupid. At some point, Erin called her mom to ensure that Doris could hear Erin state, "If you don't get out of this room, I am going to call 911. You are acting this way because you are off your Lamictal! You are a sneak and a liar." She had shifted from, "I love you" to "I am going to call the cops on you," in less than forty-five minutes!

I finished the yard work, showered, and was off to what would soon become my new home away from home, the Springhill Suites. Exactly three months later, I learned that the only person stealing money from our marital account was Erin, complicit with Doris. Erin was dropping the "passive" from passive aggressive. Her now theatrical and public displays included at least twice violently accusing me of thievery. I started to realize she was pushing me to put hands on her in a violent manner. That is not my nature! I am sure she made Katie and Billy aware of Dad's new behavior and outbursts.

The final straw occurred on March 30. Erin told me that she was going to work out at the Y, and I said that perhaps I would see her there. I showed up about an hour after Erin, and was surprised to see her car still in the parking lot. Her "cardiac" issues limited the length of her workouts. Any more than forty-five minutes, her blood pressure would spike, and she would lose her voice. I entered the Y and was going to say hello to Erin, but I could not find her. I looked everywhere. I became increasingly curious as to where she might be.

I worked out for an hour. When I left, her car still sat empty in the parking lot. Where was she? At this point, I was becoming a little pissed. I went home, and when she arrived back forty-five minutes after me, I inquired as to where she had been. She got defensive. Out of spite, I suggested that perhaps somebody picked her up at the Y for a little hookup.

"I was working out in the women's locker room," she explained. "I sat in my car when I arrived and checked some e-mails." The excuses started flying. I have kicked myself for this incident many times. I should have hidden out somewhere. *Something* was shady with this whole situation. What an idiot I was! I checked, and the Y does not have workout equipment in the women's locker room. Shocker, she called her attorney, and our separation was back on.

In 2015, Easter arrived early. Given our version of March Madness, it should've been no surprise that Doris didn't include me in the family gift. A large box from Doris arrived on our doorstep addressed to Erin, Katie, and Billy. No Danny! I let Erin know it bothered me, and once again, she reminded me to "not take any shit from my mom."

At some point during my nine days in psychiatric lockup, Erin had reached out to our church. I never asked why, but she started seeing the deacon. Erin and I previously met with this deacon on a few occasions. He was outstanding, as he had some personal experience with marriage conflict. We met with him again on April 17. He was very direct with both of us and asked Erin if she still loved me. She said yes. He then asked if she wanted to stay married.

She said "yes, but," and he jumped in to remind Erin this is a yes/no question, acknowledging that it comes with conditions. She said yes. I answered yes to both questions as well.

He then addressed her anxiety about Katie. Of course, her story was that she was there to protect our daughter who fears me due to my mood issues. The deacon acknowledged her anxiety but reminded Erin of her obligations. "Your obligations are to God, your husband, and your family." It would be the last time Erin and I would see him together. We agreed with the deacon that separation might be a good idea but that it should be a step toward saving the marriage, not the first step to divorce. I found comfort in that and, based on Erin's responses to his questions, my naïve self once again had hope.

On April 23, I returned home from a business trip to Dallas. After some conversations over the previous few days, Erin and I had decided to get a hotel room together Friday the twenty-fourth, Katie's prom night. We were also intimate the night I returned. It had been four months since we had been together. We never revisited the concept of separation following our visit with the deacon. Perhaps I was avoiding the inevitable, but I honestly did not want to bring it up. It was not what I wanted for our marriage or our family.

The evening of the twenty-fourth, we enjoyed watching Katie light up throughout her prom pictures. We had a nice dinner, a few drinks, and an evening at a hotel. I think we enjoyed each other's company. However, our physical affection was entirely different from all the times that we were intimate throughout our marriage. I continued to walk on eggshells, doing my very best to try to reconnect with Erin.

Katie would not be home the following evening, as she decided to spend the night at a friend's house. She was never around much on weekends. Maybe this was because I still lived at home, or she just wanted peace, wanting to avoid the typical weekend fireworks. Looking back now, I don't blame her one bit. Quite surprisingly, since we had the house to ourselves, Erin suggested that we "have another night." Erin decided she would go shopping for some new lingerie, and she went out on a limb and bought some temporary tattoos. This creativity was 100 percent Erin's idea, but I did not object. Disclaimer: As you gawk at the next paragraph, please know I am probably thinking the same as you . . . who was the one with all these new ideas and new bedroom moves? Clue: Not Danny.

Erin was gone most of the day shopping and would occasionally send some text pics as she was trying on her new apparel. Erin settled on some beautiful white lingerie. While she was gone, she asked me to get the upstairs set up for "our night." There is no need to go all *Fifty Shades of Gray* on you, but our evening involved an air mattress, old sheets, Erin's laptop, speakers, an LCD projector, and baby oil. Thus, the need for old sheets. I will let your imagination fill in the blanks.

Al and Jane would later dub this evening as "slip and slide" night. Yes, I have been very open and transparent with them. Unfortunately, our night was brief. After all the anticipation and setup, it was quite a letdown. Erin passed out after having less than three drinks. I was always a beer drinker, but Erin had grown quite fond of vodka and V8 Fusion. Anytime Erin had three or more drinks she typically ended the night in a fetal position next to the toilet. I would be right there waiting for the vomiting or dry heaves to stop so I could put her in bed. I always thought it was her fibromyalgia meds. That night, I carried her down the steps, got her in the shower, got her dressed and put her in bed.

The following morning, Erin and I made yet another trip to the emergency room. Her bowels stopped working and she was in tremendous pain. Her surgery had been over two months ago, and this should not be happening! I thought she was just dehydrated, a combination of her meds and drinking two evenings in a row. Erin's explanation was that she took too much Imodium. Post-surgery, her doc recommended that she take two Imodium tablets daily to help control the firmness of her movements. "I took six tablets because I did not want to shit all over you," was Erin's comment to me.

As she lay in the ER bed, me holding her hand, she gushed, "I love you, and I don't want to separate." The flood of relief her words brought me! Despite everything, I still loved her and was inexplicably committed to her. April was a reasonably good month for us, and I thought things were going to work out, especially if we could demonstrate this to Katie.

Erin had yet to be retested for HIV. The six-month window, per her OB/GYN's alleged policy, had not yet expired.

# CHAPTER 9
## *Just a Week or Two*

The trust of the innocent is the liar's most useful tool.
—*Stephen King*, Needful Things

5/5/2015

Dear Al and Anthony,

I wanted to share a report I received months ago from the Division of Health Service Regulations Department of North Carolina. After many attempts discussing Dan's release from Holy Hell with two of his doctors and the hospital, I took it upon myself to call the health department.

The first call I made was a complaint in regards to bed bugs. The health department was there within 3 hours, swarming the hospital using their protocol to ensure the environment was free from bed bugs.

The second call I made was about the deficiencies in care, treatment, and my feeling that Dan had been admitted to that facility unjustifiably. The acute certification team at the health department assigned my complaint to a health team; however, I never thought I would hear back from them. Despite my doubts, I received this letter in the mail that I wanted to share with both of you.

Not only did I get this letter, but the head nurse consultant also called me personally the day the health department arrived unannounced . . . They spent a week at the facility, and these were their findings.

This has been hanging over my head for months. I feel since you are family and were a huge part of his support system while he was in the hospital and of course, now at home, I thought it was absolutely necessary to share their explanation and findings of the unannounced visit.

I realize there are MANY emotions, possible judgments and opinions in regard to Dan and his well-being. I do love your brother and ALWAYS WILL. I have always supported him throughout our 21 years of marriage, whether it's his career choices, our relocations, his health difficulties, counseling . . . . . . . . He has always been there for me throughout all of my tribulations in life as well. This support is NEVER taken for granted. I am not sending this letter to rustle any feathers or start any confrontation. I felt this letter was necessary for both of you to have because you have been such a big part of his support in this horrific dream. We all want to put this behind us. This is my way of doing so.

Sincerely,

Erin

*She loves me, and all will be okay*, I thought. (Thanks, Al, for hanging onto this letter.)

Erin never shared with me the above letter that she sent to Al and Anthony. They verbally shared it with me a few weeks after they received it. The North Carolina Department of Health & Human Services investigation could not substantiate deficiencies in care. They did acknowledge the bedbug infestation. Erin quickly provided me a copy upon receipt of it.

The week of May eleventh, I was in sunny San Diego for work and returned home late on Friday the fifteenth. For the first time in a long time, I was looking forward to a weekend with Erin, as I felt we were finally making some progress restoring our marriage. There had been no recent discussion about separation.

Katie continued to struggle with me being in the house. I was oblivious to Erin's subtle and ever-present manipulation of her. Now and then Erin would tell Katie, "Dad and I are the adults, and we will decide what is best for us and our marriage." My guess is Erin manufactured her eloquent statement with no small amount of coaching from Doris.

Saturday, May 16, Erin and I went to dinner and a movie. We invited Katie, but she declined. Erin had grounded her that weekend due to "disrespect" she was showing Mom, regarding me continuing to live in the house. I stayed silent, as I did not feel comfortable doling out discipline. I'd given up my right to do that during the course of the last year. Regardless, Erin and I had a reasonably regular evening together.

What a difference a day makes! The next morning Erin was upstairs having a conversation with Katie. I was not privy to the conversation and never asked Katie for details. Suddenly, Erin, happily bouncing down the stairs, looked me in the eye and said, "I finally see the look of belief in her eyes. She finally believes that I will protect her. I have grown tired of being called a liar by our daughter. Why don't you go to a hotel for just a week or two until she calms down? It is easier for you to go than Katie and me."

WTF! I was dumbfounded. When I gently reminded Erin of what our deacon said about her obligations, she dismissed it, saying, "He doesn't know the whole story."

"Why don't we give him the whole story then, Erin?" was my response. I also countered, "We have been getting along fairly well the last several weeks. Is it a 16-year-old's place to dictate what happens in our marriage?"

"We were not making progress; we went and saw a movie." Erin mocked.

With that, I agreed to go to a hotel for a few days prior to heading to Pittsburgh in the latter part of the week. I numbly threw some clothes in a bag and was off to spend more Marriott points at the Springhill Suites. I don't remember even saying goodbye to Katie.

After dropping my stuff at the hotel, I headed to mass. I texted Erin to let her know and offered that she was welcome to join me. Surprisingly, she showed up. Her presence, coupled with the tears we shed as we held hands the entire mass, gave me a sense of hope once again. I rationalized that I would be the bigger person and could handle a few days at a hotel. It would be a good break for all of us!

As church ended, I walked Erin to her car where we hugged for a while. I kissed her on her cheek as the tears were rolling down both of our faces. We apologized to each other and stated how sorry we were that all this had happened. Again, I felt renewed.

As I was pulling up to the hotel, Erin called me. "You are never going to believe the text that I just got from our fucking daughter!"

The text was from a girlfriend of Katie's that said she saw us in church and apologized to Katie that she did not get a chance to say hello. I asked Erin to review her phone and texts to understand the full context.

"No, I won't do that," she told me. "You know how you did not like that when I did it to you."

It appeared to me that Katie was calling Mom out for sneaking around and going to church with me. The irony of all ironies is that we stood in church, wept, held hands, and recited the Our Father together. It's a prayer I have recited thousands of times throughout my life. However, the words in the prayer never had as much meaning or impact as they do now.

As I pray it daily, the words resonate with far greater conviction. In particular, a few key phrases: "Thy will be done . . . As we forgive those who trespass against us . . . Deliver us from evil . . . Amen." The irony is that I was holding the very hand of the evil that I would soon be delivered from.

. . .

On Monday the 18th, Erin informed me that I needed to stop by the house to review a non-abandonment agreement she had just received from her attorney. It is a relatively simple document addressing the intentions of the parties in regard to one party moving out of the marital home. It also asserted that Erin could not file a claim of abandonment against me for moving out. I was familiar with the concept of this agreement, as it had lain on top of our refrigerator for months collecting dust. However, this was a revised edition. Her attorney, Brenda, had modified the agreement adding language requiring me to leave $700.00 a week in an envelope in the mailbox for incidental expenses.

My first question to Erin was, "I thought we were talking 'just a week or two?' What is this all about?"

Erin coyly replied, "It is to protect you. To prove that you did not leave home and abandon your family."

I ultimately agreed to sign the fundamental form without the $700.00 stipulation. I did not have an extra $700.00 a week to give. That afternoon, we drove separately to Brenda's office and individually signed this agreement. I arrived back at the house to get some clean clothes. As Erin and I stood in the kitchen, I shared my hope that we could soon return this agreement to the top of the fridge to resume collecting dust. With her back to me, she tearfully stated, "I hope so too." I did not have an attorney at this point (big mistake), and I did not fully comprehend the impact of signing this agreement. Continuing to trust Erin was yet another stellar move on my part, as evidenced by the additions her attorney attempted to make to the standard agreement. We were both working hard . . . me in San Diego and Erin behind my back to manipulate me out of my home. In legalese, the term is "malicious turning-out-of-doors."

After four nights in the hotel, I headed to Pittsburgh for Memorial Day weekend. My father's health had continued to decline, and I kept telling myself how much this trip would help him and my mom. In reality, they were helping me. I needed to be around happy families, as mine was falling apart.

In my many trips to Pittsburgh, my home away from home was Al and Jane's home, number 810. For several years now, I'd hijacked their life. Their whole family graciously welcomed every visit without judgment. Summer camp at 810 was full of love, support, Sammy's comfy bed, gifts, and always, wonderful food. This particular trip I went to Keystone Lake. I returned to the spot where Erin and I shared our first meaningful kiss. My thought was to fill a jar with sand and call it "new beginnings." I asked the lifeguard if I could have some sand, only to be told that it couldn't be removed from the beach. I said, "Okay, look the other way then." I filled a one-gallon freezer bag and left.

I returned to North Carolina on the twenty-sixth, as I had scheduled time with our deacon. I began to see him on my own, as Erin had temporarily moved on from him. His counsel was to focus on myself and to do my best not to worry about Erin's responses and reactions going forward. He also suggested I keep my wedding ring on and to read the book *Be a Man! Becoming the Man God Created You to Be* by Father Larry Richards. Coincidentally, Father Richards has strong ties to Pittsburgh. The book caused me some conflict as I wrestled with whether to stay away or continue to show up and help around our home that was for sale. Al and Big G were concerned about the possibility of me being arrested. I decided to continue being the man God created me to be, doing even more than my share around the house. In months to come, I would seek clarity on one quote in the book that I struggled with: "You only love God as much as you love the one you like the least."

On May 28, I attended a conference in Florida. Erin and I spoke on occasion and, sadly, every conversation spiraled into arguments. I had quickly tired of living out of hotels, suitcases, and my car and wanted clarity on how we were going to proceed. To my detriment, I continued avoiding attorneys. I hoped Erin would allow me some money from our emergency fund so I could find a place to live for at least a few months. I had asked many times about the ability to stay in Billy's room until the house sold, but as was typically the case with Erin, I got no answer. Talking by phone the evening of the twenty-eighth, she remarked, "I am not your puppet." Click! She hung up on me. So says Geppetto, Pinocchio's puppeteer. I was the puppet! The following morning, I finally contacted an attorney, Olivia Esquire, and set up a meeting for June 3.

I returned "home" on May 30, as Billy was coming to town. What an indescribable feeling to drive up to your own home feeling unwelcome and leery of every potential confrontation. As soon as I walked into the house, Erin asked when I had time to get sun. She pressed her fingers on my arms while making comments under her breath.

We had dinner with Billy, accompanied by Erin's unrelenting digs. As she headed toward the laundry room, I followed her, to avoid arguing in front of our son. There, the finger-pointing began in earnest. Erin suggested that I was sitting by the pool instead of working. Erin left the laundry room, and instead of just letting it go, I followed her to the bedroom, pulled up our meeting agenda on my computer, and set it on the dresser.

I wanted Erin to see that Friday morning was open, so I sat on my balcony doing work, and yes, the sun happened to be in my way. She didn't care. She left the house to fill up Billy's car, and I got busy replacing some bedroom blinds our dogs had been using as chew toys. Upon Erin's return, Billy left to head back to Charlotte. I gave Erin her space the rest of the evening. Earlier, Erin had invited me to stay overnight, but after her tirade, I thought it best to go back to the hotel.

Before I left, I went upstairs to get a few things out of my office and found that Erin had locked herself in the upstairs bedroom. As I walked to

my office, she darted out of the bedroom and ran downstairs. After retriev-
ing what I needed from my office, I walked downstairs. Erin stood at the
front door with her hand on the knob as I asked, "Are you getting ready to
run out of the house?"

"Yes, you are being irrational and are following me around the house."

Not sure where she got that from, I grabbed my computer bag and left.

After my June 3 introductory meeting with Olivia, I retained her as my
new attorney. My focus during the initial get-together meeting was to find
a way for Erin and me to get through this amicably. I also wanted access to
our emergency fund to secure a place to live. I told Olivia that I still loved
Erin and wanted to work things out. Our first mediation would occur July
7, 2015.

I found out that "just a week or two" for me to be out of the house
actually meant, "You are not coming back into this house." Erin's attorney
e-mailed me to let me know that Erin was interested in moving forward
with mediation. "We can do this through the courts as well, but the court
system is backlogged." She instructed me to e-mail her with a list of things I
needed from the house. I started to limit my communications with Erin but
pleaded with her to place my belongings in the garage. I did not want the
neighbors to see my stuff. Erin was in charge now! I was evicted, and she
would be calling the shots. Despite my plea, my shit was in a laundry basket
on the front porch. The house was on lockdown with Erin and Katie inside.
Not reaching Erin on her cell, I called the home phone. Erin answered, "I
am not even supposed to be talking to you." I asked her very nicely for a
bigger suitcase. "Fine, I will put it in the garage."

It gets better and better . . . *The next morning,* I awoke to Erin's text
asking me when I would be by to cut the grass and to pay the carpet cleaner
while I was there. Really? By now, all of you have to be asking yourselves,
"What the hell is wrong with this guy?" I have asked myself that same
question hundreds of times. But there my dumb ass was, at the house by 8
a.m., one day after collecting my stuff off the front porch. Erin texted me

she would not be home, but there she was.

I walked upstairs and unintentionally startled her as she came out of the bedroom closet. She wasted no time starting in on me about lying about my HIV test, ogling women on TV early in our marriage, her lack of trust in me, so forth and so on. Same old shit, different day. I calmly and simply told Erin that I was not debating this anymore and that I still loved her. The earbuds went in, my jams went on, and I immersed myself in yard work. Upon completion, I initially left the house but returned ten minutes later, as a call for work was canceled. After I finished the lawn, Erin had given me a lengthy list of other things to be done, so now I had time to take care of those. I arrived back at the house, opened the garage door, but the door into the house was locked. I gently knocked, and Erin opened the door just a crack. She was on the phone with Doris in another strategically placed call.

"What do you want?" Erin bellowed at me (and into her cell). "You are not even supposed to be at the house!"

I had no response. I was speechless. Besides, I had to get to a follow-up appointment with my oncologist that afternoon.

I spent nights and weekends checking out apartments, Craigslist ads, and extended-stay arrangements, uncertain how long I would need a place. A short-term lease of three to six months was out of my financial reach. And I wouldn't put a dog in an extended-stay place. The two dark and dingy units I looked at for $60.00 per night were flat-out depressing. Erin's attorney had suggested the extended-stay arrangement as an option. I checked out a place I found on Craigslist and initially was excited about it. The ad stated, "Master bedroom, kitchen, living room, and free Wi-Fi." I showed up and introduced myself to the owners, a young couple from Upstate New York. They seemed nice enough, but in a matter of minutes, I started wondering if I was getting a taste of my future . . . I almost lost it emotionally. "Here is the living room and kitchen that you will have access to!" she stated so cheerfully. I then asked her, "So where do you live?" She pointed to the right and said, "We live in this room. Don't open the door as we don't want to let the dogs out." We proceeded upstairs so that she could show me "my room." My interest in this arrangement was already gone, but I obliged her by heading upstairs. We arrived at the top of the stairs, and she stated, "The guy that lives in this room does not come out very much!" *"Unless he wants to kill someone," I thought.* I graciously declined their offer and headed to my car. I called Erin and told her about this visit, and her comment to me was, "I am so sorry you had that experience."

Four short days after Erin remarked, "You are not even supposed to be at the house," she called me while I was in Nashville, Tennessee. I was at the airport when Erin invited me to stay at the house on the evening of June 9. "Katie is not home so you are welcome to stay at the house."

I had already had a hotel reservation and told her I would think about it and call her back. I foolishly decided that it would be nice to sleep in my home and canceled my hotel room. As usual, with the way my luck had been lately, my delayed flight caused me to arrive back in Wilmington after midnight. I was having serious second thoughts about staying at the house. I began to tremble as I entered our subdivision, and it became more pronounced as I headed up the driveway. Fearful of pulling up to the place I once called home, I said to myself, "If the door is locked, I am not knocking or calling Erin." God was watching over me; the door was locked. I sent Erin a text to let her know that I could not get in and that I would be going to the hotel. Erin had previously told me that the door would be unlocked. What were her intentions for inviting me to the house that night? Was she trying to get me arrested? Was she trying to seduce me? Only Erin can provide the answer to what her motivations were. I arrived at the hotel, and unfortunately, there was no room at the inn. Taylor Swift was in town, so they'd sold my room after I canceled it. I sat outside on the patio for a few hours trying to process, yet again, what had occurred that evening. I slept in my car that night. ("Don't worry. You may think you'll never get over it. But you also thought it would last forever." –Taylor Swift)

Erin called the next morning, inquiring as to why I did not come home the night before. I explained to her what happened and reminded her that I sent a text. She denied receiving it, so I re-sent the text to her. She also claimed that when she woke up, the house alarm system was off. "Are you suggesting that I entered the home, turned off the alarm, locked the door from the inside and left the house?" I asked. She did not answer my question, so I called our alarm company to see if they could tell me when the system was armed and disarmed. They could not as we did not have that feature on our very basic system.

It was back to Nashville the following week for work. Sure, it was more nights in a hotel, but the change of scenery was a blessing. My colleague Russ picked me up at my hotel on June 16. As I got into his car, I noticed something that he had taped to his dashboard. It read, "God is after something. Let nobody judge you or define you but God." This powerful quote hit me hard. I had let my wife and mother-in-law judge me and define me. I allowed this! God was indeed after something, and God wanted me to hang in there as long as I did post–Holy Hell because he had plans.

I was excited to return home on June 18, as Billy would be in town for Father's Day weekend. I could not wait to see him. The civility between Erin and me was short-lived, however, as she began her taunting remarks. "You know, Danny, as the primary account holder, you could check my texts and phone calls at any time."

I responded, "That is great, but I have never accessed those records."

June 20, 2015, Happy Father's Day! Erin graciously agreed to spend the night at a hotel to afford me a night at home. We attempted to have dinner together before Billy returned to Charlotte. Katie did not join us but came downstairs to wish me a Happy Father's Day. I don't recall what we ate or whether there were gifts, but I will never forget his card. As I read it, the tears started flowing. Erin could not look at me as she stared out of the kitchen window with tears rolling down her face. I am not sure if Erin bought the card for Billy or not, but the front of it read, "All of us wanted to be sure to wish you a Happy Father's Day. Of course, we always wish you happiness, but on days like this, we like to put it into words . . ." The inside of the card stated, "It's just our way of saying, you're special to us all year round. Wishing you every good thing you deserve today and always." My tears really started flowing when I read Billy's words:

Dear Dad,

I just wanted to wish you a Happy Father's Day. Thank you for always being there for me and guiding me throughout life. You've shown me many good qualities such as being hardwork-ing and motivated. I wouldn't be where I am today without you. Attached is some cheesy pendant I found while detailing cars; it says "Count your blessings," and I figured it was a sign from God when I had found it. Hope you have a great day. I love you!

Billy

Billy had held onto that pendant for a year! That gift and card meant so much to me that I had the pendant's words tattooed on my right shoulder on the one-year anniversary of my release from Holy Hell. Erin had *always* signed my Father's Day cards, but not this one. I would ask Erin about this later only to have her reply, "You're not my father."

Erin had to make her best attempt to ruin what was a nice evening at home. As she prepared to leave, she inquired, "Danny, do you happen to know a bartender at a Mexican restaurant?"

I laughed out loud. "What are you talking about?"

"Now that you are drinking more, I thought you might have met this bartender. She just sent me a LinkedIn request," said Erin.

As we prepared for our July 7 mediation, the financial discovery process began. Let the legal cash registers start ringing! Thank the Lord, I remem-bered a new bank account Erin had opened three days after I got out of Holy Hell. It was through those records that I discovered that Erin had indeed been stealing money from our joint account. Doris had also been making deposits into the new account, and Erin was depositing money she took from our marital account into her pet-sitting business account. At this point, Erin had taken about $1,200 from our marital account and made significant cash withdrawals without my knowledge. It was not all deposited into her accounts, so what was she doing with all that cash? More hypocrisy! Yet, she lay in our daughter's bed on March 28, and snapped, "and get more money too!" She was the one stealing! I was in Vegas on business when I made this discovery. I calmly brought this up to Erin.

She was pissed! She was caught. "How did you know about that?"

"I received your financial records from your attorney today. I believe it's a standard part of the financial discovery." It was all I could do to keep a straight face . . . finally, an ounce of redemption.

While in Vegas, I texted Katie to say goodnight and to tell her that I loved her. She texted me back that she did not trust me. She did not believe me one bit and said that I should not call her. I called Erin to ask what that might be about, and she stated that she might have an idea.

"Katie thinks that you are smoking marijuana."

"I don't smoke marijuana; could you please tell Katie that I do not smoke marijuana?"

"I just listen, Danny," was all Erin said. Erin had been filling our daughter's head with the fact that Dad was doing drugs. She attempted to spin the same story with Billy.

After flying all night, I returned home on June 25, my fiftieth birthday. Erin was in Pittsburgh visiting Doris and I would be staying at our house. In addition to caring for our four dogs, I had a nice long list of chores to complete. Katie did not want to be at the house with me; instead, she would stay with her best friend Emma and her family.

I arrived at the house to find a card and a little gift bag on the counter for me. Initially, I was touched that Erin made an effort to get me something. I waited until later that evening to open the card and gift. She got me a Nike t-shirt and a dozen golf balls. With money so tight, I thought about returning them, but I decided to keep the gift. The card started well and was quite humorous. Then I read this:

> Dan, what a day! This comes at a really bad time for you. I
> know that the kids would have wanted you to have something
> to open. Perhaps your birthday next year will be better. Try to
> make it a decent day.
> Love, Billy and Katie

Do you remember the Easter box from Doris that ignored me? Erin had a great mentor for subtle emotional abuse. Like mother, like daughter—she did not sign the card.

I ended up spending my fiftieth birthday alone but enjoyed the peace, quiet, and space that the house afforded me. I'd started feeling like a caged dog at the hotel. The next evening, Big G and little g began a tradition that continues today. For my birthday, they took me out for dinner and a movie. I have strengthened many friendships during this nightmare, and this couple in particular have become terrific friends. They are beautiful people with huge hearts.

Communication with Erin was limited to an occasional text or brief phone call. I called her on the morning of the twenty-eighth. I wanted to say hello and for some reason, wanted to hear her voice. I mentioned the dinner and movie with Big G and little g and her comment back to me was, "Who else was there?"

I replied, "Nobody."

"I thought maybe they would have fixed you up with someone."

I reminded her, "We are still married, and I love you."

Of course, this led to Erin going down the worn-out path, "You say that you love me and that I am beautiful. Then you turn around and ogle other women. I can't trust you. We have never had trust in our marriage because of your sneakiness and lies."

I reminded her about recent events and her getting caught stealing money from our marital account. "Yeah, I am sure that you have taken five bucks here and five bucks there and are putting something in your cigarettes, up your nose, or up your butt," was Erin's comeback to me. No kidding, word for word. I laughed so hard, and then I hung up on her and ignored her repeated attempts to call me back.

July 3, four days before our mediation, Erin agreed to stay at the hotel in the room I had reserved. My ignorance allowed her to stay at my place. It had gotten to the point that we rarely crossed paths. I would text when I arrived or left the house. She sent me a text asking me to have the sheets changed at the hotel for her stay on the third. You guessed it. I called and had the sheets changed. July 4, as I returned to the hotel, this text exchange occurred.

*Erin: "Thx for help."*

*Me: "Ur welcome. Did you get my prescriptions?"*

*Me: "Never mind I found it. Thx for getting."*

*Erin: "In with your condoms."*

*Me: "Lol"*

*Erin: "No Lol"*

*Me: "R u serious? There are none. That was pretty mean. Thought you were joking."*

I had been sitting outside the hotel when these texts came in. The shakes began again, and I ran upstairs to my room and tore it apart. I thought perhaps Erin had planted a condom in there and took some pictures to use against me during our mediation. I ripped off the sheets, went through all my clothes and checked the room top to bottom. I called Al, and rightfully so; his response to me was, "Why the fuck did you let her stay in your room? You need to stop all communications with that crazy bitch!" He was right. I did not respond to the multitude of texts that came in from her, and I threw out the prescriptions she had picked up for me. She had Katie call me to ask, "Why aren't you responding to Mom?"

"I have my reasons, and I am not going to discuss them with you," was my reply.

The last of her string of texts on July 4 began, "You say you are an

HONEST stand-up guy. You truly disgust me with this phrase. You are anything but! My ring is off forever. I can't wait until Tuesday."

I was doing my best to ignore her texts, and I had not yet mastered or even thought about blocking her. On July 5, she texted: "It's not going to be pretty Tuesday. Just prepare yourself. Not that I know the specifics, but I am sure some things aren't going to set well with either of us.

"This is very, very sad. I am angry disappointed and deeply hurt. Two beautiful children, they are going to get the worst of this and 25 years here and gone. You said you are prepared for Tuesday in a tone I took as a threat. My attorney has been ready for a year, and I just became very prepared last week.

"My number one priority is the children. This year 'mama bear' has been front and center and she still seems to be there. I guess it's easier to say goodbye when things are ugly. I've owned my part in this nightmare; however, this nightmare has just got worse for me. It's VERY hard to see any sunlight through those clouds. I am at peace inside. I am going to take myself off the Y membership in the a.m. It should be pretty cheap for you. There is a lot of good in you, Dan; however, there are two simple things I want from you that you can't give.

"There are some new issues that are causing all my anger, and I don't forgive you. Goodnight."

# CHAPTER 10
## *The Third Gift*

Someone I loved once gave me a box full of darkness. It took me years to understand this too, was a gift. —*Mary Oliver*

The evening before our mediation, I sat out on the little back patio of my hotel. It was a typical Monday. Most of the guests were business travelers. I had gotten to know several regulars and most of us who hung out usually gravitated to the front patio. Tonight, the back provided me the solitude I was seeking. I received several phone calls from my family, offering me their love and support as I headed toward tomorrow's uncertainty. My sister-in-law's call provided a most profound statement, leaving an uneasy feeling in the pit of my stomach. She suggested, "You know, Danny, the guilty are usually the accusers." At 10:13 p.m., I initiated the following text exchange:

Me: "I have a question for you that I am going to save for a couple of months from now. I hope you can get some sleep."

Erin: "I have questions for you. Night."

Me: "I have answered all yours over and over and over. Night."

My uneasy feeling prompted me to reach out to AT&T. It was July 6, 2015, and this was the first time, but certainly not the last, that I would ever examine Erin's phone records. I had no clue how to do it, but would later become very proficient. The folks at AT&T were accommodating, and they informed me that someone had made Katie the primary account holder. "She is sixteen years old!" I told them, and they switched the account back to me. I initially did not spend a ton of time in the account, but a Texas area code jumped out at me. There was heavy text and talk traffic between Erin and this number. I assumed it belonged to Erin's ex-boyfriend in Texas. Erin recently reminded me of his location in the spring of 2014 following a nice lunch at the Cheesecake Factory. As we were walking to the car, she remarked, "Because things have not been going so well in our marriage lately, I looked up Chris on Facebook. I did not friend him or anything, just looked him up."

I made a misstep at 11:30 p.m. and called that number. I was shaking as I dialed, not prepared should anyone answer the phone. Fortunately, it went to voicemail. Unfortunately, it was the number of a woman named Tiffany, who I'd come to think of as the "phone friend." Erin became very close with Tiffany after I moved out of the house on May 17, 2015. (More to come on "phone friend.") I did not leave a message but knew that I might have to explain this call at some point.

I tossed and turned all night.

The sun did come up the morning of July 7, 2015, as I headed to downtown Wilmington all by my lonesome. In North Carolina, mediation is an attempt to avoid the backlogged family court system. I would occupy one unit of a condo-type arrangement with my attorney, Olivia. Erin and her attorney, Brenda, were in another unit. Our mediator, another attorney, would go back and forth between the rooms. Both Erin and I arrived early. We parked away from each other and remained in our cars for a little while. She entered the building first, and I sent her a text, *good morning you look nice.* I was not expecting a response, but it was my way of attempting to let her know that I still cared for her. I still loved her and prayed we could make an amicable arrangement: separate for a while and work things out. I get it now! I *was* the idiot that Doris used to refer to in her text messages.

Olivia was very clear that they were going to try to take off my arms, legs, and any other available appendages with their first offer. In our meetings leading up to mediation, Olivia had me prepared for the fact that their initial alimony number could be significant given the length of our marriage (almost twenty-two years). She came highly recommended, and I trusted her to do her absolute best to minimize that number. She was well versed in how my stay at Holy Hell transpired. Olivia had received from me a ton of documentation outlining all that I had endured in the form of mental and emotional abuse post–Holy Hell.

Nevertheless, Erin had been painting her mosaic with Brenda since September 5, 2014. I had bipolar, was crazy and abusive, had anger issues, and Erin and Katie feared me. Erin had to deal with all of this in addition to her fibromyalgia and other ailments. Oh yeah, lest I forget, Erin had sacrificed her career to stay at home and be the primary caretaker for our children. Her story was tight and convincing. She played the hell out of my mental health diagnosis and my time in psychiatric lockup. I knew this would be the story, and it played out just as Al, Jane, and everyone else predicted.

At 11:30, Robin Wright, the mediator, arrived with their first offer. I was doing all I could to breathe deeply.

- Husband is to maintain the yard and the outside of the home in showing condition. He is not to enter the house.

- Wife to have sole legal and physical custody of the daughter. Daughter to see father by arrangement between father and daughter.

- Husband to maintain health insurance policy for wife for sixty months following execution of mediation agreement. Neither party to file for divorce before June 1, 2020.

- Husband shall maintain a life insurance policy with a death benefit of at least $1,000,000 on his life, with wife as primary beneficiary and children as secondary beneficiaries, for the next thirteen years.

Suffice it to say, combined with their alimony request and proposal for the division of the pension and 401K, they found their extra appendages. I have worked hard since I was eleven years old, received many blessings and good fortune, but Erin was looking to add master's degree in financial destruction to her doctorate in mental and emotional abuse. They were asking for more money a year than I make.

Mike Tyson's uppercut hurt like hell, but I did not see his overhand right coming. It was a damn good thing that I was sitting down.

Nonchalantly, the mediator, Robin Wright, added, "Oh, by the way, Erin wanted me to let you know that you gave her herpes 2." She dropped the results, dated June 16, 2015, from Erin's OB/GYN on the table.

"What the fuck! I gave her what?" I screamed. I then looked at the results. I did not examine them as closely as I would later, but I did notice the big, "Positive Abnormal" for HSV2 circled and signed by her OB/GYN.

"When did I allegedly give her herpes 2?" I blurted. "Perhaps this is a false positive, and I would like for her to get retested." I knew damn well that I had not been with anyone but Erin in the last twenty-six years.

"She said you gave it to her while you were in Holy Hell."

"Really? Erin only visited me twice, and they did not allow conjugal visits. Do you mind getting further clarity from her on this?"

Robin returned with clarity that I gave it to her in December of 2014. I do not recall what I had given her that Christmas, but it wasn't herpes 2! It became clear to me that somebody else had been sliding down her chimney that Christmas. *Dirty Santa!* Our request for Erin to be retested was met with a big "hell no" from the other side.

Knocked down, but not out. Somehow, I managed to get up! My blood pressure, usually healthy, was through the roof. This mediation was over, and I was on my way to my family practitioner to be tested.

My mind racing, I remember nothing about the drive to my appointment.. One thing was clear: Erin had been running around on me, yet had beaten me up for six years about being a liar and a cheat. The woman supposedly raised to be about family, truth, honesty, and transparency was anything but. My mind then pivoted to our "slip and slide" night and the two nights preceding that. She was trying to infect me, and my immediate concern was that she might have accomplished her mission. "He is mentally ill, abusive, angry, addicted to porn, addicted to drugs and he gave me herpes," was the story she was attempting to write.

My appointment with the family practitioner was not until 3 p.m., so I had two more hours to allow my thoughts to spin in a million directions. I attempted to refocus by applying what AT&T had taught me the previous night, but my trembling hands prevented me from working the keyboard effectively. I called Olivia's paralegal, Abby, and I gave her my AT&T password and requested her to start pulling phone records. We also retained the services of a private investigation firm.

Inexplicably, my emotions toward Erin were not angry ones. Hypocrisy, betrayal, and disappointment left no room for anger. I had flashbacks to the verbal assaults and death threat I received from Doris in June of 2014. I reflected on my nine days in Holy Hell, the beautiful letter Erin had written, and most recently, in April and May of 2015, her affirmation of love for me. I was disappointed in myself. Why was I so blind? Why did I allow others to judge me and define me? How did I lose sight of who I was as a man, husband, and father? To think, just a few short hours ago, I had sat in the parking lot of Robin Wright's office still expressing my love for her! Thank you, Lord, for the smack of your hand across my face, and for shouting loud enough for me to finally hear, "Son, your marriage is OVER!"

Faster than Natty Light at a frat party, twenty-two years of marriage, gone!

I took my wedding ring off and almost threw it out the window! I am glad I didn't, as I would later sell it for $400.00

I swear the clock seemed to tick backward, but it finally read 3 p.m. I was escorted into an exam room and greeted by the medical assistant, "Are you okay? Your face and neck are beet red!" I explained the situation, she took my blood pressure and not surprisingly, it was significantly elevated.

"The doctor will be with you shortly. In the meantime, you better not tap that anymore." Referring to being intimate with Erin. My doctor arrived and opened with this statement, "If Erin has it, you are going to test positive." The same physician that involuntarily committed me to Holy Hell in September of 2014. He did a full examination of my genitals. I share this because it will be a topic of much discussion and debate. I had my blood drawn and was comprehensively screened for not only herpes 1 and 2, but every known STD.

I headed to church. I wanted to thank God for the strength he had provided me thus far and for the beautiful people he had put into my life. I prayed that he would bless me with negative test results so that we could put some closure to this horrible dream. I'd had enough! Billy and Katie had as well. I no longer asked God "why" but simply said, "Let your will be done." I stayed for about an hour, and my church's surroundings helped me calm down and clear my mind.

I arrived back at the Springhill Suites with reality staring me in the face. For the near future, I would likely be spending a lot more time at this or some other hotel. I spoke to Al, Jane, and a few of my other family members throughout the day. I was on the phone with one of my brothers (it was not Al for a change) when another call came through at 5:04 p.m. Doris was calling me! I hung up with my brother, and I took her call.

I know, what was this guy thinking? For the life of me, I will never understand why I took her call. Let's chalk it up to giving this woman way too much regard. She certainly wasn't calling to wish me a belated happy fiftieth birthday. The peace and tranquility I felt in church vanished.

"How dare you to attempt to make your son an ally and a pawn in this situation. You are a slimeball!" Doris hung up on me and shot me an ugly text.

Like the dumbass I continued to be, I fell into a texting exchange. I typed that she does not know the truth, does not have all the facts. "I have 18 pages of very well-documented mental and emotional abuse that I have endured from your daughter," was in the body of one of my texts to Doris. I promised her the truth and told her that I did not care what it cost me. I communicated that if she knew the facts, she might have significant concern about her daughter and her well-being.

She fired back, "You are self-important and need professional help." She closed with the promise, "Soon Erin will no longer be your concern."

When was I ever going to learn the difference between blood and water?

In a matter of minutes, an e-mail arrived from Olivia reminding me of her instructions not to have *any* contact with Erin or Doris. She forwarded an e-mail from Brenda, Erin's attorney, stating that due to my mental instability I was no longer to go to the residence but that I would have to pay for the lawn care. "He has been harassing Erin's mother via text," she also stated. No mention of the fact that Doris shredded me and initiated the contact. I informed Olivia about the warm phone call I just received from Doris, but there was no response from Olivia. It was becoming clear that she was not interested in engaging in the petty B.S.

Hypocrisy was another talent Erin inherited from her mom. Who was genuinely attempting to use our kids as allies and pawns? Text message evidence would later reveal that both Erin *and* Grandma were guilty as charged.

In spite of our collapsing marriage and the events that unfolded on this day, Doris had no issue with reaching out to my brother-in-law to do some significant work at her home. She had quite a bit of water damage and needed floors, cupboards, and doors repaired and refurbished. It begs the question as to who is self-important, entitled? Half-jokingly, I asked my brother-in-law to cut her doors up and throw them in her driveway . . . maybe I was only a quarter joking.

A famous novelist once penned, "Adversity does not build character, it reveals it." I am tremendously proud of my extended family, my many siblings, nieces, nephews, and the way that they have conducted themselves throughout this nasty divorce. They undoubtedly could have barraged Erin with electronic assaults or hang-up phone calls, but they did not. Al, Jane, and Anthony had plenty of reason to take the low road after witnessing all I had gone through over the past year, but they always took the high road. That is how people with real character conduct themselves. Conversely, Doris's lack of integrity would become more and more apparent as this mess moved forward.

The evening of the seventh, I sat alone on the curb in the back of the hotel. Naturally, I was struggling to comprehend the events of the day. All that occurred over the past six years seemed to crash down on me at that moment. I was devastated, shocked, and grateful, all at the same time—indeed, an emotional roller coaster. Once again, I looked up at the star-filled Carolina sky and thanked both God and Erin. I thanked them for my two beautiful kids and what I now call the "Third Gift"—the gift of clarity about Erin's role in wrecking our marriage and the drive to search for answers to all those unanswered questions. I no longer would torture myself about my role in our marital demise. Naturally, new questions would occupy my thoughts. "How could she do this to me? Who is the evol woman I gave 24 years of my life to?" Thank you, Erin!

My mind's fog started to lift, and certain things came into focus. Erin's "positive abnormal" herpes 2 test, conducted on June 16, 2015, was four days before the infamous Father's Day dinner on June 20, 2015, when she could not look at me as I sobbed, reading Billy's beautiful card. She stared out the window with tears rolling down her cheeks, knowing what she was about to drop on me! She had a grenade in her pocket and would soon pull the pin.

It was nine days later, on June 25, that she would leave me the gifts and the card for my fiftieth birthday, signed only "Love, Katie and Billy." I remembered the text exchange that we had on July 4 regarding condoms. "No Lol," she would state. "No Lol" indeed, Erin! On July 5, she texted me, "There is a lot of good in you, Dan; however, there are two simple things I want from you that you can't give." The text should have read "two simplex" things . . . but I digress. I received clarity on what those two things were . . . herpes 2!

July 5 text flashback from Erin: "It's not going to be pretty Tuesday. Just prepare yourself. Not that I know the specifics, but I am sure some things aren't going to set well with either of us." She knew the specifics!

Then, on the same day Erin was having lesions DNA tested for herpes 2, I read this on the dashboard of my colleague's car: "God is after something. Let nobody judge you or define you but God." God was indeed after something, and He is just!

Erin's revelation on July 7, 2015, enabled me to begin to re-establish who I was as a man and as a father. I was no longer a husband, but I was not the cause of our matrimonial collapse. If she had not played this card, God only knows where we would be today. Trust me, it is not a financial gift, but an emotional reward. I more than likely would have continued to hold onto a marriage that was a lie. I would have continued to "dig deep" into myself, searching for flaws that explained the brokenness of our relationship. I might still be holding onto the allegation that my lies were the reason for the lack of trust in our marriage.

Erin's story was near perfect! She thought she had me, but her story started to unravel when she played one card too many. Many unanswered questions remain, but I am okay with that. I have all the answers I need. Erin used to tell Katie, "Your dad has me on a leash." In reality, I was on the leash. But on July 7, she cut me loose. I went from being her little puppy, getting my nose slapped with a rolled-up newspaper because I wet all over the floor, to a big dog who would develop a fondness for digging deep, but this time in a different part of the yard.

What was it in Erin that kept her from confronting her role in our unhappiness? Was it greed, was it evol, or did she merely lack the courage to come to me and tell me that she was no longer happy in our marriage? These questions aren't for me to answer. Only one person knows the truth, the whole truth and nothing but the truth, so help her God. Family, Trust, and Honesty! Why hadn't she lived up to her supposed values?

I'd received an answer to Erin's e-mail to me on March 2, 2015:

"Is this something that can ever change? I don't know.

I look forward to seeing what our therapist has to say. Just know that I do love you, and I pray every night that the Lord will somehow intervene. One thing I will ask you, 'If you fell to your knees, (not counting pre-separation plans), would you trust me, hands down, no doubts that I would be there when you landed?'"

Erin, your prayers were answered. God did intervene, and no, *I don't trust you!*

# CHAPTER 11
## *3 Clicks*

He who is devoid of the power to forgive is devoid of the power to love.
—*Dr. Martin Luther King, Jr.*

After a catnap on the evening of July 7, I was off to "summer camp at 810."

I left my hotel about 5:30 that morning. My ten-hour drive would enable me to clear my head and attempt to prepare for what lay ahead. Barely thirty minutes down the road, logic sprang forth. "If she has herpes 2, she *must* be on or have taken some medication for it!" I pulled the car over, took out my iPad and in *three clicks*, I had access to Erin's pharmacy claims through our insurance company's website.

My, oh my! I did not need to "dig deep" at all, three simple clicks, just a couple of rips in the wrapping paper allowed me to peak at the gift that Erin handed me the day before.

As is usually the case, the employee who is paying the medical and pharmacy bills has full access to medical and pharmacy claims. Therefore, specific to Erin, I was her "employer." I was paying the bills for all of her medical and pharmacy claims, so as a result, I had full legal access to these records. This "idiot" did not realize it until a half hour on my way to Pittsburgh!

"What the hell is this?" As I looked at Erin's pharmacy claims, two prescriptions every month were marked "private." I had yet to familiarize myself with treatment options for herpes 2 (or any STD for that matter). Initially, I assumed she needed to take these "private meds" chronically to treat herpes 2. This thought vanished as quickly as it had popped into my head when I continued to scroll through her enormous list of pharmacy claims. I accessed five years' worth listed in chronological order, most recent prescriptions filled through those dating back to September 1, 2010 (the day my benefits for my current employer began). There was a ten-day supply for valacyclovir 500 mg that Erin filled on June 16, 2015, and a thirty-day supply of valacyclovir 500 mg filled the following month. I Googled "valacyclovir" and learned this medication is an antiviral used to treat herpes 2. All of her other pharmacy claims had the name of the drug clearly displayed, the strength of the medication and the number of pills dispensed. Unfortunately, these claims did not identify the physician who prescribed them. Additionally, what were these "private" pharmacy claims dating back to January 5, 2011? How was this designation established? Did the physician write it on the prescription? These were among the questions flooding my mind. Despite so much work ahead of me, I was energized by the gift that would keep on giving (like herpes) in the coming weeks and months.

My initial discoveries only took about fifteen minutes. I wanted to get on the phone with our insurance company, Al, Big G, or anybody that would listen, but it was only 6:15 a.m. My mind kept coming back to Erin's "private" prescriptions and wondered if they were narcotics. Could this explain her mood swings, hostility, outbursts of anger, and slurred speech? Tempering my excitement was self-disappointment. All this had been right at my fingertips the whole time, and I never looked. I wanted the Clinic or someone to evaluate Erin's medications as a contributing factor to her health issues. However, their evaluation would be inaccurate, since Erin never fully disclosed all that she was taking. But at least I now had the complete list for her lawfully prescribed meds the last five years. Previously, the only thing

I ever looked at on my new favorite website was whether we were close to hitting our deductible or out-of-pocket limit.

Big G kept me company via cell phone on the long ride up to Pittsburgh, and it was his suggestion for me to call our insurance company regarding the "private" designation on Erin's pharmacy claims.

As soon as the clock struck 8 a.m., I was able to reach someone from our insurance company. One would think my head couldn't spin around many more times, but once again, I was surprised to learn that Erin had set up the private designation in her profile.

"We have several classes of drugs that we allow our members to designate as private," I was told.

"Would that include narcotics and medications to treat STDs?" I inquired.

"Yes, it would," she responded. Stunned by Erin's deception and sneakiness, I did not think to ask what the private prescriptions were and who wrote them. I recalled that on more than one occasion, Erin would unexpectedly say, "I don't even have a username or password for our insurance company." Really? Then how could you manipulate your profile to establish private settings on your medications? Why did I not look before? Could I have avoided much of what Billy, Katie, and I had to endure?

3 clicks . . . Damn.

After multiple calls to our insurance company, I connected with an individual willing to provide me with the information I was desperately seeking.

"I am the primary cardholder for our family's insurance coverage," I explained. "I am paying for the medical and pharmacy costs, and want to know what these private prescriptions are and who wrote them."

"Okay, sir. I would be happy to assist you."

I damn near wrecked the car.

"Those private prescriptions, for Adderall and Adderall XR, were written by her psychiatrist. We have had to reject many of her prescriptions because she is trying to refill them too quickly."

"Can you clarify that, please?" I asked.

"There are quantity limits on these prescriptions, and she is utilizing them in a manner that is not in line with how the prescription is written. We have sent several letters to her physician regarding this issue."

As I sat parked on the side of the road, I feverishly scrolled through the claims on the iPad. I did not want to push my luck but was curious about a five-day prescription for Vicodin filled on May 18, the day Erin and I signed the non-abandonment agreement.

"Do you mind telling me who prescribed five days' worth of Vicodin for her on May 18?"

She obliged. It was our dentist. It must have been one painful cleaning. What a system! Is it any surprise that our nation has an opioid crisis?

Erin was abusing amphetamines with her prescriptions for Adderall! She had been doing so behind my back since at least January 5, 2011. This discovery did not elicit any joy, but great sadness. I loved this woman, who had been a picture of health back in May of 2010, the last vacation we took alone together. She was not experiencing any cardiac issues; she had yet to have any stroke-like events. She was healthy, and her mind and cognitive abilities were intact.

Erin was looking for something to fill the emptiness she was feeling. Sadly, the family we built together could not fill that void.

You do not need to be an MD or a pharmacist to understand the risks that come along with amphetamine use. They are classified as Schedule II substances for a reason: they are highly addictive and dangerous. At this point, Erin had been taking them for at least five-and-a-half years without legitimate (or adequate) medical oversight.

I was beginning to understand the genesis of her unexplained cardiac issues, elevated heart rate, uncontrolled blood pressure, slurred speech, and the cause of her two stroke-like events in April and November of 2011. She put herself and our family through all of the stress of multiple cardiac exams and emergency room visits without ever mentioning that she was taking these medications. When I say cardiac exams, I mean that they evaluated her with all manner of technology, including cardiac catheterization—nowhere near a benign procedure! Nothing was found to explain her cardiac issues. They ultimately settled on the fact that she has a hard time maintaining volume. Among many other side effects, amphetamines can cause dehydration. Did this, along with her other medications, contribute to her bowel issues?

WebMD reports the incidence of adult onset of ADHD (attention deficit hyperactivity disorder) in the U.S. is 4 to 5 percent, and approximately 60 percent of children with ADHD can carry this condition into their adult life. Erin was never diagnosed with ADHD or ADD (attention deficit disorder), either as an adult or as a child. Erin graduated with a 3.9 GPA when she was eight months pregnant with our daughter, Katie, without the assistance of amphetamines.

According to the National Institutes of Health (NIH), "Addiction is defined as a chronic, relapsing brain disease that is characterized by compulsive drug seeking and use, despite harmful consequences."

Erin was an addict, and I was beginning to scratch the surface of all that she had hidden from me. I was left wondering if she had also been doing illicit, or street, drugs in addition to her lawfully prescribed medications. For years, Erin had accused me of addictive behaviors. I sadly realized now this was pure psychological projection. The more thoroughly I dug into her medical *claims*, not medical records, the more heightened my interest became.

. . .

GPS failed me, I made a wrong turn or two, or perhaps my discoveries consumed and distracted me. I somehow ended up in Ohio on my trip, driving right by the exit for the town where Erin was born. I believe a higher power was guiding me. Never in my life had I taken that route to get to Pittsburgh. I pulled into the driveway at 810 at about 7:30 p.m., arriving at my home away from home. The shaking that I experienced practically the entire fourteen-hour drive stopped, only to be replaced with love, acceptance, and a sense of family that I thought no longer existed for me.

# CHAPTER 12
## *Surf's Up!*

The only thing worse than a liar is a liar that's also a hypocrite!
—*Tennessee Williams*

On my first day at Camp 810, two things overwhelmed me . . . the outcome of my pending STD results, and where to begin.

Al, Jane, and Diane, my niece, left for work and college early that morning, so it was just Colonel, their old chocolate lab, and me. Al named him after Colonel Tom Parker, Elvis's manager. When Colonel wasn't racking on the couch, he was right by my side with his head on my knee. His once-sweet puppy breath now revealed the essence of kibble, moldy cheese, and foot sweat. Regardless, I loved his old soul, and I appreciated his unconditionally loyal company, as I do with most dogs.

The pouring rain made it a perfect day to position myself at the long, antique kitchen table and get to work. Ready or not, it was time to tackle the pile of Erin's phone history, pharmacy claims, and medical claims. My PIs had begun their investigation into Erin's phone records, starting with May 2015. I too started in on her phone records—but in July of that year. I was particularly interested in July 7 and the days preceding our first mediation.

There was heavy text traffic between Erin and a local number. It began at 7 a.m. on the seventh and continued through our mediation and late into the night. There was a one-minute phone call between Erin and this number that day. Who was this character . . . what was their connection . . . why were they so engaged in our personal lives . . . or more accurately phrased, engaged in our affairs? I paid $4.95 for a trial membership in an organization that would enable me to look up any phone number and identify its owner. When I found it, I did not recognize the name, but was pretty sure the owner was male. I had never heard the name, Erin had never mentioned him, and my senses were undoubtedly tingling given the volume of texting on the day of our mediation.

Evidence that great minds work alike: Thirty minutes later, I got an e-mail from the PI firm with a list of names they uncovered from Erin's May phone records. They asked that I get back to them with names I did *not* recognize. Sure enough, "Dexter" (the texter) was on their list too! I replied immediately with the names I did not recognize and informed them that I too had identified Dexter via another resource. They clearly instructed me to "not attempt to contact this individual." Pumped at yet another revelation, I realized I need to clear my biggest hurdle; a negative herpes 2 test had not yet happened.

The daunting process of revisiting Erin's medical claims began. I created an Excel file containing her medical claims from September 1, 2010, to July 7, 2015. Sweet Mother of Pearl, I had a ton of work ahead of me. In this five-year period, she visited seventy-two doctors! While multiple visits occurred with several prescribers, the list of seventy-two did not include the scores of physicians who saw Erin in her numerous emergency room and Urgent Care visits. I was aware of the ER visits, as I was right there with her, but she was on her own for the Urgent Care visits. I was a novice with the insurance company's website but, with a little guidance, I became quite the surfer.

Jane stopped by the house to bring me lunch. With barely an appetite, I absentmindedly nibbled on the massive sandwich. I briefly shared some discoveries from my morning efforts. As Jane, a nurse, headed out the door to return to work, she advised, "You should also check the explanation of benefits attached to Erin's medical claims." This did not require three clicks, only one! I simply had to click on the "details" button next to a claim and *voila*, the full details appeared. If not literally spelled out, a billing code could easily be deciphered to determine every charge and specific test or procedure tied to the claim. My motivation was further increased. As luck would have it, I was very well versed in billing codes for both hospitals and physicians. Over the years, I had conducted several workshops for my colleagues on hospital and physician billing. They are universal codes used by every physician and every hospital in the country to receive payment.

Immediately, I began evaluating Erin's visit on June 16, 2015, with her regular OB/GYN. She had been a patient since 2004. This physician had diagnosed her with herpes 2 as revealed to me in the form of a mediation grenade on July 7, 2015. Sadly, this was just the tip of the STD iceberg for Erin. It became very evident as to why Erin was so concerned about my HIV test in December of 2014. There is no doubt in my mind that she was trying to infect me with something December 30, 2014. Billy and Katie were away skiing while Mom sat in the bathtub and popped the question, "Do you want to have a night?" Perhaps it was Erin's issues "down there" that stoked the rage that she unleashed on me that evening.

As I researched Erin's records, I had not yet become educated about herpes 1 or 2, how it was transmitted to someone else, incubation times, or any of the other specifics about the gift that keeps on giving. So I wondered, had she been trying to infect me on our three nights together on April 23, 24, and 25? Is that why she suggested we have "another night" on April 25? Was she successful? Her issues in the female region would have already been apparent to her on June 9, 2015, the same evening she invited me to stay at our home. Thank God, I turned away when I discovered the locked door.

Before the day at 810 was over, I'd also discovered Erin's tests for multiple STDs in the spring of 2014, two days before Big G and little g's wedding. It

was yet another OB/GYN, not familiar to me, who conducted this evaluation. I dubbed him Dr. One-Time Visit. I was supposedly "ogling" women
at this wedding, while Erin was being tested behind my back. Somebody
was doing more than "ogling," and it wasn't I! These discoveries revealed
so many secrets, intensifying my already sky-high anxiety regarding my
pending test results. What had she been up to? The plot would only thicken
from here, and the dramatic intensity of our divorce proceedings would
build. Remembering Al Pacino's quote in *Scent of a Woman*, I thought, "I'm
just getting warmed up!"

Late that afternoon, personal e-mails popped up alerting me that new
test results were available in my electronic chart. My mouth went dry, the
shakes began, and the blood pressure was heading north. It was still raining
pitchforks and hammer handles outside as I got on my hands and knees and
began to pray.

I accessed my electronic health record, and the results of the curable
STDs were in! I was negative for trichomoniasis, chlamydia, syphilis, and
gonorrhea. It was time to breathe deep and to give quick thanks.

Wait, where was the herpes 2 result?

I was the pathological liar, cheat, slimeball, scumbag, and addict. I was
incapable of giving Erin the two simple things she had asked for: truth
and honesty. I had endured so much abuse and so many verbal insults from
Doris and Erin, yet she was the one out collecting STDs.

As I sat in Al and Jane's kitchen with the rain continuing to fall and
Colonel by my side, I began to see why Doris threatened my life on our
beach trip in June of 2014 and suggested that I was addicted to porn and
drugs. She had been played . . . used and lied to by her own flesh and blood.
Erin had been recruiting her as a negative advocate for months.

Or perhaps she was all too familiar with what her daughter was all about.
After all, she had been cleaning up her messes dating back to Erin's prom days!

I hope you are beginning to see why I consider such clarity The Third
Gift.

As the clock struck 5:04 p.m., it was still just Colonel and me at Camp 810. My phone rang, and I could barely look at the screen. *Why is my family practitioner calling so late? It can't be good news,* I thought. The last call I received at 5:04 p.m., two days prior (from Doris), was not full of good news or well wishes.

"Your results for herpes 1 and herpes 2 are negative," he announced.

"Thank you! Thank You! Thank You!" was all I could manage.

Very soon after this call, Al, Diane, and Jane arrived home. There were hugs all around, and we celebrated a little that evening. It was going to be a long month waiting for our next mediation on August 12, but I hoped the end was in sight.

As the winds of our storm picked up, many people were sucked into the eye. JG and Mary would not be able to avoid it. They were the first two people we met when we moved to Wilmington in 2001, as they lived across the street. JG called me in mid-June 2015 and invited me to play some golf with him. I had not seen him in a few months. I held off until the tenth hole, and then I sprayed him down with all that had been going on. Fore! JG's question prompted the conversation, "Are you feeling all right? You have lost a ton of weight." At this point, my weight loss was impossible to miss. I was down to 155 pounds from 225 pounds. The size 38 waist was gone, and I was now a size 32. Thanks, Erin.

In exchange for JG handing me another ass-whupping on the golf course, I received many free therapy sessions. In all the years that we have played, I only beat him once. He is an outstanding golfer and an even better friend. Their house would become my surrogate mailbox. I would pick my correspondence up there (after Erin opened and scrutinized it, and then taped the envelopes shut).

Phil and Claire, my other brother and his wife, were two more wonderful and generous people that were always there for me, and they soon found their way into the eye of the storm. I had to reach out to the Bank of P&C (Phil & Claire) because I needed their credit card to pay my PIs. My credit card statement was still going to our home, and Erin was opening it. Without ever a hesitation, they obliged. It was no small ask, as the PI firm's initial fee was $2,500!

"Just let me know if you need me to stroke you a check," was Phil's saying. They opened their home many times to our vast family to host dinners during my many trips to Pittsburgh. These occasions provided me with a nice mental distraction and a sense of normalcy.

Mid-July, I returned to Wilmington. My stress was high as the financial and daily pressures continued to mount. I was still working full time, but added a host of new daily routines: dealing with PIs; maintaining my review of medical claims, pharmacy claims, and phone records; and checking our marital account four to six times a day. Erin had no regard for the bills that were due, and she was moving money in and out of our account. In July alone, Erin took over $2,800 from our joint account. Initially, it was $800.00, but her grand finale was when she took the remaining $2000. We had a negative balance of $450.00. She called Billy to inform him of this negative balance and to alert him to the fact that his parking at school was probably not paid. "Your dad has run up a negative balance in our account," she told him. Of course—"Dad did this." I made a trip to the bank to freeze this account at the end of July. I removed the overdraft protection so she could not continue to drive up the negative balance. I also placed a hold on Erin's debit card. I would then receive this e-mail from her via my work e-mail:

"CORRECT THE NEGATIVE BALANCE IN OUR CHECKING ACCOUNT NOW!!!"

By July 20, I had reached a boiling point and texted Erin:

Me: "How dare you put 900 dollars on your credit card bill? I hope you realize we have about a thousand coming out for bills this week."

Erin: "How dare you put as much as you have on yours. Definitely more than me. How dare you spend $110 at dinner, golf, movies, taverns, and a pack of cigarettes a day at $9.00? You've taken how much out of Billy's college account before we signed. You started after you read the agreement.

Two of which not in the checkbook. Your bonus checks not recorded. I have many clients this week that I have already planned to put in that account."

Erin: "I've really done nothing except clean this house, work outside, work my business, and take care of our daughter . . . (Who you haven't contacted for almost a month. Shame on you)."

It would take many months and therapy sessions to attempt to disengage from her. Her delusions, paranoia, and cognitive impairment were only getting worse. I did spend $110 on dinner. I paid for the meals for my parents and two of my sisters. I also played golf with my dad and a few of my brothers during this trip. It was the last time that my father would ever play golf. I am so thankful that I was with him the last time he played nine holes of golf. Six hours to play nine holes, but six hours for my brothers and me to spend with our father.

As I'd previously learned, her financial manipulation, deception, and thievery were not limited to July 2015. I received a call from our financial firm that I needed to come into their office immediately as Erin had power of attorney over my IRA.

"What? When did this occur?" I was incredulous.

"This happened on September 24, 2014," was the reply. The day *after* I got out of Holy Hell! The discoveries kept coming. I headed to their office to have this rescinded. It was my signature on the form, but Erin had filled out most of it. I do not remember signing it! With each passing day, I struggled more and more with the fact that I really did not know the woman to whom I had given twenty-four years of my life.

As the month was ending, the male "friend" from Erin's mysterious texts was identified. He was married with two little kids. The PI firm had placed a GPS tracker on Erin's car and began limited surveillance based on her whereabouts. Now, I began enjoying real-time updates regarding Erin's location and travels. They proved the falsehood of her claim via text that all she'd really done was "clean this house, work outside, work my business, and take care of our daughter." She found plenty of time to go to the neighborhood pool.

Erin's private prescriptions continued flowing without her knowledge of the discoveries that I had made the morning of July 8. I kept my small inner circle of trust informed every step of the way. My niece Diane (aka Diane Sawyer), was working her magic on social media and was assisting my PIs with pulling information on Erin's "friend" from Facebook. On one particular evening, the situation overwhelmed her as she stood in the kitchen and sobbed. I hugged her and tried to reassure her that it was all right because I had received a gift. "I don't like that this is happening to you," she sobbed.

My newfound stressors certainly weren't helping my weight issues. I still had no medical explanation for the irregularities in my blood work. My oncologist and another specialist assured me that stress was not the cause of the abnormalities in my liver enzymes and significantly elevated creatine phosphokinase enzyme. Jane and a specialist believed Erin had been slowly poisoning me. I dismissed this until I discovered further information on the education and background of Erin's "friend." It seems almost unimaginable, but he had the education, degrees, and livelihood to offer Erin counsel on how to poison someone. I know, I know. You might be thinking, "C'mon, Danny, really?" But let's face it, after everything I'd been through to date, I put nothing beyond the realm of possibility. While I was still residing at home, Erin was quite infatuated with the contents in my protein powder. Multiple times, she would question me about the powder's ingredients. Looking back, Erin frequently removed the container from the cupboard to scrutinize the product label, and I would hear, "You are putting something in your protein powder." Now I cannot help but wonder if she was putting something in there with (or without) assistance. Perhaps this was more taunting from Erin. Catch me if you can, Danny!

Upon my return to Wilmington on August 4, I underwent an analysis for arsenic and heavy metals poisoning. A follow-up hair-and-nail test revealed that I indeed had been the victim of long-term exposure to arsenic! Arsenic is odorless and tasteless. Was Erin putting this in my protein powder? Admittedly, I am a creature of habit . . . not prone to trying new things. That includes what I eat and drink. I am a boring meat-and-potatoes kind of guy. Protein supplements suggested by my son were literally the only change I had made to what I ingested on a routine basis in the past couple of years (other than being unenthusiastically put on meds described in previous chapters).

I found myself reviewing Erin's actions from a new viewpoint. Had she taken a sudden interest in our financials—in particular, life insurance coverage for me—because she was planning my death? That interpretation certainly fit her interest, as well as her desire to gain power of attorney over my IRA.

My exposure to arsenic was confirmed, so now it was a matter of determining a source. The most common cause for chronic arsenic poisoning in the world is tainted drinking water, but I had not traveled to Bangladesh or West Bengal in recent memory (aka never). I was also relatively positive I had avoided living near strip mining operations where arsenic may have seeped into the water supply. Acute arsenic poisoning, rather than chronic, is much more dire, with overt issues including vomiting, watery diarrhea, and dying, so that is unlikely in my case.

Therefore, chronic exposure it was. The bitch of it? The height of my naivete included my pre– and post–Holy Hell time spent at home. By the time I was kicked out and reduced to begging for clean clothes, toiletries, and any personal effects that might be granted, the last thing I thought about was asking for my damn container of protein powder! So by the time my heavy metal exposure was confirmed, the arsenic was isolated, and my discoveries of Erin's multitude of treachery and deceit became known, the container of whey protein and I had long been removed from our marital abode. No way to test the powder, no way to move beyond my suspicions . . . damn (again).

Moving on, only seven more days until we'd get to drop our grenade on their side.

# CHAPTER 13
## *Former FBI*

Goin' to be a good day, Tater. —*Sluggo*

After a few more days at the Springhill Suites, I moved to a new hotel for five days, courtesy of Al and Jane. I had yet to secure longer term living arrangements but needed to do so shortly. Anthony and Jackie had given all they could in Marriott Reward points and, even though I was now getting the military rate at the Springhill Suites, money was drying up. I will be forever grateful to so many folks for their love, support, and generosity.

Whether in Pennsylvania or North Carolina, dark clouds seemed to loom on the sunniest of days. As much as I love North Carolina, even those skies appeared to dull whenever I reached the state line. It had been almost three months since I had been evicted from my home, leaving me to endure living out of only a few suitcases. The house I was still paying for was less than twenty minutes away, yet I did laundry on coin-operated machines. Eventually, the hotel provided me with complimentary detergent.

Based on my discoveries I became concerned for my safety. I had no idea what my wife of almost twenty-two years had been up to, or with whom she had been running around. Perhaps she was doing illicit drugs to complement her lawfully prescribed medications. Is that where all her cash withdrawals were going? Given the scope of her STD testing, it crossed my mind that she could have been trading sex for drugs. My PI fueled this speculation, sharing information regarding other clients and the compromising situations he had witnessed firsthand. He referenced current data around increasing Adderall abuse, primarily by moms. We also discussed that prescriptions in their children's names were a means to supplement the abuser's supply.

I was long overdue for a haircut and with my continued weight loss, needed some new underwear. I no longer went to my barber, J squared, as his shop was too close to areas that Erin would frequent. I settled for an inferior haircut and was off to Kohl's to buy some new skivvies. My new drawers set me back $23, cash! I know, I was living on the edge, but I would soon have to defend this purchase. My mistake was how I responded to the cashier's question about Kohl's rewards card. "My wife has a rewards card," I answered. I provided our home phone number and my license so that Erin could get credit for my purchase. I am such a giver! (Kohl's cash, not STDs.)

August 5 was the beginning of Erin's ever-changing mobile numbers and cell phones. As part of my new daily routine, I noticed that the activity on her previous phone number stopped completely. I checked Billy and Katie's records and saw texts they both were receiving from the same phone number. I called Billy, and he confirmed that Mom had changed her number. Erin told both of our kids that I had dropped her from the family plan. She also shared this with our financial advisor, JG, and Mary. I certainly had done no such thing, as I enjoyed having access to her records. It was yet another attempt by Erin to make me look like a crazy a-hole. What was she hiding? Why change your number, Erin?

Is it August 12 yet?

August 7 was moving day, and I headed to my new hotel. My hero, Al, flew into town and we began the process of looking for a more affordable, stable housing situation. Sight unseen, I paid $3K that I couldn't spare for a one-month living arrangement. Complete with rental furniture and in a lovely area, it sounded perfect. We grabbed some lunch, and Al wisely suggested we try to check out this arrangement. Thank God we did! Although located in a very upscale area, this particular unit was on the backside of the building and was terribly outdated. The fantastic balcony view they promised turned out to overlook a dumpster where restaurants unloaded their trash. The ancient rental furniture included a bed that appeared to be the last resting place of the previous tenant. No kidding, the mattress was stained with what appeared to be an outline of a body. I immediately called the rental office, instructing them not to charge my card.

"How did you get into the unit?" they asked. "We have other properties we can show you."

I somberly let them know I was not interested. Back to the short-term housing drawing board. We then visited a brand-new apartment complex I had checked out in June. I gave them a verbal commitment for a 2-bedroom apartment, even though at that point wasn't sure where I would find the money.

While Al was in town, he joined me for an appointment with my therapist, Kasey Lockwood. It was good for Kasey to get a different perspective on me. I also wanted Al to meet some of my friends that had been providing me with tremendous emotional support. Al and I met Big G and little g for dinner and a few "slanks." A slank, Al's creation, is Captain Morgan and root beer. That evening, little g topped the slank off with a scoop of vanilla ice cream. An adult root beer float. It was great to laugh and enjoy a drama-free evening for a change. (I bet you never imagined reading a book about STDs and slanks.)

At last, I was (hopefully) one day away from ending this! The evening of August 11, Al and I had dinner with a friend of his and his wife. Arriving early, I jumped out of my car and called Billy. As I paced back and forth in the restaurant parking lot, I thanked him for standing by me and believing in me. I wanted him to know that I loved him and to assure him that the truth would arrive tomorrow. Despite my minimal communication with Katie, she was in my thoughts every second of every day. I missed her terribly. We once had been so close. Both kids had endured so much over the last year. It was time for the madness to end!

After a nice dinner, Al and I returned to the hotel. Another fitful night lay ahead, so we hung out for a while at the hotel pool before turning in.

Cock-a-doodle-doo! After a few hours of sleep, it was time to shower, put on the new clothes and shoes Al and Jane purchased for me so I could finally pull the pin on our grenade. Al snapped a picture of me in my new outfit so that he could share it with Jane. As I departed, I hit Al with the following: "Goin' to be a good day, Tater." The remark was based on a joke by comedian Ron White. Ron describes putting M&Ms in his English Bulldog's jowls as he sleeps. As he awakes, the Bulldog licks his chops and remarks, "Goin' to be a good day, Tater." This nickname has stuck, and Al and Jane now refer to me as Tater.

Downtown Wilmington, here we come! I arrived at Robin Wright's office with my certified negative results in hand. It was the same setup as last time. After some obligatory small talk, my attorney, Olivia, revealed to Robin that I had tested negative for herpes as she handed her the envelope containing the certified documents.

We also gave Robin an earful on our discoveries regarding Erin's amphetamine abuse, her private prescriptions dating back to January 5, 2011, and her multiple STD tests by Dr. One-Time Visit OB/GYN in April of 2014.

"How did you get access to all this information?" Robin wanted to know.

"I am the primary cardholder for our insurance," I delightedly admitted, "and had full legal access to Erin's pharmacy and medical claims."

Before revealing these results to Erin and her attorney, Brenda, we wanted Robin to pose the following question: "Danny is very embarrassed by this whole herpes situation. How many folks have you discussed this matter with? How many people have you told that Danny gave you herpes?"

We were setting Erin up for potential defamation charges in Superior Court.

Robin returned to share the following, "Erin has told her mom, two girlfriends, and your two kids that you gave her herpes 2." I was shocked that she told our children and that she'd done it weeks before I revealed my negative results. My hand was so unsteady as Robin told us this that I was unable to write down the exact words she relayed. The gist of it was, "I have undeniable proof that your father has cheated on me. He gave me herpes 2."

Even though they are young adults, I can't imagine our kids knew much about herpes—either 1 or 2! Hell, at fifty years old and, primarily out of sheer panic and desperation, I had just become knowledgeable about the disease. Erin's behavior made me snarl an internal question, "Who is using our kids as allies and pawns, Doris? Who is the slimeball?"

It was time for Robin to return to the other side's unit and reveal our negative results. Walls and a decent distance separated us, but you could hear the gasp coming from the other room. Robin came back to inform us that Erin challenged my results. All Erin could remark was, "There are a lot of different types of tests out there, and I don't believe these results."

Robin returned to their room sharing our knowledge regarding Erin's STD tests for trichomoniasis, chlamydia, and gonorrhea on April 3, 2014, performed by Dr. One-Time Visit OB/GYN (2 days before Big G and little g's wedding). We also wanted Robin to inform them that we had identified her male friend and to question Erin as to why she changed her phone number on August 5.

Robin ventured back with Erin's answer, "I had something going on 'down there' in April of 2014 and thought Danny was cheating on me. I changed my phone number because I was having issues with my e-mail on my phone and Danny had turned off my data."

Robin then surmised, "She thinks you are fucking around on her!"

Yes, those were her exact words. Her language was salty and direct, but I was way beyond taking offense. "With all due respect, you both are married women, and if you are supposedly faithful, how many STDs do you get tested for before you go to your husband with some questions?" was my rebuttal to both Olivia and Robin. There was no response from either, as they correctly guessed mine was a rhetorical question. Robin then asked for the phone number for Erin's male friend. Of course, we obliged.

I sensed that this was not ending anytime soon! After dialing the number we provided, Robin returned playing a voice message from a female friend in our neighborhood. I recognized the voice. Katie had been a grade school best friend with their daughter. These folks were more neighbors than friends. "What the hell is going on?" was my reaction. My PIs were 100 percent sure that they had identified a male attached to this number. My research confirmed the same. There was little doubt that this supported Erin's claim that I was crazy and made this shit up.

I got on the phone with my PI. At this point, I was into him for $6,300. I was not pleased with their shoddy investigation.

"Something is wrong here," he countered, "and she is involved somehow. This has never happened to me. I have used the same firm for my research for the last ten years, and they are all former FBI."

"You have put me in a terrible spot and have made me look even crazier to the other side," I retorted. "Fortunately, I have some medical evidence to lean on. We are going to need to revisit your fees. I will be in touch!" I hung up.

My next call was to the neighborhood friend's husband. Erin and I had known them for fourteen years, and I needed to determine how long his wife Candace had had that phone number. He already had some knowledge of what was going on in our marriage. His recollection was that she had that number for at least ten years.

Candace, who went by Candi, is another stay-at-home mom who had "sacrificed" so much to support her husband. (Recognize the sarcasm here.) I was not aware that Erin and Candi were close. Then again, there was much of which I was unaware. If it was indeed Candi's phone number, why was she so interested in what was going on during our mediation? Why was Erin texting Candi at 2 a.m. during her hospitalization for her bowel surgery in April of 2015? Why did Candi respond at 6:15 a.m. the next day?

I was right there by Erin's side, and Candi never visited. Why was that? What were these two stay-at-home moms up to? Candi and Erin never did anything socially that I was aware of, and Erin occasionally remarked how weird Candi was! This might have been part of her plan to cover things up.

Our second attempt at mediation came to an abrupt halt. In spite of denying our request for a retest following our first mediation, Erin headed off to have the same blood test that I had.

To say that I left the mediation dejected would be a gross understatement. Thank God, Al would be at the hotel upon my return. I was devastated, but had much work to do and needed to stay focused. I called the apartment complex and secured a nine-month lease. I made a trip to the bank and opened a new checking account. I could at least relieve one stressor of having to watch our marital bank account four to six times a day. It *wasn't* a good day, Tater!

August 13 was a busy, depressing day. Al had to head back home soon, and we had a lot to do. My move-in date for the new apartment was a couple of days away, and I had none of the basics. Off to Target we went. I could not think straight. We had an attorney-arranged "pick-up" to make at the house by noon, but Al and I proceeded to fill two shopping carts, losing track of time. We had to leave the shopping carts parked in the corner of the store and return later to finalize the purchase.

At the house, we found that this time Erin was kind enough to put my additional belongings in the garage. Nobody was home, and the house was on lockdown. It was hotter than the hubs of hell that day, so I looked in the garage refrigerator for a bottle of water. What do you know? In addition to the water, there also was a nice twelve-pack of Leinenkugel's Summer Shandy. It seems the rules had changed in Dad's absence; it was now okay to have some beer in the fridge. Katie would later inform me that Phone Friend Tiffany liked Summer Shandy. I should have taken the beer and case of water, but instead I just left my garage remote and departed. There would be further pick-ups to come.

Upon completion of the pick-up and a return trip to Target to finalize our initial purchase, I hurriedly took Al to the airport. I hated to see him go. Following the day's events, I dreaded being alone.

After bringing my suitcases and Target essentials into my apartment, I sat down on the floor and lost it. This mess was supposed to be turning around after the twelfth. But there I was, fifty years old, alone, and in a barren flat. The worst part was that I had not seen Katie in three months, and whatever communication we did have was less than civil. Somehow, I needed to find the strength to keep moving forward. Just when I thought I could not feel lower, the Man Upstairs lightened my mood. Well into the night, as I stared at the ceiling from my freshly inflated air mattress, the love symphony began. My new next-door neighbors welcomed me with a raucous session of boot-knock-ing. Not only were the walls thin, but the apartment layouts also had our bedrooms butting up to each other. There was no way to ignore the festivities, so I turned up the ceiling fan as high as it would go, put in my earbuds, lay there, and laughed. As it would turn out, this couple had no happy medium in their relationship. They were either having sex or fighting. I was living next door to Ike and Tina! Proud Mary, keep on burnin'!

August 17, I headed to Music City for work, thankful for the opportunity to get out of town for a few days. The night before, I had worked at the apartment complex clubhouse, since my apartment Internet access had not yet been activated (somehow, I still had a job). I was clearing out e-mails and preparing for the upcoming customer visits in Nashville. Lo and behold, an e-mail appeared from Erin with the subject line "Sorry":

Dan,

I see you were in my electronic chart. Sorry, your cheating plan window is closed. My mom has that. Back at you.

Erin.

Her cryptic e-mail was suggesting that she had herpes 1 and not herpes 2. Herpes 1 (cold sores) is not considered a sexually transmitted disease.

The mental abuse was continuing, even over the damn web! I immediately called Jane. Was it possible that she could have tested negative for HSV2 with her recent blood test? Jane, always reassuring, said that Erin was messing with me. There was no way she could have tested negative! We'd determined that Erin had filled forty days' worth of valacyclovir, and the treatment started two days before the test results came in on June 18, 2015. I blocked Erin from my work e-mail, and informed Olivia of the communication I had received.

The time in Nashville was quiet, and I thought, silence is golden. Not so fast, Danny. When I arrived at the airport on the twentieth, I received an e-mail from Olivia with Erin's certified results indicating she is positive for herpes 1 but negative for herpes 2! I wondered how in the hell is this possible? There was no way, was there? Something was not right. I sent Olivia a lengthy e-mail beginning to lay out my findings from Erin's medical and pharmacy claims, explaining that this herpes 2 is not an isolated case. Erin had been running around on me for years.

Quickly, a second e-mail from Olivia arrived alerting me to the fact that Erin had filed a civil summons against me. Going forward, Erin would be the plaintiff, me, the defendant.

The civil summons is as follows:

The Plaintiff [Erin] is a fit and proper person to have the primary care, custody, and control of the minor child [Katie] and it is in the best interest of the minor child that her primary care, custody, and control be placed with the Plaintiff.

During the parties' marriage, the Defendant [Danny] committed several acts of marital misconduct as defined by NCGS 50–16.1A, including but not limited to the following:

a. The Defendant has engaged in verbal abuse of the Plaintiff and the minor child and has terrorized the Plaintiff and the minor child with his erratic, irrational behavior on several occasions, which resulted in the Plaintiff being forced to call law enforcement to intervene.

b. The Defendant has withheld love and affection from the Plaintiff and has been emotionally neglecting, rejecting and abusive toward the Plaintiff.

c. The Defendant has unilaterally decided to stop attending marital counseling.

d. The Defendant refuses to spend time with the Plaintiff.

e. The Defendant abuses alcohol and prescription drugs.

f. The Defendant is controlling, constantly following the Plaintiff, reviewing her phone and home security records, and even accessing her private medical records.

*At all times throughout the marriage, the Plaintiff has been a faithful and dutiful wife to the Defendant,* and actions described above and conduct of the Defendant have been without justification or adequate provocation on the part of the Plaintiff.

An unequal distribution of property (in favor of the Plaintiff) would be fair and equitable in this case, considering the factors set forth.

The Plaintiff is entitled to recover her attorney's fees incurred in the prosecution of her claim for post-separation support and alimony.

My legal knowledge at this point was nominal, and I did not understand what all this meant. All I knew was that a hearing would take place on October 6, 2015. We would have to answer these claims as laid out in the summons and eventually file our counterclaim. August 12 had come and gone, and this dance was anything but over. It was just beginning!

I was raised to defend myself and taught to fight my own battles. When you come from a large family, your parents don't have the time or energy to fight your battles for you. I would be meeting with Olivia in four days, and had a lot more digging to do.

I was going to need a bigger shovel.

# CHAPTER 14
## *Nothing But Faithful*

Happily ever after is not a fairy tale. It's a choice. —*Fawn Weaver*

Events unfolding the week of August 17 staggered me once again. Somehow, Erin pulled a rabbit out of a hat, or more fittingly, out of "down there." I had barely scratched the surface of her medical claims. I had three days, prior to meeting with Olivia, to examine five years of medical and pharmacy claims. I took a day off from work, hardly a vacation! I needed to document what I believed was a pattern of infidelity on Erin's part. It certainly did not help our cause that we had yet to identify any love interest(s). However, I was encouraged by my initial work that began the morning of July 8. To this day, I believe that Candi was somehow involved. I needed to convince Olivia to retain the services of a medical expert that could explain the differences in Erin's two tests.

Priority number one was to get back on the phone with our insurance company. I hoped to gain access to additional history for Erin's explanations of benefits (EOBs). They were like finding a pearl in an oyster. (No pun intended) The concierge told me that she only had access to two years' worth of Erin's EOB's. So the call was a bust, since I'd already found those records myself.

Next up, I revisited the conflicting results from Erin's two herpes tests. Though I am not an expert, my line of work exposed me to many different lab reports and their terminology. I had a substantial network of clinical colleagues who generously provided their knowledge. I had not examined Erin's first test since the day it rained down on me like a collapsing building. All of a sudden, a light bulb flickered. The designation after her first test was different from the blood test she had the second time.

The classification on her first test was HSV2 NAA. Most of us may be familiar with "HSV2," which stands for herpes simplex virus 2. But, "NAA"? It stands for nucleic acid amplification. I was certain that NAA is a DNA test, and I validated my thinking via the Centers for Disease Control (CDC) website. The only way to perform the analysis is by swabbing one or more active lesions and testing specifically for the virus. I dug deeper into their website to figure out why her two tests would be mirror opposites. Her first test was positive for herpes 2 and negative for herpes 1 (cold sores, not necessarily sexually transmitted). These results were inverse on her second test (the blood test); Erin was negative for herpes 2 but positive for herpes 1! If Mom indeed infected her, why did I not have herpes 1? Her team was prepared to claim that Erin did not come into the marriage with either herpes 1 or 2, having retrieved her medical records from the OB/GYN in Louisville that delivered Katie in 1998. Routinely, women are tested for herpes before delivery. It makes sense, as the child could contract it during vaginal birth. My early work with Erin's phone records revealed that she made multiple calls to the OB/GYN's office in Kentucky in June of 2015. I could not resolve this but felt that this would warrant at least a conversation between Olivia and a medical expert. We needed an STD expert, an infectious disease expert. The clock was ticking, and it was way past time to get moving on this!

For the time being, I ignored her private pharmacy claims and focused on all of the other medications she had taken dating back to September of 2010. I inhaled deeply after realizing that there were 641 rows on the spreadsheet to review. I eliminated the medications that I previously knew Erin had taken. The number of drugs I was not familiar with *significantly* outnumbered those. Over the course of a five-year period, Erin had been prescribed seventy different medications, the majority of which were not for ongoing use. Unfortunately, in the pharmacy claims data, you cannot determine who the prescribing physician was. So now the work began. Painstakingly, I cross-referenced prescriptions with potential medical claims in an attempt to narrow down the individual prescribers. I was especially interested in all of the antibiotic prescriptions, medications for yeast infection, urinary tract infection, vaginal burning, itching, etc.

I found that over a forty-five-month period beginning September 6, 2011, Erin had filled twenty-three prescriptions for antibiotics. That is an antibiotic prescription almost every two months. I realize that antibiotics have many uses and are not just used to treat STDs, but where were the corresponding medical claims indicating that she had visited our family practitioner or an Urgent Care for an upper respiratory illness? What about her rheumatologist for her neuropathy?

They did not exist!

Erin filled eleven prescriptions to treat urinary tract infections, eight for yeast infections, and five for burning and itching "down there." Lest we forget, she had filled prescriptions for forty days' worth of valacyclovir for her latest door prize, herpes 2.

Forty-nine prescriptions in forty-five months! All related to her issues "going on down there," dating back to September of 2011. This did *not* include all of her fibromyalgia medications and private prescriptions. I thoroughly evaluated those medications, and there was no connection between them and her issues in the female region.

Somehow, I emotionally disconnected while slogging through this three-day analysis. Getting lost in these cumbersome spreadsheets, I worked hard to avoid the reality that these disturbing discoveries were emerging from the records of my wife.

The patterns became very clear to me. Erin had been boarding all sorts of dirty buses outside of our marriage. Still, she taunted *me* on July 4, 2015, about finding a condom in my hotel room. The irony is now pitiful. Her trips on public transit brought her to syphilis (ville), chlamydia (burg), trichomonas (town), gonorrhea (opolis) and, last stop, herpes 2 (field). Erin's cutting remarks to me over the last few years now sliced even deeper, reminding me that hypocrites wield much sharper blades:

"Danny, perhaps you are angry and are drinking more because your relationship went south."

"I know how important sex is to guys. If you want somebody else just let me know."

"Trust is the foundation of a marriage. One lie is all it takes to break that trust."

"You say that I am beautiful and then you turn around and ogle other women."

"If you were to ever cheat on me, we would be done."

"There is a lot of good in you, Dan, but there are two simple things that I have asked for that you just can't give."

"Telling the truth would be a huge step forward for you, Danny."

*Erin* is evol. I have experienced her deception and evol firsthand. She is the one addicted to real-life porn, sex, and drugs and has attempted to project all of that on me!

I have previously shared the letter that she wrote to my psychiatrist on October 6, 2014, less than two weeks after my release from Holy Hell. The following letter is "well-documented proof" of her trying to blame me for all of her issues in her female region. My psychiatrist briefly alluded to this correspondence during one of our visits but did not share the full letter. However, when my medical records were subpoenaed in April of 2016, it came into my possession. The unedited version is as follows:

9/14/2014

Dear Dr. [psychiatrist] and Dr. [family practitioner],

On Saturday evening, I called your offices after hours, and I am so very grateful to speak with Dr. [family practitioner] and the doctor on call at Dr. [psychiatrist's] office. (I apologize for not remembering her name) I would please ask for you to keep this information confidential. I just want you to have a better understanding of the other major issue throughout 21 years of marriage that may affect what his only prognosis is now. Dan knows TRUST is the foundation of any relationship and we've never had it. The cycle of our life since day one is he continually lies, I get upset, distrust him, and then he will say it will never happen again, he says he feels bad and overcompensates with gifts, dinner or be overly affectionate. Dan is aware that he is being dishonest and deceitful, but for some reason, he just doesn't care or understand why he is lying. He will get caught over and over. He admits to this but doesn't have an answer for it. The answers are "I don't recall, or I don't remember why I said or did that." I've told him, it is better to be absolutely, consistently true to me and possibly hurt my feelings then tell lies that just set our relationship/family, back even further in trust. When I met Dan, his ex-girlfriend said he was a pathological liar. At the time I just brushed it off as jealousy losing him. There is no REMORSE OR [CONSCIENCE] at all after being untrue! He can tell me or the children something he has lied about and lay his head down to sleep. I can't go into detail on everything that he has hidden or lied about over the last 22 years, but I will just give you an idea of some examples I am mentioning. If he can't tell the truth about everyday things, how can I trust him with the bigger situations that are sneaky. When Dan tells a lie, it is extremely well thought out, "story-like," and absolutely believable to ANYONE, including some professionals along the road. If you question his answers he gets VERY upset and VERY defensive. He has a quick and complete answer for everything that I feel in my gut just doesn't feel right. I realize this was long ago, however these examples of what started all of the mistrust. When he went on a business trip and when out drinking, he could have told me he had too much to drink and was hung over. Instead he comes up with such ELABORATE stories that I know in my heart aren't true. I call him on it; he gets [angry] and defensive and then confesses. He said he quit smoking but our family knew he was still smoking he denied it, got angry. This went on for months; he covered himself every time with another [lie] each time we would ask. He yelled at the kids about accusing him. I found a lighter in the washer and he still tried to lie out of that until I just didn't give up and finally came true. He doesn't remember lie from lie. He denies any questions you may have with a situation he may possibly be untruthful about with such conviction looking straight into your eyes and when is caught has NO REMORSE OR [CONSCIENCE], actually jokes after. As for reasons for feeling that he has had affairs would be: going up to his office and suddenly shutting his computer laptop down. (I asked why and he said it was reflex) He would get texts early Saturday am and when I would walk around the corner he would shove it in his pants. He blames it on not wanting to explain who it is all the time . . . He always leaves and goes to the gas station or the store at a whim. One night lately it was the middle of the night. I got a vaginal infection about a year ago like I told you on the phone and unfortunately, I was on antibiotics for 10 days given to me by my family doctor. I went to my ob doctor and he did a swab and it was negative. He said I needed to come in when the discharge was present and not while on antibiotics. The infection was already gone. He said it was probably trichomoniasis, sexually transmitted disease. (Green discharge). He is always 10 steps ahead of me when it comes to sneaky situations . . . I also felt he became more adventurous in the bedroom, doing things that we never did before. I was pumping gas at a gas station and he saw me and made a drastic U-turn and got back on the highway. He admitted to avoiding me. He said he was going to have a cigarette and saw me and made a major U-turn. I know he smokes, he smokes at home. There was NO REASON for him to have to do that, he admitted he had no idea why he did it.

This weekend was the last straw!!! I told him I will be here to help him through this as long as he promises to be honest all the time and be willing to help himself while I myself get counseling. I have done my part and continue. He now says HE DOESN'T HAVE BIPOLOR AND HE DOESN'T BELIEVE THE DOCTOR'S, IT'S [VOODOO]. DR. FP TOLD HIM NOT TO DRINK ON THESE MEDS AND HE DID THIS WEEKEND AND MADE ME SCARED WHEN HE UNLOCKED MY DOOR AFTER I TOLD HIM TO LEAVE ME ALONE, YOU'VE BEEN DRINKING. HE STILL OPENED THE DOOR AND WAS TALKING IRRA-TIONAL AND SAID "WITH ANY LUCK THE GOOD LORD WILL TAKE HIM TONIGHT AND I WON'T HAVE ANYMORE WORRIES." I LEFT THE HOUSE AND CALLED THE POLICE. HE FIRST WAS CALM, THEN BEGAN TO SHOW ANGER AND WAS PACING BACK AND FORTH BLAMING ME

FOR ALL THIS AND I DON'T HAVE BIPOLOR. . .
. .IT WASN'T PLEASANT. I STAYED AT A HOTEL
THAT NIGHT DUE TO THE OFFICERS ADVICE.
HE CONTINUES TO LIE, LIE IN FRONT OF MY
DAUGHTER ALL THIS WEEK. SHE FEELS UNSAFE
AND WANTS TO LEAVE.

I DO LOVE DAN AND WAS WILLING TO HELP
HIM. HE DOESN'T WANT HELP!! I CAN'T LIVE
WITH SOMEONE WHO I CAN'T TRUST ANY-
THING THAT COMES OUT OF HIS MOUTH. I
HOPE THIS HELPS YOU BETTER UNDERSTAND
OUR SITUIATION. IF YOU NEED FURTHER
PEOPLE TO SPEAK TO IN REGARD TO HIS BE-
HAVIOR, THEY HAVE WITNESSED IT AND WILL
HELP IN ANYWAY.

Erin [married name]

It is imperative to reorient you regarding the date and timing of the letter. It was on the evening of September 13, 2014, that Erin called our family practitioner, my psychiatrist's office, and then the Wilmington PD on me. The following morning, as I traveled to see Billy in Charlotte, she wrote the above letter. Monday, the fifteenth, with Erin by my side, I was involuntarily committed to Holy Hell by the family practitioner in less than two minutes. God only knows what other communication Erin had with him.

Erin set me up! I was broken down emotionally, psychologically, and set up by my wife!

After three mentally exhausting days, my discoveries crushed me. Disappointment, betrayal, and gratitude accompanied my newfound clarity. There was no joy in my findings. Erin had been a busy young "lady" from 2011 until May 2015 when she finally threw me out of the house. Only Erin knows how far back her infidelity went.

Enlightenment led to additional questions, but I embraced the fact that I now at least had some answers. What I uncovered would cause me to speculate that the painful intercourse, patchy hair loss, mouth sores and swollen lymph nodes Erin experienced in 2012 and 2013 were not a result of the fibromyalgia she never had. All of this was due to untreated or possibly a secondary stage of syphilis.

From the Centers for Disease Control (CDC) 2015 STD Treatment Guidelines:

> Syphilis has been divided into stages based on clinical findings, helping to guide treatment and follow-up. Persons who have syphilis might seek treatment for signs or symptoms of primary syphilis infection (i.e., ulcers or chancre at the infection site), secondary syphilis (i.e., manifestations that include, but are not limited to, skin rash, mucocutaneous lesions, and lymphadenopathy).

In plain English, they are referring to mouth sores and swollen lymph nodes. Erin had all of these symptoms. Every single one of them! The majority of STDs (except herpes) are treatable and curable with one or two doses of an antibiotic. I *am* thankful that Erin took these meds, albeit behind my back, as I never once contracted any of the STDs that she brought home to our bed.

Again, referring to the CDC 2015 STD Treatment Guidelines:

> Penicillin G, administered parenterally, is the preferred drug for treating persons in all stages of syphilis. Data to support the use of alternatives to penicillin in the treatment of primary and secondary syphilis are limited. However, several therapies might be effective in non-pregnant, penicillin-allergic persons who have primary or secondary syphilis.

Regimens of doxycycline 100 mg orally twice daily for 14 days and tetracycline (500 mg four times daily for 14 days) have been used for many years.

Erin is *allergic to penicillin!* Of the twenty-three antibiotic prescriptions Erin filled in a 45-month period, four of them were for doxycycline 100 mg. Filled prescription fills dated as far back as September 6, 2011, and as recently as April 9, 2015. There is no doubt that she was having unresolved issues in April of 2015, the month that we were together three nights in a row (the twenty-third, twenty-fourth, and twenty-fifth). Coincidence? I think not! Perhaps this explains her tests for syphilis in December of 2014 and again in June of 2015 when she was diagnosed with herpes 2. These are CDC recommendations. You must be retested to see if the penicillin alternative has cured the disease. Again, I had no access to her explanation of benefits before August 30, 2013, and therefore had no knowledge of previous syphilis testing in 2011, 2012, and 2013. However, the pharmacy claims, combined with her symptoms, led me to deduce that she indeed had contracted syphilis from her dalliances. Syphilis was one of the many door prizes she brought home to me, Billy, and Katie!

Did her relationship(s) outside of our marriage have some meaning? I hope they made her feel special, because she wasn't these individuals' only interest. Did she take the wedding ring off or did wearing it add to the thrill for all parties involved?

She'd been a very busy volunteer, gone many nights . . . all night! She also claimed extended Y workouts, but Elvis never seemed even to make it *to* the building. She was following a pattern of other stay-at-home moms in our neighborhood whose husbands caught their respective wives in bed with other men . . . in their own homes! I have mentioned gratitude for many things, and I am thankful I never had to experience that.

The many hours that I invested "getting educated" served me well during my meeting with Olivia. She agreed to begin searching for a medical expert.

# CHAPTER 15
## *You've Been Served*

Lies don't end relationships; the truth does. —*Shannon L. Alder*

For the third time in less than two months, Erin and I would sit down to mediation. Per Olivia's advice, I agreed to this mediation to avoid the October 6 hearing that resulted from Erin's civil summons. Olivia counseled me that if we ended up in court, the judge could hurt me badly on post-separation support. This is interim support provided prior to alimony being awarded or denied, previously referred to as temporary alimony. In North Carolina, proof of infidelity is not a bar from post-separation support but could prohibit him or her from being granted alimony.

I was delighted with how direct Olivia was with this negotiation. She countered their first request for post-separation support with a meager number, less than 15 percent of what they were asking. It was our final offer, and it was accepted.

I would be obligated to pay Erin a small monthly sum and child support based on a sliding scale. Prepared with statements to back up what I was making compared to my financial obligations, I only had so much to give. I, for one, was going to do whatever it took to make sure I delivered on the promises Erin and I made to our kids regarding their education. Legally, since Billy was no longer a minor, I had no financial obligation to him. Morally, I would not leave him hanging. He was working, but he still needed support. Erin agreed to cover our home's utility bills, and beginning on January 1, 2016, she would be responsible for her own medical expenses. I would no longer have to subsidize her addiction to lawfully prescribed medications and the medical costs that accompanied her complications.

Based on our mediated agreement, communication between Erin and me would be conducted via a website called Our Family Wizard (aka "the Wizard"). Text messages were allowed for emergencies only.

Erin utilized this new platform to continue to assault me with all sorts of delusional accusations. I was not innocent either. I would send a few taunts about her "friends," her lies to our kids, and her hypocrisy. My restraint was a work in progress, and I received steady coaching and guidance from Olivia, Abby (Olivia's paralegal), and my therapist (Kasey Lockwood) to limit my responses.

"They think you are crazy, and I don't want you to give them any more ammunition," warned Olivia.

Kasey rhetorically asked, "Would you engage with an intoxicated individual in a bar? Would you attempt to carry on a conversation with a mentally ill individual on the street?"

By this point, I had already completed four sessions with Kasey; she was outstanding. She believed, as others would also come to see, that Erin had a mental illness called borderline personality disorder (BPD). Erin's prescription drug abuse further exacerbated this disorder. Kasey's insight was spot on. She accurately predicted all that would happen. The books that I read about BPD provided further validation and led to several "Holy shit" moments. I literally put the book down and uttered those words countless times. This was especially true with the book *I Hate You, Don't Leave Me*. I had been living this life for the past six years!

The week of September 7, 2015, was hellacious. The one-year anniversary of my involuntary commitment approached, and I was unaware that I had yet to reach rock bottom. Erin continued to assert control over my possessions, the house, and Katie.

That day, as part of our settlement, I was to pick up additional items at the "marital residence." I never made these trips alone, and this time JG, our former neighbor, joined me. We arrived to a driveway completely filled with cars. Katie had had several friends over the previous night. I was happy that she had friends over, but I was embarrassed to think that her friends would be witness to her crazy dad coming to collect his stuff. "My stuff" was on the back porch. Against her attorney's wishes, Erin had been kind enough to leave some of my Red Sox paraphernalia on the porch. Her attorney insisted on appraisal before handing it over. It was worth maybe $300. Erin also left some of the utility bills for August with a strongly worded note that they needed to be paid—NOW! I left those bills right where they lay, as she had quickly changed the accounts into her name. JG and I were there maybe fifteen minutes. He graciously offered to assist me in unloading the items at my apartment, but I declined. My impositions on JG and his wife, Mary, were beginning to mount.

Erin fell way short of giving me all that I was supposed to receive. Although a small collection of basics including towels, blankets, silverware, plates, cups, and the one television that we agreed I should have would have been nice, several missing items hurt me deeply. Our agreement stated that I was to receive half of our kids' photos and half of their sentimental Christmas ornaments and childhood art creations. I received six sentimental ornaments (five of Billy's and only one of Katie's). None of their artwork and relatively few photos were included. Yes, I counted them! We had boxes upon boxes of albums, and I got only seventy-five photos! To add insult to injury, I received an empty picture frame that had once contained a beautiful Father's Day letter that Katie wrote for me when she was eight years old. It was titled, "My dad and why he rocks!!!!!" Erin packed our wedding photos, several cards that she had written to me over the years, pictures of her, and her lingerie. You read that correctly—lingerie. Stuffed in a plastic bag in the bottom of a laundry basket was her lingerie. I opened the bag but did not touch it, as I could not guarantee what might jump out at me. I called Jane and shared a good laugh with her. I did hang onto it for a few days as I thought it might be of use for legal purposes. Kasey suggested I get rid of it; "No judge is going to want to see that." I sent Erin the following message on the Wizard:

> "Thanks for my stuff. I would have liked the letter Katie wrote me years ago for Father's Day. I see someone took it out of the frame. It is so nice having pictures of the kids!"
>
> Erin: "I didn't see any Father's Day letter. You will have to ask her that. That frame that said Happy Father's Day was a picture of Billy and I. Thought you might want the frame."
>
> Erin a matter of minutes later: "The picture had me in it. That is why it is empty."

The fun and games were just beginning!

The next day, the stupidity started with the Time Warner Cable equipment in my home office. I went to TWC early that morning to sign over our joint account to Erin. I agreed to pick up this equipment from JG and Mary's on September 11 (our twenty-second anniversary) any time after 2 p.m. It was also on the eighth that Erin sent a message on the Wizard that Katie was not feeling well, so she was taking her to our family practitioner. Our family practitioner called me when Katie was a no-show for her scheduled 4 p.m. appointment. I reached out to Erin over the Wizard and received a cryptic response, "It was her ovary." That was it! I deemed this to be an emergency, so I texted but received no response. I sent Katie a text and gained some peace of mind that she was all right. It was a ruptured cyst. My baby girl was in the emergency room for abdominal and pelvic pain, and I heard nothing from Erin about this!

We closed out the week with more frustration. The cable equipment I was supposed to pick up at JG and Marys' to return to TWC never made it. Erin had informed me the day before that it would be there. I stood an hour in line at TWC to notify them of the situation. $45 later, I closed my account, and the equipment and their respective late charges were now Erin's concern. Aggravating e-mails from Erin's attorney helped to make the week complete. Brenda stood by every word that came out of Erin's mouth, pushing every allegation along to Olivia. Without any apparent discretion, she forwarded bills to Olivia demanding immediate payment. Two examples of frivolous requests were from AT&T collections and our lawn care company. The AT&T collections notice was not for our family plan account. It was for an account Erin set up with entirely different account numbers. The $350 lawn care bill was not a bill but an estimate for aeration and over seeding.

Nevertheless, they made their way to me with the demand for immediate payment. Olivia's tremendous composure wasted no energy or emotion reacting to any of these requests. She merely handled them and kept me informed. Olivia was a great role model for me to emulate. Not all of Brenda's ranting was about money. Several of her e-mails that week spanned all manner of insinuation. Accusations that I had hacked Erin's e-mail, checking account, Wi-Fi, and routers, shut off her cable, and was using her credit card for purchases. Brenda's closing remark (for this week's onslaught) was, "I hope he is taking his meds. Somebody needs to speak to his psychiatrist!"

Happy twenty-second anniversary, Danny!

As if that weren't bad enough, I wound up making it worse. That evening, after such a long week professionally and personally, I decided to have a few slanks. Liquor is rarely an option you should choose, but it was that evening. I had a few too many slanks, got slunk (as my late uncle once remarked) and made the mistake of texting Erin. Based on our mediated agreement, those texts were a violation of our contract. No excuses, I made a mistake. My text messages were as follows:

"You need to know that I still loved you. On July 7th, you tried to destroy me. I hope you have found happiness."

"For the sake of our children, make the right decision. If you are with your boyfriend, respond when he is gone. Stop the games, Erin!"

I am not sure why I was expecting a response, perhaps it was the Captain in me, so when I did not receive one, I sent an additional text:

"If you are not with your boyfriend, can you call me? After 22 years of marriage, I get no response."

On my one-year anniversary of being involuntarily committed to a psychiatric facility, I decided it was time for a little ink. Erin and Doris had beaten the concept of Family, Trust, and Honesty into me, so I thought I would make it official with a tattoo. I had a beautiful cross with the words "Family, Trust, and Honesty" emblazoned on my chest over my broken heart. (Can I get an aaaaahhh?) It also contained Billy and Katie's initials.

Katie's seventeenth birthday was fast approaching, and our relationship was almost nonexistent. I had missed her sixteenth birthday and vowed I would never again miss a chance to do something on her special day. My little girl was always in my thoughts. I missed her and the relationship we once had. I shared with Kasey, my therapist, an idea of delivering cupcakes, a card, and a letter to Katie's school. I would not attempt to see her but wanted to ensure she received them. I was confident that if I mailed anything to the house, Erin would make sure it never found its way to the birthday girl. Kasey read the letter before I delivered it to Katie.

9/12/2015

Dear Katie,

It truly breaks my heart to have to miss another one of your birthdays. I know your 16th birthday was not what you deserved, and I hope your 17th birthday will be a little better.

Katie, I want to acknowledge my part in this whole nightmare. I will forever regret the fear that I caused you last July, and I know that saying I am sorry again are just empty words. I used to be a man that kept all his emotions inside and never opened up or discussed what was bothering me and the way I reacted to the issues Mom and I were dealing with was entirely inappropriate. I should not have been drinking as much as I did, and one should never drink out of anger. I know I have hurt you, scared you and have negatively affected your teenage years. I truly miss you and often think about the last time we did anything together. It was last March when we went shopping for Emma's birthday, and you hugged me and said, "It is nice to have my normal Dad back." I assure you that your normal Dad has been back for some time. I have been getting much professional help so that I can process all that has happened and to come to terms with the destruction that has taken place in our family. I want you to know that I was not suicidal; I was simply in a bad emotional state of mind. I have so much to live for and being here for you and Billy is all that matters to me. As I said in my text, I can't even begin to imagine how you at the age of 16 can process all of this, because I struggle some days with this whole situation. We all need to move forward somehow and begin to heal because life is short. You deserve happiness, peace, and the ability to be a teenager truly. Mom and I should not have involved you, Billy, and so many others the way we did. It was wrong. My faith in God has become much stronger, and accepting that everything happens for a reason has helped me to try to move beyond trying to understand why this has happened. I no longer ask God "why" I simply say, "let your will be done."

I have never stopped loving you, and I think about you every day. I will respect your wishes to stay away, as you do not deserve any more pain or hurt. I will continue to pray that someday you and I can begin to take small steps towards rebuilding our relationship. I am willing to wait as long as I have to and in the meantime will hold onto and cherish the memories of you and me from the past. I often think about Big G and little g's wedding and snuggling with you on the couch as we watched the basketball game. I have the picture of you and I standing in the ocean hand in hand, and my goal is to redo that picture someday hopefully. It will be a much skinnier version of me.

Katie, I am genuinely sorry and Love you so much. I am proud to call you my daughter. All your aunts, uncles and cousins love you. They often ask about how you and Billy are doing with this whole mess. I will not ask for your forgiveness but would ask for an opportunity someday to earn your forgiveness. I will continue to pray for a chance for you to see that the man I used to be is a better man and will be an even better father because of this. I believe that there is good that can come out of this. My offer still stands for you to sit down with someone and discuss your feelings. If it is just you alone, then I am ok with that. I would be happy to facilitate this and of course will pay for it. Billy is in counseling, and he says it is helping him.

In spite of this situation, I hope that you can make your 17th birthday a good one. I know Mom will do something nice and that your friends will surround you.

Happy 17th Birthday Katie!
Love always,
Dad

On her 17th birthday, I delivered the card and cupcakes to the receptionist desk at school.

The receptionist did inquire, "Is Katie expecting these? Do you want me to call her down to the lobby?"

I responded, "No, I would like these to be a surprise."

As I left the school campus, I tied a balloon to her car and texted Katie a picture of it.

The weekend of September 25, I flew to Pittsburgh for the christening of Al and Jane's first grandchild, Hannah—the first great-grandchild in the family. Being part of the good times and blessings that were occurring in my extended family provided me with a semblance of sanity.

The joy of this occasion was dampened by a call I received from the New Hanover County Sheriff's Department. I thought they were calling to inform me of something happening to Erin due to the lawfully prescribed drugs she was abusing. I was wrong!

"We have some papers that we need to serve to you," the officer remarked.

"For what?" I retorted.

"Your wife has filed a domestic violence protection order against you," he stated.

"I have not seen her since May 30. What is she accusing me of?" I asked.

"We don't read them; we just serve the papers," he replied.

A year ago, the law was transporting me to a psychiatric facility, and now they are serving me papers for domestic violence. Panic stricken, I reached out to Olivia to try to make sense of all of this. She was pissed that the opposing counsel did not inform her that a Domestic Violence Protection Order (DVPO) had been filed against me. Olivia did not handle this type of case, so I would need to find another attorney and do so quickly. My hearing would be in four short days after I returned from Pittsburgh.

The baby's beautiful baptism brightened the darkness of what occurred on Saturday. Again, I leaned on Al and Jane in an attempt to process all that was going on. In my struggle to find peace, this weekend provided me a little. The support of friends and family had been fantastic, and their kind words meant so much. Jane's mother leaned over to me in church and whispered to me, "I hope you find peace." I have carried those five simple words with me since that day.

I talked to Billy Sunday evening. So he could focus on his studies, work, and life, I had previously committed that we would no longer discuss my marital situation. It was an impossible promise to keep since Erin continued to attempt to manipulate our children against me. I could sense that he was upset. Of course, Erin had made Billy aware of the current situation: "The next time you talk to Dad he may be upset. A sheriff will be serving some papers on him because he is harassing me about a boyfriend."

# CHAPTER 16
## *You Got Caught*

If you're going through hell, keep going. —*Winston Churchill*

Monday, September 28, I was duly served at my apartment. Erin had filed these orders on the twenty-fourth at the courthouse. In her filing, Erin had asked that these orders for protection be *ex parte*. *Ex parte* is Latin, meaning "without a hearing." She was asking that the order for protection occur without the judge hearing the case. Thankfully, her request was denied. Erin's accusations were detailed in the filing:

> Defendant has accessed my e-mail and bank accounts using my personal identifying information without my knowledge or consent. The Defendant contacted me by phone and text. This is despite the provisions of our family court agreement stating that he shall not do so. Defendant has been unable to stop harassing me since our separation and has repeatedly attempted to access various accounts of mine including my internet and phone accounts.
>
> During the time we resided together the Defendant ex-

hibited erratic and unstable behavior. He followed me from room to room in the house, abused alcohol and other drugs, and terrorized my daughter and me to such an extent that on one occasion we were forced to lock ourselves in a bedroom and call the police to intervene. Subsequently, the Defendant was hospitalized in Holy Hell Hospital for an extended period, and after that, we separated. During the marriage, the Defendant was excessively controlling and emotionally abusive such that I became fearful of setting him off, and became emotionally anxious and depressed and am seeking treatment for these conditions. The Defendant refuses to accept responsibility for his actions and continues to harass me.

The Defendant has continually texted the minor child, attempting to place her in the midst of the parties' conflict, despite the child's explicit direction to the Defendant that she does not want his contact. The Defendant showed up without invitation at the minor child's school to attempt to force a conversation with her.

The minor child is scared of Defendant's acts as he continues to text her relentlessly despite her asking him to stop.

The Defendant made threats to commit suicide prior to his being hospitalized at Holy Hell in September of 2014.

I want temporary custody of our minor child.

I want the Court to prohibit the Defendant from purchasing or possessing a firearm.

I want the Court to order the Defendant to surrender to the Sheriff his firearms, ammunition and gun permits to purchase a gun and carry a concealed weapon.

I want the Defendant to be ordered to have no contact with the minor child except through therapy as requested in the custody order.

The only allegations that had any merit were the texts I sent Erin on our twenty-second anniversary and the visit to Katie's school for her seventeenth birthday.

P.S. I have never owned or possessed a gun.

After calling several attorneys Olivia recommended, I retained the services of Frank Slade.

The efforts I put forth to review Erin's pharmacy and medical claims would be invaluable in painting the picture for Frank. Her pattern of STDs and prescription drug abuse would be a useful topic of discussion in court. I was not overly concerned about the outcome of the hearing until Frank remarked during our two-hour meeting, "She can call the police at any time and tell them you have been at the residence or following her. They would have no recourse but to arrest you," he replied. Then the nerves kicked in!

During this same time, Doris was also texting Katie, encouraging her to speak to her mom's attorney: "Mom's Attorney, Brenda, may call you to introduce herself. No big deal. Mom is driving so she could not text you herself. Love U!"

On September 29, I was meeting with Frank Slade, unaware that my fan club was thriving as Doris penned a letter:

September 29, 2015
To whom it may concern:

Erin [Maiden-Married Name] is my daughter and was married to Dan for 21 years. I will be the first to admit that Dan had me fooled for about nineteen of those years. I now realize that he is a master at his craft of lying, control, manipulation, and verbal, mental, and emotional abuse. Little did I know what a toll of 21 years of his behavior had on my daughter until she began to open up to me?

The issues escalated within the past one and ½ years and with this escalation came increasing anger and abuse from Dan.

I have been on the phone with Erin when she and her daughter, Katie, are locked in a bedroom because they were afraid that he would harm them. On another occasion, I was also on the phone with Erin when Dan had been drinking. Dan has been diagnosed with bipolar and is (supposed to be) on medication (and not drinking), and his increased agitation rose to the level that Erin had to leave the house so quickly that she did not even have time to put shoes on. The police were called, and Erin was advised not to stay in the home that night. Luckily, on that occasion, Katie was not at home. In addition, Katie has unlocked the window in her bedroom so she could escape if his actions escalated at any time. Dan has hit Erin hard enough to leave a handprint. She has photographs.

Erin has had the courage to file for divorce, and although Dan is not in the home anymore, he continues to harass Erin and Katie through texts, written letters, phone calls, using the phone and internet to track her every move. Dan has already violated the mediation agreement and disregards any instruction by attorneys to not have any contact directly with Erin. They are using Wizard only for communication about their two children, but Dan uses it to continue to harass and verbally abuse Erin. She lives in fear of this man and what his next action against her will be. She has stated to me several times "that he is going to kill me."

Until now, Dan has been able to manipulate the system and ignore all the rules without penalty. I am asking that the law will protect Erin's and Katie's safety and rights and that there will finally be a penalty for Dan if he violates it.

Sincerely,

Doris [Self-Righteousness]

I never put my hands on Erin in a violent manner. The alleged photographs containing handprints were yet another revelation that I was previously unaware of. She pulled out all stops to set me up in all sorts of ways.

Two days before the hearing, I received Erin's subpoenas. She subpoenaed her therapist, a representative from ADT (our home security system), a representative from an AT&T retail outlet, and our daughter! She also had documentation from the loss prevention department at Kohl's alleging that my men's underwear purchase occurred with her credit card! There was no evidence of a Kohl's credit card statement reflecting my charge of $23.00. But all that was trivial compared to seeing Katie's name in a subpoena. My flesh and blood was going to testify against me! Once again, in addition to my full-time job, I had an impossible amount of work to do to be as prepared as I could be.

The events of the day did not stop there. That evening, ADT contacted Billy. Our Realtor, Kay, had triggered the alarm during a last-minute showing of our home. She did not know the passcode and ultimately, the Wilmington PD arrived at the house. Erin had added Billy, Katie, Candi, Doris, and Tiffany as emergency contacts. Initially, Billy ignored the call, but returned it later. What was he to do, three-and-a-half hours away in Charlotte? Erin's cognitive impairment was becoming even more evident not only to me but to others. The Adderall was less than effective in improving her focus and recall.

I was amped up and angry the evening of the thirtieth, pissed at Erin for her continued attempts to alienate me from our children, with the ultimate insult being her dragging our daughter into court. The subpoenas for Kohl's, AT&T, and her therapist, for that matter, did not concern me. What would Katie have to say? What would the allegations be regarding our security system? I called them to prepare for the hearing, as I wanted to understand the capabilities of our system. I was relieved to hear that our basic system did not allow for remote operation. My name was still on the bill, and I was paying for the system, yet Erin had already instructed them not to provide me with any information. They informed me about Erin's six calls in the last few weeks, and offered to speak to my attorney. I was not very complimentary about Erin as I commented to the customer service representative, "She is fucking crazy!" Remembering that the calls are recorded, I caught myself and apologized for the language.

October 1, Anthony arrived in town, following a trip out West with his family for a wedding. It was another personal sacrifice to support me. I was as prepared as I could be for the events of the following day.

In the pouring rain, we arrived at New Hanover County Family Court relatively early, for the 9 a.m. calendar call. All in the name of love—or evol!

As we sat in the church-like pews, Brenda approached and asked, "Are you with AT&T or ADT?" We chuckled a bit and simply said no. I had never met her before then.

Shortly after that, my heart sank as Katie entered the courtroom with Erin and Tiffany. As she took her place a few pews in front of us, she briefly looked over her right shoulder and glanced at me. I had not seen Katie in four months. Tiffany quickly embraced her with her right arm as if to provide protection. Thank the Lord that before calendar call the bailiff removed Katie from the courtroom. She was only seventeen, and the judge did not allow minors in her courtroom. Frank had arrived before Katie's removal, and he was pissed that she was even there. He leaned over and remarked, "How dare she drag that child into this courtroom?" I saw his anger as a positive emotion for our team.

We would be the second case heard that morning. Rightfully, DVPOs are of high priority. Each side would have thirty minutes to present their argument.

. . .

In the allotted thirty minutes, Brenda would call Erin, her therapist, and the representatives from ADT and AT&T to the stand. The therapist's rhetoric was pretty much what I had expected.

"She's exhibited a lot of anxiety and fear around her personal safety, her daughter's safety, the environment in the home before the separation. She's lost weight. She's had trouble sleeping, trouble concentrating, and confusion in making decisions from time to time. Erin was looking forward to the separation creating some space and some peacefulness in the household with her and her children. But since then, there have been ongoing texts that I have seen, phone messages, coming by the house, driving up in the driveway at nighttime, the thought that maybe he had been in the house when she wasn't home, some issues with her credit card and her AT&T cell phone, possibility of maybe having some spyware on her computer."

Frank's cross-examination effectively clarified to the court that I had only met this therapist one time, for forty-five minutes, ten months ago.

"You managed to form all of those impressions drawing from one joint meeting with my client for a grand total of forty-five minutes," he stated. "That is the only time you have had any contact with him, correct?"

"Correct."

Frank's focus shifted to Erin's Adderall use.

"Are you aware of the medications Erin is taking? She takes Adderall. Correct?"

"I am not aware of that."

"Matter of fact, she has two different Adderall prescriptions."

"I am not aware of that."

"So—I mean, with those drugs, if she was also taking the Adderall every day, would that cause her to be anxious and paranoid, do you think?"

"I'm not a medical doctor. I don't feel qualified to speak to that."

Brenda's brief direct examination of Erin was difficult to watch. I had not seen her in three months and her appearance was alarming. Her noticeably slurred speech caused Frank to lean over to me and inquire, "Why is her speech so slurred? Is she intoxicated?"

"It is the Adderall, Frank," I replied, "along with all of her other medications."

The story she told was all too familiar to me. She and Katie are afraid of me. I won't stop harassing her. I have accessed her e-mail, bank accounts, and routers and have broken into the home. I have used her Kohl's credit card to purchase men's underwear and have recently harassed her about having a boyfriend.

As she was rattling off her list of accusations, Frank covered the microphone on our table and remarked, "She is willing to say anything about you. She is gaslighting you!"

"What does that mean?"

"Look it up," he replied with a smile on his face.

Brenda and Erin's only surprise was when they asked to play a voicemail that I had left Erin on our twenty-second wedding anniversary. I did not remember making the call, as I had a little too much Captain in me. I leaned over, apologized to Frank, looked back at Anthony, and shrugged my shoulders. Frank, Brenda, and Erin would step into a room so that Frank could hear the recording. I was concerned not knowing what message I had left.

As Erin returned to the stand, she attempted to play the voicemail but had difficulty getting it to work. She handed her phone to Brenda to figure it out.

The recording began. "Erin, this is Dan. Stop the charade."

That was the extent of my message. I certainly was relieved that it was nothing more than that.

The highlight of Frank's cross-examination was the following exchange with Erin:

"You testified just a minute ago that you were—that the defendant was accusing you of having a boyfriend and it wasn't true, and you haven't dated anybody and all this kind of stuff?"

"Absolutely."

"Do you recall—you went to mediation, and you produced a medical report showing a positive test for herpes and used that to argue that he was committing adultery, right?"

"That's what I was told."

"Okay. And then Dan produced a report that was negative for any venereal disease, right?"

"Correct."

"Okay. So, it wasn't Dan accusing you of anything. You were accusing him and *you got caught.*"

"This is what I was told by the lab, which was a misdiagnosis."

The ADT and AT&T representatives barely had time to get comfortable in the chair on the stand. They had nothing inflammatory to offer. There was no evidence of my tampering with Erin's accounts. Neither of them was particularly pleased to be there but had no choice.

When Frank directly examined me, he was able to clarify exactly how much communication I had had with Erin post the date of our mediated agreement. It amounted to one phone call and three texts that all occurred on our anniversary.

"I have been devastated by this whole situation. I used poor judgement making that call. I made a mistake."

Then it was over, and the judge rendered her verdict: "Based on the information and the testimony I have, I am going to dismiss the Complaint for Domestic Violence Protection. I've heard a lot of evidence about the contact. It's clear that there are phone calls and communication, texts. If I find out that you willfully violated the order, I can put you in custody for up to thirty days, or I could put you on supervised probation. That will not be good for your job. So you need to follow the order. Do you understand what I am saying?"

"Yes."

Anthony, Frank, and I were the first folks to leave the courtroom with an escort from the bailiff. As we stood waiting for the elevator, I looked around hoping to see Katie again, but she was nowhere in sight. Tiffany came buzzing around the corner and quickly made a U-turn when she saw us. Anthony and I thanked Frank for his excellent work.

"I did not think it would be that close," he said, "but we were successful. Make sure you look up *gaslighting*!"

The emotion that I experienced was relief, not joy. Once again, it saddened me to see what had become of the woman that I once loved. It was traumatizing to see our daughter physically dragged into this mess by appearing in court, but I was thankful she did not take the stand against her own father.

One hurdle cleared!

# CHAPTER 17
## Now Comes the Defendant

In every difficult situation is potential value. Believe this,
then begin looking for it. —*Norman Vincent Peale*

In early September, Olivia located an infectious disease specialist with incredible credentials who was willing to provide insight into Erin's conflicting herpes test results. We had indeed found a national STD authority. Olivia provided our expert with the test results from Erin and me, along with my extensive compilation of her medical and pharmacy claims. At the beginning of October, Olivia heard back from our expert via e-mail, and the brief e-mail was very encouraging: "I have some firm opinions about these results and would be happy to meet and discuss further."

Perhaps momentum was beginning to shift. I was thrilled to get this meeting scheduled. In the meantime, we finally started to swing the hammer that Erin handed me on July 7, 2015, the date she accused me of giving her herpes 2. We filed a litigation hold notice asking Erin to preserve all electronics (phones and computers) and documentation from January 1, 2014, to October 31, 2015. A week later, they returned the favor with a similar notice for me.

Erin went silent on the Wizard for ten glorious days following the conclusion of our domestic violence hearing. I enjoyed the electronic calm. The quiet ended on October 12, when I landed in Houston. I received a communication that the contact information on my bank account had been changed. Perhaps her frustration from the outcome of the hearing led her to do this.

October 21, 2015, Olivia and I met with our expert. Almost twenty-three years before, on October 22, 1992, Erin and I were engaged to be married, and now I was about to sit down with a national STD authority. Although I was confident heading into the meeting, I was getting better at tempering my emotions and expectations. Although our meeting lasted two hours, in the first five minutes we received the explanation that I had hoped for. According to the expert, "She has both herpes 1 and herpes 2, and she did not get either of them from you. Her conflicting results are easily explained. On her first test, which was a nucleic acid amplification test, she had a DNA swab of either a vaginal or rectal lesion. It is nearly 100 percent reliable. It was an 'incident' or recent infection and she more than likely contracted herpes 2 sometime between February and the first week of June 2015. The second test was a blood test that is identical to the test you had. These tests are done to detect antibodies that are developed to fight the virus. It takes eight to twelve weeks for the antibodies to develop. Erin had been prescribed 40 days of valacyclovir, and this would further delay the development of antibodies. That is why she tested negative for herpes 2 on the blood test. Her OB/GYN that diagnosed her started her on valacyclovir two days before the test results were received from her DNA swab so he must have seen something that caused him concern."

Our expert believed, as I had, that there was a pattern of STDs as evidenced by Erin's multiple visits to her routine OB/GYN and to Dr. One-Time Visit, coupled with a large number of prescriptions Erin had for antibiotics because of vaginal burning, yeast infections, and urinary tract infections.

Furthermore, the expert stated, "I won't be able to confirm this pattern without reviewing her medical records definitively. However, women over the age of twenty-five are not routinely tested for STDs unless there is something seen on a physical exam. The types of antibiotics that she was prescribed are consistent with those used to treat many of the STDs according to the Centers for Disease Control (CDC) guidelines."

For how much of our entire marriage had this behavior been happening?

As Olivia and I prepared to leave, our expert advised, "Brace yourself; she will burn the village down." All of my professional help had been exact with their predictions and assessments. So far, the village idiot has made it out alive. Not only an MD, but also a prophet!

The timeline for Erin's "incident" or recent herpes 2 infection confirmed my suspicion that Erin was trying to infect me when we were "together" three nights in a row in April of 2015. She must have been confident that she was successful or she would not have played the herpes card at our first mediation. I will never be able to reconcile the fact that I was married to someone this calculating, manipulative, and evol.

The cheating plan window that Erin stated had closed— "My mom has that. Back at you."—remained wide open. Sorry, Erin.

On this journey, I became accustomed to the fact that every day could bring new emotions. On the twenty-first, my feelings were ones of encouragement and hope. On the twenty-second, they swung to disbelief and despair.

With over two months of apartment living under my belt, I found myself blessed with my neighbor Copper, also in the middle of a divorce after a very long marriage. I like to think that we provided each other with free therapy. Unlike me, he was at a loss to explain the end of his long marriage. His divorce cost him very little to finalize, and I was burning through money faster than I could make it. I recruited Copper to go with me for yet another pick-up at JG and Mary's. This pick-up resulted from Olivia's very strongly worded letter to Brenda reiterating all of the items that I was obligated to receive because of our mediated agreement in August. The thing I most longed for was Katie's Father's Day letter (the one that used to reside in a frame but had mysteriously disappeared). Erin continued lying to Brenda, claiming there was never a letter. JG and Mary were not home, but on the porch was a single black garbage bag . . . damn, I was pissed. Copper, on the other hand, was amused, "Twenty-two years of marriage and that's all you get?" The bag contained some pots and pans (but no plates or cups), two towels, and three small blankets. I was supposed to get half the towels and blankets. And if you thought that was awesome, two of the three blankets were the ones we used for our dogs when they sat on the couch. I left the dog blankets and took the third, which my mom made for me for my fortieth birthday. I soon discovered all manner of stains ruined it, so I sadly had to throw the quilt out. Once again, I received very few of the kids' pictures and only a couple more sentimental Christmas ornaments. I took photos of the stuff with my iPad and e-mailed Olivia with a request to file a motion to show cause for contempt against Erin.

One result of our litigation-hold notice was that both Erin and I had to have our electronic devices imaged. Items such as deleted texts and e-mails can be retrieved, unless you restore your phone to factory settings, aka "wipe" your phone. So, there I was, Mr. Compliant, carrying my computer, iPad, telephone, and a jump drive to downtown Wilmington so an imaging expert could extract all of the data. After five hours, the expert also retrieved $1,800 from my wallet! Erin attempted to manipulate even this process by having a spare five-year-old computer and only one of who knows how many of her phones imaged. Sadly, we also requested images of Katie's phone and iPad. Ultimately, Erin did have *all* her phones and her three computers imaged.

On October 26, we provided Erin's attorney with our answer and counterclaim to the civil summons they filed against me in August of 2015. Long story short, we denied every allegation that they had made and closed with our counterclaim that read:

Assuming Plaintiff [Erin] is a dependent spouse and Defendant is the supporting spouse pursuant to NC Gen Statute 50–16. 1A, Plaintiff should be precluded from receiving an award of spousal support as Plaintiff has committed acts of marital misconduct, which include, but are not limited to: illicit sexual behavior, abandonment, malicious turning-out-of-doors of the Defendant and other indignities rendering the condition of the Defendant's life unbearable and burdensome, including, but not limited to: withdrawing her love and affection and ignoring the Defendant."

The meeting with our STD expert was significant and provided Olivia with the ammunition to file this counterclaim. In the great state of North Carolina, if there is a proof of infidelity, the dependent spouse (Erin) could forfeit alimony. It is a North Carolina law. The DNA evidence was clear that Erin had stepped outside of our marriage. We would now just have to wait for our date in court with the hope that the law would be upheld.

As October ended, I had my final appointment with my psychiatrist. It was a good day, Tater! I was no longer taking any medication, and there was no need for me to continue to see a psychiatrist. I did not have bipolar after all! He stopped short of an apology and reiterated, "I thought you had a unique form of bipolar with irritation and agitation."

Life continued outside of my turbulent world. My parents continued to battle health issues. Dad's dementia took a stronger hold with each passing day and my mom, an incredibly strong woman, had just survived a four-and-a-half-hour cardiac procedure. She'd had chest pain for four weeks and told no one. Her pride runs deep!

November 4, I boarded a plane in the early evening, as things appeared to be dire for her. Arriving in Philadelphia, I received a text message from AT&T that someone had accessed my account. C'mon, man! I had extra security on this account after all the games Erin had been playing. A quick call to AT&T corporate informed me that Erin had accessed my account while in a retail store. Erin was attempting to use my account to get Katie a new phone. The day before, Erin had sent me a message on the Wizard. "Katie cracked her phone and I was going to get her a new one since you had an upgrade available." I did not respond to that message and certainly was not going to address Katie's phone issue now.

Erin wasted no time in lighting up the Wizard as I was completing my travel to Pittsburgh.

Erin: "I am sorry to hear your mother is in the hospital. I hope she is okay and recovers quickly. I asked Katie to text you the picture [of her broken phone], she is cutting herself [on it], and she can't wait any longer."

Erin: "I did pray for your mother last night and the strength for your family to endure whatever God has already planned for her. If the prognosis is poor and is of course not what you planned, hold her hand, talk to her and let her know if it's to join her family, okay to let go. I am sure your mom will fight for her life because of her family. Despite all the ugliness that is going on, I still think of her as a survivor and 'one hell of a strong woman.'"

I had done the best I could not to wallow in self-pity or feel like a victim. After all, Erin had given me the Third Gift. Most days, I was successful. On Thanksgiving, I volunteered at a local mission and helped feed 1,500 families. I was humbly reminded of all my blessings amidst the madness: I was employed, had my health and two beautiful kids.

But the evening of Thanksgiving, self-pity crept in. As I sat in my apartment alone, I thought about the lovely home-cooked meal Erin, Katie, and Billy were enjoying in the house I was paying for. Doris was in town as well, and the "family" was together.

When you think things are as bad as they can be, God sends examples of others confronting far worse challenges. Sadly, my son provided me the example. Billy arrived at the apartment the day after Thanksgiving, and his body language told me something was wrong. It turned out that Erin had verbally attacked Billy on Thanksgiving and accused him of being involved with me in hacking her information and committing fraud and identity theft.

I felt terrible about the emotions I had experienced the evening before. While I was feeling sorry for myself, Billy's mother was accosting him. After cursing her out, Billy went and sat outside by himself for close to two hours. Mom offered a weak apology, excusing herself because Billy did not understand what she had been going through. Billy also revealed that during this visit Mom and Grandma had him check out her computer to look at the suspicious word document that was logging all the security scans done on her computer. He is very tech savvy and explained, "Dad, this is a routine document produced by the anti-virus software Mom has on her computer." More than likely, this was the genesis for Erin's allegation that I put spyware on her computer!

In spite of our revelation at the domestic violence hearing, Erin continued her use of Adderall and Adderall XR. That is what addicts do, and it continued to fuel her paranoia and delusions.

I reconnected with my PI in the first part of December. His staff had been harassing me for payment, and I was firm that I would not be paying another dime until I received some explanation for their shoddy phone work. He had the impression that my legal journey ended with a mediated agreement.

"Oh," I told him, "it has not been resolved, and the mistakes that you have made are going to cost me dearly with additional legal work."

"There is something wrong here," he assured me. "I believe that Candice is involved somehow. I have used the same agency for ten years. He is a former FBI agent, and this has never happened before. I want to rerun the number and will do so at no charge."

He wanted to clarify the ownership timeline for the phone number he believed belonged to Erin's love interest(s). That evening, I revisited the PI's file. I had previously overlooked that Erin's name was on the TWC account that Candice and Tom had for their home phone. Erin's name was on the account dating back to December 7, 2011. Why was that? This aligned perfectly with when Erin's issues "down there" began. I would sit on this information until I heard back from the PI.

December 14, my dad's eighty-fourth birthday. I exchanged a string of e-mails with my PI that had me celebrating.

PI: "I knew I was right. Candice is deeply involved. Confidential source. Cellular Line History for Candice was 6/26/14 to present. The previous owner was "love interest" until 6/26/2014.

. . .

A belated Christmas gift arrived on the twenty-sixth. We finally sold the house. In a hot market, we sold it at a slight loss, but it mattered little. I was relieved to be out from under the mortgage. I had been working much closer with our realtor on the sale, as I did not want to leave this asset in Erin's hands. Our Realtor, Emma's mom (Katie's best friend), was becoming concerned about Erin's state of mind and competency.

I could not afford it, but I decided to join Al and Jane in Punta Cana, to ring in the New Year. In the meantime, Erin twisted this against me with Katie and the folks in her camp. "He can go off to Mexico (her words) but cannot provide any support for me to attend Katie's competition in Orlando." She was a master spinner. The reality was that she could not attend Katie's competition because she had several doctor's appointments in late December. Based on our mediated agreement in August, Erin would be responsible for her medical expenses beginning in 2016. She needed to load up on her medications before the New Year as they were currently costing her nothing!

Following the sale of our home, I sent Erin the following message on the Wizard resulting in a lovely sendoff text from Doris.

Me: "With the house now being sold I would like to know what your plans are to find suitable housing for our daughter. Forty-two days will fly by, and January will be a busy month legally as well. I will work through my attorney to gain access to the home, as I am sure there are possessions that I do not have. It is time for you to think about our daughter's well-being and your continued financial impact on your mother. Time to tell the truth, Erin! I think you know that we won't be done legally by Feb 11 unless you come clean. Tell the truth, and you can move on with your new life with your "friend" or "friends" you met four or five years ago. January is going to be a hectic month for you. I have already texted Katie to let her know that I have a place for her. February 11! What a day! It is going to come at a really bad time for you!"

Erin: "No worries about housing. I have a plan in motion, my daughter and my son's well-being is always a top priority. Nothing to hide, Dan. Your accusations are delusional and have no basis."

My jab regarding February 11 coming at a bad time for Erin was in response to the fiftieth birthday card that I received from her in June of 2015. "Dan, what a day! This comes at a really bad time for you . . ."

Erin forwarded my Wizard message to Doris and Katie. (Let's keep the kids out of this?) Doris texted me in response:

"You have crossed the line. You threaten my children or grandchildren, you threaten me. They are a gift from God, not a burden, and I have earned the right to support them in any way I see fit. Your lack of respect for my family is appalling. You are wasting your time and money in your attempts to 'fabricate' a reason for Erin to divorce you. She has been nothing but faithful in her marriage. Her reasons have not changed . . . you refuse to accept your diagnosed illness, the documented verbal, mental and emotional abuse, controlling behavior and anger. Perhaps if you could have accepted these issues, the picture would be different. You will apparently go to any lengths to not step up to the plate and man up to your issues. . . . we all have issues . . . it is how we deal with them that is important. Should you continue with your empty threats, you are sealing your own fate. The behavior you exhibit is indicative of a state of mind that is troubling. Your underestimation of Erin's strength," (the text ended there)

You are correct, Doris—we all have issues and what is important is how we deal with them (or choose not to). Doris lacked meaningful context in this whole situation. Acquiring context requires one to open their mind. An open mind would mean that you might have to confront the real issue. It is far easier to project one's issues onto other people. "Nothing but faithful in her marriage!" LMAO! Erin's increasingly erratic and paranoid behavior is indicative of a state of mind that should have been very troubling to Doris.

New Year's Eve with Al and Jane was the best New Year's I had had in a long time. During the last six to seven years of our marriage, I often rang in the New Year by myself. Erin would be fast asleep due to the combination of amphetamines, benzodiazepines, sleeping pills, and "exercise" outside of our marriage. Of course, during those years I believed she was exhausted from her "disease."

# CHAPTER 18
## *Lawfully Prescribed*

Narcissists do not feel guilt or remorse for what they have done. Since a
narcissist has no conscience, there are no limits to the pain and destruction
they can cause. Not only will they not feel guilty about what they have
done to you, they will most likely blame you for it! —*Author unknown*

Although the Dominican holiday provided me with a needed respite, it
would be short-lived. As we barreled toward our trial date, we faced months of
emotional ebbs and flows. I became adept at taking things one day at a time.

I reached out to Erin on January 5 via the Wizard to try to get some
clarity on living arrangements for Katie. Previously, all I had received from
Erin was, "I have a plan in place, and I am running with it." Erin's new
response was as follows:

"We will have our own place. No worries. My life has been and always
will be my children. If she chooses to reside at your residence, that is a choice
she will make on her own. (The therapist will also have a say in that) I've told
her whatever her decision may be in regards to you, I am 100 percent behind
her, however, I truly don't think that will come to fruition at this time. Your
best interest was not apparent when she was the only one at the competition

without a mother there to hug her when she was done with her performance. You sat in the sun in Cancun laying in the sun while I got messages that made me cry. Your best interest was not apparent when Billy got Christmas presents, and she did not. Your best interest is only about Danny."

Profoundly trusting Kasey's advice and judgment, I had followed her counsel. Though painful to me, I did not get Katie anything for Christmas, as she was not in my life. Regardless, Erin continued attempting to smear me by gleefully sharing my lack of generosity to anybody within earshot.

I abandoned all hope that Erin would do the right thing for the sake of our kids and "own" what she had done. Mama Bear was not about her children. She was only interested in herself and deflecting any accountability for the destruction of our marriage. She could not take back the herpes card she'd thrown down. Kasey did an excellent job of keeping me grounded concerning this. She also provided me hope that one day Katie would see the light and appreciate the truth of this entire mess. Kasey also accurately predicted that it would not be long after I was out of the picture that Erin would begin to turn on our children. That was evident when she attacked Billy at Thanksgiving.

As Billy was preparing to head back to college, Erin once again accused him of conspiring with me to "mess" with her electronics, e-mail, and bank accounts. Erin demanded that Billy speak with Brenda to inform her that he did not call ADT or TWC. Billy refused, telling me later, "If she was smart enough to get through law school, then she can figure it out. Katie needs to be left out of this as well."

Katie tried to engage Billy regarding this, but he told her, "I don't want to discuss it. I am headed back to Charlotte."

Katie replied, "Welcome to my world. You are so lucky not to have to live here." Katie began to cry and Billy, ever the big brother, embraced her. One of the many unseen benefits in our darkness, Katie and Billy have become even closer.

In the coming days, Erin's legal team would submit subpoenas for phone records for both of us. She was hoping to prove that I was playing around with the home security system, Internet, and routers, so they wanted all calls and audio recordings of the calls that occurred with ADT and TWC. Why in the world would she subpoena her phone records? Olivia believed that she was trying to prove that she had not made the calls to TWC and ADT.

The closing on our home was less than a month away, and Erin controlled everything. She violated our mediated agreement, unilaterally making healthcare decisions for Katie. She selected a therapist for her and attempted to have a psychiatrist initiate medications for her without my input. On the occasions I challenged Erin, I would be told, "Making decisions for our children is called parenting." Similarly, she took it on herself to arrange for an auctioneer to sell most of our possessions.

Early one Saturday morning, I got a call from this auctioneer. "Your soon-to-be-ex-wife asked me to call you regarding an estate sale at your former residence."

"We were supposed to make this decision together. I need to speak with my attorney, and I will get back to you," was my reply.

"She said that she was in charge and that she is not allowed to speak to you. She also stated that she had you banned from the home." I got a kick out of that.

After consulting with Olivia, I decided to move forward with Erin's auctioneer. I called him back to gather more specifics on the sale and to have him begin the process. He closed our conversation with, "Do you mind if I deal with you directly from now on? Every time I speak with Erin, she sounds like she had a bottle of wine in her."

In a short period, all of our possessions appeared on the auctioneer's website. I thoroughly reviewed all of the items as Erin was attempting to keep many things that she was not entitled to. My emotions spiraled seeing all that we had accumulated over twenty-three years up for sale. Erin used every medium she could in her attempts to taunt me. My dresser was on the site prominently displaying a sign that read, "Let your faith be bigger than your fear."

I would not challenge Erin on the therapist she selected for Katie. She needed to speak with someone, and I did not want to delay this any further. January 17, Billy's twenty-first birthday and the night before I would meet with Katie's therapist, my mind was in overdrive. My boy was becoming a man, chronologically speaking. It pained me no end to see how fast he'd had to mature with all we had put him through the last few years. Now, the next day, my baby girl would be counseling with a stranger to help her deal with the collapse of our family unit.

Before my meeting, I spoke with Katie's therapist on the phone, and was informed that they would be doing a thorough evaluation of Katie, including assessments for both ADD and ADHD. I began to wonder about Katie's prescription history for ADD medications (stimulants). In grade school, I recalled that she had tried Adderall but did not continue taking it as she hated the way it made her feel. Thank God! So, it was back to my favorite website. I had never considered either of our kid's pharmacy records before. As soon as I accessed Katie's pharmacy claims, I damn near fell out of my chair. What were the medications in her claims marked "private"? I took a few deep breaths and then looked at Billy's. Holy Toledo! Bunches of his claims were marked "private"! Who was the sneak in our marriage? If I could prove these private scripts were what I suspected, it would be evident that Erin was using our kids to supplement her supply of amphetamines. My PI had mentioned the increase in parents utilizing their children to gain access to amphetamines. It certainly looked like this was happening here with my ex.

Immediately, I revisited Erin's claims. I had done a lot of the heavy lifting already but needed to compare her private prescriptions refill dates with the kids' records. I confirmed that every private fill, whether for Erin, Billy, or Katie, was for a form of amphetamines. I could not believe what my analysis revealed!

Assuming Erin was taking the volume of amphetamines she was

filling, she began her use (abuse) on January 5, 2011. I genuinely believe her use began in 2009. In April of 2011, three days before her first stroke-like occurrence, I believe she began supplementing her supply with Katie's amphetamines that were lawfully prescribed by our illustrious family practitioner—the same doctor who had me involuntarily committed. In May of 2011, she began tapping into Billy's supply. Billy, diagnosed with ADD in fourth grade, started taking Adderall as he entered fifth grade. He stopped taking it at the end of his sophomore year in high school (May 2011). Our family practitioner never evaluated Katie, but perhaps assumed that since her brother had it, so must she. Alarmingly, all of Erin's buried deceptions were rising to the surface. In totality, Erin had twenty months of gaps in her fills for her private medication beginning in early 2012. She used our kids to gain access to 600 days' worth of amphetamines. Twenty months!

She spread her deception equally between Billy and Katie, utilizing their names for 300 days each of amphetamines. No wonder Erin was so pissed when Billy was denied another prescription for Adderall his freshman year in college (October of 2013). She was running out. This same family practice group had previously allowed refills for their medications over an eighteen-month period without seeing the supposed patients. I fully evaluated both Billy and Katie's medical claims and confirmed this was the case.

Billy was no longer a minor, so I did not worry about getting his private scripts unblinded, as I knew what they were. Katie was only seventeen, so I filled out the necessary paperwork to get her private prescriptions unblinded, I also requested her full medical record from our family practice office. The information confirmed my suspicions. Sight unseen, this office was allowing refills over an eighteen-month period of a controlled substance. The only new revelation was that Katie's prescriptions weren't for Adderall but Ritalin LA, a long-acting version of the amphetamine Ritalin. Erin had been taking Adderall, Adderall XR, and Ritalin LA on top of all her other medications. No wonder she had had two stroke-like events and was having unexplained cardiac issues!

October 29, 2013, six days after Billy was denied a refill, Erin settled in with a new psychiatrist. She was evidently more than happy to write for whatever Erin requested. Erin was very effective at doctor shopping. Oddly enough, this psychiatrist was in practice with a psychiatrist that Erin saw for only a few visits in late 2011. I can only guess that he was not as accommodating with her prescription requests as his colleague would be. At the same time, Erin's "miracle worker" was running into some issues with the North Carolina Medical Board and DEA (Drug Enforcement Agency), so she turned to our kids. Addicts will do whatever is necessary to get their fix. Mama Bear was using our cubs to get her "honey."

At the end of January, we got the results of our subpoenas for Candi's cell and home phones through TWC. The results were disappointing. The Verizon records showed that Candi had owned that phone number since 2006. Time Warner Cable (TWC) leaned on cable privacy laws and stated that a court order was required to provide the information. Money was drying up; we had DNA evidence that Erin had cheated on me, so we reluctantly decided not to pursue this matter. We will never know why Erin's name was on their home phone account. There is even more that I will never know, and with each passing day, I became more comfortable with that.

I had been looking to buy a little townhome or small house for several months as a means to access a line of credit. I was maxed out on two credit cards, and the legal fees were only escalating. Olivia not only set me up with a great therapist, but she also aligned me with a very knowledgeable CPA. Her expert guidance on managing my finances and debt was life-saving. It was her suggestion to buy a place so that I could then gain access to an equity line of credit. Once again, Phil and Claire opened their large hearts and checkbook. All other banks had denied me, but the Bank of P&C came through again. With their generosity, I was able to put a down payment on a new townhome. My payment would be the same as my rent, so it all made sense. Nevertheless, I would have to defend this purchase.

Two months into the New Year, the legal intensity increased. Erin was tardy in her submission of her answers to the interrogatories (questions) we posed to her because of the civil summons she had filed against me in August of 2015. Olivia addressed this via a stern four-page letter giving Brenda until noon on February 15 to fulfill our request and produce the delinquent documents. Failure to comply would result in us filing a Motion to Compel Discovery of medical records and other missing documentation. Olivia directly stated, "Erin cannot assert that she cannot work full time due to her health issues without providing proof. She has tested positive for an STD, and therefore her medical records and prescription history are discoverable."

The very same day we sent that, we received their subpoena information from ADT, TWC, and AT&T. Another weekend engulfed with more legal work. In a matter of four months (September to December 31, 2015), Erin had called ADT twenty-two times and made seventeen calls to TWC. Seventeen hours of audio recordings to occupy my spare time. I needed to know the specific accusations against me. Abby would also listen to these calls and we would compare notes. Over the course of listening to more than 1,000 minutes, I experienced the full range of emotions from sadness to laughter and fear.

Erin's delusional and cognitively impaired allegations included:

"He has hacked into my phone and is keylogging my computer. He is listening to my calls, has hacked into my bank account as well. He has cameras on the roof of the house, in the doorbell and he has placed a listening device somewhere in the home."

"He is banned from the home, but I know he has been here. He is probably getting in through the doggie door. He is leaving little clues that he has been here. He has also messed with the alarm sensors in the kitchen windows. I have had a tech come out, but they could not find anything wrong."

"I am seeking further documentation from you guys because I am working with a detective at the Wilmington Police Department. I used to worry about losing his income, but I don't care anymore. I have enough evidence to put him away in federal prison. Once I move, I am going to need to learn how to use a gun to protect myself. I may also get a German Shepard as he is afraid of those dogs."

"He still has a PI following me, and they must have a garage door opener. Last night, I came home and closed the garage door behind me, but twenty minutes later it was open again."

"My mom has some mob connections as her late husband was Italian. She is going to send somebody down to North Carolina to scare him. They won't hurt him but scare him."

The seventeen calls to TWC were equally disturbing. She accused me of cutting phone lines and the power to the house and attaching a suspicious-looking box on the side of our home. It took an hour-long call for TWC to figure out why the landline was not working. At the end of the call, the representative quietly asked Erin, "Is the phone line plugged into the wall jack?"

It was not! Erin had changed out the router out of fear that I, or somebody, had hacked into it, and she forgot to plug the cord into the wall. The suspicious-looking box on the side of the house was a box that TWC had installed eight years ago.

Her paranoia and delusions were real! My predominant emotion was sadness. Erin, once an intelligent woman, had fried herself with all manner of medications. I shed a few tears as I listened to these calls, as Erin sounded incapacitated and inebriated. Her conversations were marked with slurred speech. Her cognitive impairment was so severe that she did not recall adding Billy and Katie as emergency contacts to the security system. She did not remember the Wilmington PD arriving at the house after Kay set off the alarm due to the last minute showing. One of her many calls to ADT was to find out why she received a letter from the Wilmington PD following their visit to the home on September 30. On every occasion the ADT representative gently reminded her that she had made the very changes she was questioning. My fear spiked as I listened to her comment about learning how to use a gun . . . to the ADT rep! God help me!

Erin's final call to ADT was on December 30, 2015, when she canceled the service. "If you can't protect me, I don't need your service anymore."

"We can't protect you if you cancel your service," was the response that ended the call.

The alleged camera on the house was an irrigation sensor that had been there since the day we moved in. I never went to federal prison and never heard from the Wilmington PD regarding any of these allegations. The mob connections never showed up either.

We were only a few days into February. What a year this would turn out to be!

Erin's Wizard messages continued to flow with new accusations about me establishing master accounts for her AOL e-mail, which enabled me to control her e-mail. She would then pivot to messages about me having an affair with Mila.

Erin via the Wizard on February 15:

"Are you kidding me? Drug problem? LOL. Everything & anything I have EVER had prescribed for me by my physicians had to do with fibromyalgia and any secondary illness I had at the time. It is so easy for you to forget the pain I was in for years. Those 'RX Drugs' saved my life. Dr. 'Miracle Worker' as whacked out as he was, directed me to the Clinic, which was the beginning of my new life. You should be happy that I was gone and as sick as I was because I didn't catch on to you and Mila until later. I hope you and Mila enjoyed the Country Club in November 2011. Lovers Chocolates good? After I totally cleaned your desk, you were so worried about those receipts. You got them, didn't you? I just so happened to have someone over that can "prove" as you say they were real. Room service quite expensive. I sure wasn't present that weekend. You are trying to find something other than the REAL REASON we are where we are. You just can't handle the truth.

"Oh, there is plenty there Dan. I saw the 'guy friendship' you and Mila have. That broke my heart and made me sick at the same time. You have the nerve to say I was unfaithful. Do you know I don't get tremors anymore, Dan? I don't shake when someone pulls into the driveway. I am not on half of the meds I was on when we were together. Isn't that something?????!!! Speaks volumes. I have an interview on the eighteenth, and I pray I am their candidate, so I don't have to beg for money anymore."

Erin did not reduce her medications by all that much. I still had full access to her pharmacy and medical claims and tracked them very carefully. My access to these records would continue until our divorce would be final. The only medication that she briefly stopped was her Adderall and Adderall XR.

One short day after her Wizard message about reducing her meds, she ended up in the emergency room with more stroke-like symptoms. Katie arrived home from school to find dog food strewn all over the kitchen floor, and Mom unable to walk or speak clearly. She was in withdrawal. Katie drove her to the hospital. Katie's BFF, Emma, and her mom, Kay, met her there and stayed until one in the morning. The explanation of benefits for this visit would show that this was the first time ever that Erin was drug and alcohol tested. I did not have access to the results but could not help but wonder about illicit drug use. She had been off her amphetamines and had been out of her "downers" (benzodiazepines) for over one month at the time of the test. Her story with Billy, Katie, Emma, and Kay would be claims of low potassium, sodium, and glucose levels. Billy and Katie were beginning to know better. Billy called Erin at the hospital, and he shared with me that he could not understand what Mom was saying. I spoke with Kay a few days after this event, and she simply described Erin as a "mess."

"I had to help her with her medication list. She could not remember all of the medications that she was on."

Kay, Emma, and their entire family are beautiful people. Kay has become like a second mother to Katie as she endured all the drama that continued on the home front. That said, and despite the turmoil over the last few years, I desperately wanted to get her the help she needed but did not know where to turn.

Erin and her legal team missed our February 15 deadline. Olivia filed our Motion to Compel Discovery a few days later. Little did I know that trouble was brewing with Erin and her legal team. Like so many others, perhaps they were beginning to realize Erin's mental state.

At month's end, we conducted our fourth and final mediation with Robin Wright. We had agreed to this upon the sale of our home. Erin was feeling much better with Mom by her side.

Olivia and I discussed with Robin the entire evidence specific to Erin having an STD. We disclosed our meeting with our expert and this individual's interpretation of Erin's conflicting results. We asked her to keep this confidential, but we had a particular message we wanted her to share. So Robin delivered the following upon her return to Erin: "They are not willing to negotiate any distribution of the 401K/pension today unless you are willing to waive alimony. They are convinced that you have an STD."

Robin returned to our room with the following reply: "Erin wanted me to let you both know that your belief is crazy. She has herpes 1 and fibromyalgia."

Mediation adjourned after one-and-a-half hours.

The village is fully engulfed!

A few days post-mediation, I received this from Erin:

"I WILL NEVER ADMIT TO EVER CHEATING ON YOU BECAUSE IT JUST DIDN'T HAPPEN. YOU KNOW THAT DAN. YOU JUST DON'T WANT TO PAY ME ALIMONY WHICH BOGGLES MY MIND. I GAVE UP MY CAREER TO STAY HOME WITH THE KIDS, (WHICH I NEVER REGRET A DAY IN MY LIFE) I FOLLOWED YOU EVERYWHERE YOUR COMPANY TOOK US. I WORKED AND FINANCIALLY CONTRIBUTED BEFORE, DURING AND AFTER OUR MARRIAGE AS MUCH AS I COULD WHILE YOU WERE ON THE ROAD MONDAY-THURSDAY. Enough said. Just concentrate on the kids. Put me incognito somewhere and just love your kids."

# CHAPTER 19
## *Hi, Daddy*

The time is always right to do what is right. —*Dr. Martin Luther King, Jr.*

February of 2016, a leap year with an additional day for drama! My communication with Katie had been increasing, primarily via text. I sent both her and Billy a text on Sunday evening, the twenty-eighth, to let them know that I would be in DC for work. Whenever I travel, I have always kept them informed of where I will be. The message that I had been hoping and praying for arrived from Katie the next day. In the middle of a meeting, I received her text inquiring if I was home. I reminded her I was in DC. She texted back, "Never mind." I replied by asking if everything was okay. Katie's response brought me to tears. "When will you be home? I want to see you."

I had to step out of the meeting. Heading to the men's room, I sat in a bathroom stall and quietly cried my eyes out. Once we'd been exceptionally close, but it had been almost two years since I could claim having any real relationship with my daughter. The day that Kasey said would eventually come, had come. What a day! I told Katie that I would be back in Wilmington the evening of the first but would leave it up to her as to when she would like to see me. It was killing me, but I was trying not to push too hard.

Katie and Erin were touring an in-state college on the second. A little after 5 p.m. I got a message that Katie wanted to see me that evening. We agreed to meet at Starbuck's close to my apartment. I was nervous, anxious, and excited all at the same time. I arrived well before Katie, as I could not pace the floors in my apartment anymore. As she rolled into the parking lot, I stayed in my car until she parked and exited her vehicle. Again, I was trying to contain my excitement at seeing her. I made my way to her and Katie greeted me with the phrase that always melted my heart, "Hi, Daddy." My heart pounding, I immediately embraced her and did not want to let go.

Starbuck's was packed, so I asked Katie if she would mind going back to my apartment to visit. With her overpriced cup of coffee in hand, she followed me back to "the rock." After taking our places on the couch, I was understandably worried about Katie's comfort level being in my apartment. I simply asked, "Do you have any concerns about being here?" Without hesitation, she responded, "No." There was no discussion about the situation with Erin and me. I had missed so much of her life and wanted our time together to be about her. We spent about an hour and a half going through photos that Katie had taken over the last year. We talked about school, her plans for college, and her boyfriend at the time. I shared what few pictures I had from my trip to the Dominican Republic. Time flew by, but I was so very thankful to have had it. I was relieved that in all the photos, she looked happy. Any outsider looking through the pictures would not be able to sense a bit of trouble in Katie's world. She had a real friend in Emma and so much support from her other friends at school. As she headed out, we shared another long embrace, and I thanked her for coming to see me. I also wanted to be clear that I would follow her lead concerning seeing her again. It was a wonderfully sleepless night!

Following Katie's visit, the hostility and anger from Erin increased. Sadly, it was all directed at Katie. Erin's near-perfect story was beginning to unravel after so many chapters in the making. To date, I had had the cops called on me, was misdiagnosed with bipolar II, spent nine days in psychiatric lockup, was poisoned with arsenic, "evicted," and had my daughter wholly alienated from me.

Friday, the eleventh, Erin and Katie were headed for another college tour. I would miss another momentous and ordinarily happy occasion in our daughter's life. It was not an enjoyable experience for Katie. Erin just couldn't leave our drama out of the events of the day. "Mom keeps bringing up your situation and that you are going to drag her into court, and the court and the judge would see all of my text messages." The Wizard messages corroborated Katie's story.

Erin insisted in her messages that I needed to end this for the sake of our children. "This is killing both of our kids. You choose to drag these court proceedings despite the pain it's causing our children. Divorce is ugly. It's normal for mom and dad to bad mouth; however, if this was over, we can all move on and enjoy life. Just to make this official and on a message board submitted in court, you've decided to prolong the divorce proceedings. It doesn't have to be this way."

Katie spent the weekend with friends, and on the twelfth, I received a text message from her that melted my healing heart: "I want to come and stay with you!"

Sunday, March 13, was the first night Katie stayed at my apartment. After grabbing some pizza, we had to go shopping for bathroom and bedroom basics. Ah, the simple pleasures I used to take for granted with my kids. Spending some time with her was great. Later that evening we watched a movie together. It had been years since I had sat on the couch with Katie and done this. At this point, I wasn't sure what the long-term arrangements would be, but I didn't care. I was practically overwhelmed with relief to have her with me. I will be forever grateful to Emma and her now former boyfriend for the encouragement they gave Katie to reach out to me and potentially consider living with me.

Through the assistance of the deacon at my church, Erin was able to secure a part-time job working with adults with developmental issues. I refer to it as *my* church, because Erin joined a new church closer to her house. So, she joined a divorce support group at *her* church but needed the deacon at *my* church? Her full immersion and years of rehearsal as a victim brought her portrayal to near perfection! She had not met with him since April of 2015, the last time we met as a couple. It was during that meeting that he reminded her of her obligations: God, your husband, and family.

Nevertheless, she made her way back to him, and I was glad he helped her. I had not seen him in a few months, since I was so well entrenched with my therapist, Kasey. I reached out via e-mail, and he informed me that he was now seeing Erin. "If this were for reunification purposes, I would be happy to meet with you, but it is not," he replied.

"I fully understand," I replied, "and I hope that you can be God's vehicle to get her the help she needs."

He was well aware of all that had transpired and the discoveries that I had made, including her lawfully prescribed medications. I felt a little shunned by my own church, but I realized no one in need should be turned away.

With at least a part-time job secured, Erin immediately bought a first-class ticket to re-board the amphetamine train. She had also been out of her clonazepam (3 milligrams per day) for about six weeks. I was deeply concerned about the impact on her with this pattern of abrupt discontinuation and restarting these medications. She secured the position on March 17, and loaded up on the clonazepam on the nineteenth followed closely by her amphetamines on the twenty-fifth.

Katie continued to stay with me in March. She made our little apartment feel like a home. Inexpensively but nicely, she transformed her bedroom into a room worthy of a magazine cover.

I appreciated all of the work that her initial therapist did. She was very competent and thorough with her evaluations, but Katie did not connect with her. I desperately wanted to find someone that she could talk to. Billy had begun some therapy sessions at his college, which seemed to do him some good. As it happened, I discovered Kasey was in the same building with Ann Birch, a therapist specializing in teen counseling for high-conflict divorce. She and Kasey shared an assistant, but their practices were separate and distinct. As I waited for my appointments with Kasey, I could not help but notice how Ann's patients and their families responded to her with such warmth and gratitude. So I began the process of getting Katie an appointment. By now, Katie was pretty soured on therapy but agreed to give it a shot. Erin's continually demanding that Katie comply because it was court ordered certainly did not help her disposition to treatment. Erin and I met with Ann separately during the intake process to provide Ann with the appropriate background. I met with Ann first and Erin met with her shortly thereafter. Ann was wonderful. I was hopeful that Katie would connect with her. I held nothing back and wanted Ann to be aware of everything Katie had been dealing with the past two years. I was forthright about the drinking episode in which I frightened Katie, my bipolar misdiagnosis, and my stay at Holy Hell. I also discussed the domestic violence trial and the herpes saga. She never flinched, and I could tell that she was very experienced in dealing with high drama. I just wanted Katie to be able to share her feelings openly and honestly.

Easter arrived early in 2016. Billy did not make the trip home. In addition to his studies, he was working quite a bit. He was waiting tables at a restaurant close to campus. Katie received a generous offer to join a few girlfriends and their families on a trip to California. So, I headed to Charlotte in the midst of heavy-duty spring rain to spend a little time with Billy. In spite of everything, he continued to excel in school, but the drama of the last two years was beginning to get to all of us. Billy, wired much like me, wears his emotions on his sleeve. Following a nice dinner, as I said my goodbyes, I could tell that something wasn't right. As I hugged him goodbye, I could see the tears in his eyes. I did not address the issue immediately but called him shortly after I got on the road. I asked what was wrong and he floored me with his selflessness and compassion. "I am just worried about you, Dad, and all that you have been through. I want it to be over with so that we can all move forward." I assured him that I was doing just fine and expressed my deep appreciation for him standing by me and believing in me. I made no promises about when it would end and reiterated what I had always said to Billy, "It is in God's hands and will end when he wants it too." Both Billy and Katie's strong character were shining through all this adversity.

Erin filled her time with a telethon. Because of multiple subpoenas, we each were recipients of the other's phone records. Erin had been calling my brothers, colleagues at work, customers, Mila, and even my boss. Strangely enough, nobody ever mentioned her calls except Mila. I inquired with Al and Anthony if they had any record of Erin calling them. Erin's number did not show up on their account. All that showed up was #200. The same showed up on Mila's cell phone and her office landline. She had previously ignored multiple calls from a #200. Enough is enough. She picked up one of the calls on her office line, and it was a "gentleman" claiming to be from a Wilmington florist. He wanted her address so he could deliver some flowers. "I don't know who this is. I don't want any flowers, and I will not be giving you my address," was her response. It was at this time that she had to explain the crazy situation to her husband. As the month ended, I was so mentally exhausted I decided to take a few days off. Phil and Claire invited me to join them and their three lovely daughters for a few days in Hilton Head.

But as usual, every time I tried to escape for a few days to enjoy some normalcy, I would be pulled back in. Making my way down to HH, I received a few e-mails from Abby marked Urgent. I pulled over at a gas station to read them. It was March 30, and on this day, Erin's legal team, who had represented her for the last twenty months, filed a motion to withdraw their representation. The message that I received from Erin on the Wizard on the twenty-sixth now made sense: "You are up to something like always and believe me when I say my new attorney will take care of it! If you won't listen to me and not think about the children's well-being and stop this train wreck as I have asked, then I have no other choice to seek counsel that will stop it!"

Our August trial would be here before we knew it and now she had no representation. What did this all mean now? I exchanged several e-mails with Abby seeking some detail. Not much clarity was provided other than, "Don't have any contact whatsoever with Erin. I have spoken with their previous counsel and they will accept our discovery information and will forward to Erin's next attorney. They do not know who will be representing her, but were clear that they were done with her!"

Erin often referred to her legal team as sharks. She would not hesitate to tell our former mutual friends, "I am not concerned my lawyers are sharks." Now, reminiscent of my shark encounter at Topsail Beach in June of 2014, her sharks swam away! I speculate that either they or their legal staff listened to the same ADT/TWC audiotapes that I did and finally recognized their client was delusional and her paranoia was in the stratosphere. As Olivia once said, "She is batshit crazy."

I appreciated my island escape, but soon it was back to reality. Upon my return, I received word about Erin's new lawyer. I had seen her name before. What do you know? An attorney that shares office space and legal staff with Frank Slade was now representing Erin. Why would Erin select her? Did Erin not recall that Frank was my attorney at the domestic violence hearing? Their legal staff could not be involved in our case due to their work on my DVPO case.

Erin's new attorney was Cherrie Barr. Olivia had me speak with Frank to ensure that I was comfortable with the guardrails in place.

"Is she still fighting this alimony case?" Frank commented to me. "I spoke with Cherrie, and Erin remembered me and all the tough questions I asked her at the domestic hearing." He chuckled. "I told Cherrie not to take this case."

We could have had Cherrie disqualified from representing Erin, but August was fast approaching, and I did not want to delay the trial any longer. The legal world is far different from the business world I know. You would think that if you had representation for twenty months by another firm, the new counsel would want some insight. I know I am naïve! A check is a check; revenue is revenue. Cherrie's reputation preceded her, and there was at least $40K to $60K on the table for her. To quote Olivia, "Sometimes we have clients that we have to do our best to put lipstick on a pig."

The morning of Erin's scheduled appointment with Ann Birch, Katie's potential new therapist, I received a call from their office. Erin had left them several messages inquiring about the ability to finance the $175 fee for her visit. She played the "victim" card so well, informing them that she could not afford it. I agreed to pay the $175. In less than eight months, Erin had received $48,000 from me: money from spousal support, child support, the funds from the sale of our home, and our emergency fund. She had no money?

Prom arrived early in 2016. Katie requested that both Erin and I be there for pictures. Katie has a gift for photography, and I was thrilled that she asked me to take the pictures with her nice camera. My phone and iPad would not do the pictures justice. Katie spent prom night and the following evening at Erin's as her home was close to all of her friends. Those two nights would be the last that Katie would spend at Erin's house.

I arrived before Erin at the venue where the prom pictures would be taken. I audio-recorded the entire time spent there. Following pictures, I needed to meet with Erin at my car to have some tax preparation documents signed by her as we filed jointly for 2015. Based on her history of allegations against me, I wanted a little protection.

Erin the victim arrived after I did, with a cloud of anger hanging over her. There were multiple couples there, and we all gathered in the backyard, which housed a beautiful pond we used as a backdrop for the pictures. I went to take the first picture with Katie's camera, and she remarked, "Dad, are you okay? Your hands are shaking." I approached Katie and whispered, "I have not seen your mom since October, and I am a little nervous. I am sorry." My sense of humor quickly emerged, and I attempted to take some pictures of Erin. She turned her back to me. Figuratively, she had done the same to Billy and Katie as well. Erin and I kept our distance, but we were civil, and I believe it was a beautiful evening for Katie.

Following the pictures, Erin met me at my car to sign the tax preparation documents. Unlike last year's prom, there would not be any "slip and slide" night. We met outside of my car, and I placed the documents on the hood. Following a simple, "How are you doing?" from me, it was off to the races.

Erin asked why I kept up my legal attacks.

I promptly replied, "You filed a domestic violence charge against me, a civil summons, and contempt charges. You have backed me into a corner and have left me no choice."

Incredibly, she blamed the domestic violence charges on Katie. "There was one night that she was convinced that you were in the front yard. I kept telling her no, no, no. She would not listen to me. We had to run away, and we spent the night at Tiffany's."

"I have never been at our house alone," I replied.

"I know, she was just so scared," said Erin. "Oh, by the way, what are you telling my daughter? Her attitude toward me has completely changed since she has been staying with you."

"I have only told her that you need help," was my reply.

We made small talk about her job. I expressed my concern about her safety in dealing with these adults with developmental challenges and that they can be aggressive at times.

"Oh, I have been trained in self-defense. At the training, none of the big black women wanted to work with me because I was so strong. I guess it was my aggression coming out."

I moved on to her clonazepam use and her current daily dose. During our marriage, Erin led me to believe that she only took it as needed when her heart rate increased. I now knew that she was religiously taking 3 milligrams a day.

"You are going down the wrong path, bud. My psychiatrist will be front and center in court," was Erin's answer. She then stood there wide-eyed, like a little girl lying to her father. "I have never cheated on you. You will never hear those words out of my mouth. Mary, Tiffany, and Candi want to slap you upside your head for the false accusations you are making against me.

They have all remarked that I am not even the flirtatious type."

"I don't need to hear those words out of your mouth. Another part of your anatomy has told me all I need to know. There is a part of me that will always love the woman I thought I knew," I responded with a tremor in my voice.

Of course, we could not escape the evening without accusations of my hacking into her e-mails, phones, bank accounts, and routers.

"I know you are not smart enough to do it, but whomever you hired is really good. They are leaving a paper trail, and you will be caught," Erin ranted. "I know you and Mila were getting it on," she spat.

I felt the circular conversation coming on just as I had experienced on the Wizard, so I decided it was time to leave. As I opened my car door, I looked Erin directly in the eye and remarked, "I hope you had the decency to take your ring off."

Erin's new town came complete with a new police department. A few days post-prom, Katie and Emma ventured to Mom's to gather more of Katie's clothes. Upon their arrival, Erin informed them that she had called the cops because someone (Danny) had broken into her home. "Whoever broke in changed the locks so that they could get back in. There are scratch marks on the doors and crowbar marks on my sliding glass door." Erin would relay the same information to Billy.

The humor I used to see in these accusations was long gone, replaced by deep concern. I called the police department, and they confirmed that they had been to the home and that Katie and I were named in the incident report. I explained the situation to the officer and the fact that her paranoia is off the charts.

"There is nothing we can do, sir," they told me. "I would advise you to limit your communication and don't go anywhere near her home." Different town, different police department, same accusations.

April 29, we terminated my child support obligation, and it did not take long to hear from Erin. "Really, Dan? Again, the rules just don't apply to you. You can't just break a court order yourself without our attorney's and a judge's approval! Katie hasn't decided what her permanent plans are, so you just can't take it upon yourself to decide what you will pay and what you won't. You are emotionally hypnotizing her with your CRAZY accusations, and God knows what else. She thought I was a great mom and an inspiration before you got a hold of her emotionally. You are doing to her what you did to me, she saw it in our old home in Wilmington.

Like April, the month of May would be full of drama. I had come to expect it. There were blessings and a few happy times as well. Billy landed a summer internship with a company in Charlotte. He made a trip home to visit his mom and me before starting his internship. I was informed via the Wizard that she could not even afford to buy food to cook her son a decent meal. She added she had to take out a cash advance just to buy some basics for the meal with Billy. Once again, Erin was staying true to her "victim" character. She was working the deacon at the church as well. He provided her with gift cards and money so she could "just get by."

In North Carolina, a year of separation is required before you can file for divorce. The day arrived May 19. It was a day of mixed emotions. Katie received a call from Tiffany asking her to feed the dogs at Erin's house. "Your mom is on her way to the emergency room due to another possible stroke." Katie and Emma went over to feed the dogs. When Katie returned to the apartment later that evening, I decided it was time we sat down to discuss Mom's use (abuse) of lawfully prescribed medications. Katie asked for proof, and I shared with her all that I had pulled from Erin's pharmacy claims. She then remarked, "I am not sure how I missed it, Dad, but it now all makes sense."

"I missed it as well. It was all at my fingertips the whole time. It explains all of your mom's cardiac issues and other ailments."

Many times, one's heart gets in the way of logic. I was concerned about Erin . . . this was her fourth stroke-like event since April of 2011. She had just started back on her amphetamines and clonazepam in March, and as recently as May 4, she refilled her amphetamines. I reached out to Tiffany, her new BFF, who was with her at the hospital. Big mistake. I wanted the doctors to be aware of all of the medications Erin was taking. I started by asking how she was doing and what was going on.

Tif said, "She does not want to see you, Dan."

"No need to worry about that," I said. "She has been hiding her amphetamine use from me for the last five years, Tiffany."

"Wow, Dan, these are prescribed by a doctor. These would show up in her blood work. She told me that she has been taking far fewer meds since she no longer lives with you."

I informed her that I still had access to her pharmacy claims and that she continued to take all of her medications. I also reminded her that a doctor prescribed Prince's drugs and he is now dead. I should not have called. I sent her a text thanking her for taking my call and stated that I would keep informed through Billy and Katie.

I had not heard from Doris since her text message on December 28, 2015, but her silence ended on May 20. I did not save those texts because I had grown tired of seeing her name. It was after these texts that I blocked her. She questioned my accusations about her daughter's amphetamine and prescription drug abuse.

"You are trying to destroy my daughter, and your lack of financial support is impacting her ability to eat nutritionally. This whole situation is your fault. Period!"

I did respond with, "You have been played, used, and lied to by your own flesh and blood."

Her reply, "Don't try your manipulation on me."

I ended our little text exchange with, "You don't know the facts. Enough said!"

What happened to, "Soon Erin will no longer be your concern" (Doris's text to me on July 7, 2015, after our first mediation)?

Fortunately, Erin bounced back from this event as well. Someday she may not be so lucky, and that is my concern. It states in bold black letters in the product package insert that amphetamines can cause a stroke and cardiac arrest in adults. Three days after her event, I received the following message:

"Dan,

There are no words to describe the manic and disgraceful phone call you made to Tiffany on May 19, 2016, while doctors are telling both of us I may have had a stroke. Your only motive for the phone call was not for concern; it was only to continue your ridiculous vendetta against me. What you are doing to our children mentally by filling their heads with your delusional thoughts truly shows how sick you are. You are so obsessed for revenge that you stay up all hours of the night brainstorming these scenarios. This is when your mistakes only make my paper trail even longer. I will save the rest for August. No, I will let my attorney take care of that."

Like clockwork, Erin was back at the pharmacy on June 12, refilling her amphetamine prescriptions. It bears repeating that an addict is someone who continues to seek and use in spite of the harmful consequences they inflict on themselves and others.

# CHAPTER 20
## *Google*

I am not crying because of you; you're not worth it. I am crying because
my delusion of who you were was shattered by the truth of who you are.
—*Steve Maraboli*

At this point in our saga, Billy and Katie had started coming to terms
with who their mom was and what she had done. Katie was now living with
me permanently, and Billy began distancing himself from Erin.

Father's Day in 2016 was gloriously spent with both my kids. "Happy"
cannot adequately begin to describe my emotions. We soaked up the sun
and took a long walk on Wrightsville Beach. I had grown quite fond of
walking on this beach after moving into my apartment in August of 2015.
The countless miles I logged there, accompanied only by my music, helped
me do my best thinking and provided me with rare moments of peace. Katie
took some great pictures of us and, unfortunately, posted them on Facebook.
After our walk, we enjoyed some ice cream before cleaning up and heading
to dinner. Billy then drove back to Charlotte. That evening, I fell asleep with
a smile on my face. I thought, no matter the outcome of our pending trial, I
have both of my kids in my life.

Damn social media.

Billy had not informed Erin that he was coming to town. He wanted to make this about me and did not want to have to deal with Mom on this visit. Billy reached out to Erin on his drive back to Charlotte that evening as Erin had been blowing up his phone, curious as to whether or not he was coming to town. The pictures Katie posted would be the basis for the following text:

"I pray there will be a time and place in our lives that you can tell me why you and Katie are building this wall between the three of us. How am I supposed to fix it if I don't know what 'it' is? Grandma said there was a beautiful picture of the three of you from this weekend. She will pass it on to me. Billy, you don't have to hide situations like this from me. I am happy for all of you. I knew you were driving when we were talking, and that truly saddened me that you of all people felt the need to lie about it. I am glad you had a nice Father's Day, and I am sure Dad appreciated you making an effort to be together. I am sure it was a very touching weekend given the year everyone had. Have a nice night. Luv U."

United we stand, Erin! Billy and Katie had each other's backs when it came to Mom and Grandma. Billy forwarded to me a text Katie sent to Mom in response to the message Billy had received.

"Mom I love you, but your texts to Billy need to stop. You've put him and me at a very odd state right now. You continually put us on guilt trips for not talking to you, but it's your doing that we aren't talking. You will always bring Dad up or what has happened up or how you aren't on drugs into at least any conversation. Sure, he told you he wasn't coming for Father's Day, but there are reasons for that. I understand your upset, but you need help. We don't know who you are as a mom anymore. I love you mom but please dig down deep and try and see what you are doing to us."

Our long-awaited Motion to Compel hearing would occur at the end of June. Erin had yet to turn over the rest of her medical records and electronically stored information. In particular, we wanted to get records from Dr. One-Time Visit OB/GYN and the info from her Galaxy Samsung phone. It was Erin's phone from August of 2014 until August 5, 2015, a critical time period for my case.

June 27 was my second time in court during our journey of love gone wrong. Correction, it was not love gone wrong, it was love that may have never existed (on Erin's part). I was not as nervous as in the DVPO (Domestic Violence Protection Order) hearing in October of 2015, but it is always unsettling not knowing what the judge may decide. Our argument would be heard at 10:30. As we waited, I spent some time with Olivia and Abby reviewing some electronically stored information Erin turned over just a few days prior. It contained text messages from December 2015 and January 2016. While this was outside of the timeline that she was legally required to provide, there was nothing turned over from the image of her Galaxy Samsung S4 phone. Why was that?

Our focus was to have Erin turn over the electronically stored information from her Galaxy Samsung phone and to complete the submission of all of the medical records previously subpoenaed. The holdouts were her therapist and Dr. One-Time Visit OB/GYN, who she saw in April of 2014, two months preceding the beach trip with Doris and Erin's family. Is this the visit that she referenced in the letter she wrote on September 14, 2014, to my family practitioner and psychiatrist?

"I got a vaginal infection about a year ago as I told you on the phone and unfortunately I was on antibiotics for ten days given to me by my family doctor. I went to my ob doctor, and he did a swab, and it was negative. He said I needed to come in when the discharge was present and not while on antibiotics. The infection was already gone. He said it was probably trichomonas's, sexually transmitted disease. (Green discharge)"

Erin was not on antibiotics for ten days before this visit, only seven, but who is counting? Her STD-related pharmacy claims were burned into my memory (and spreadsheets).

Erin's therapist was holding her records until Erin paid her in full for previous therapy sessions. The judge ordered Erin to pay the $400. As

Cherrie stood behind her assigned table, the theatrics began.

She started waving her hands, and her voice modulation increased. "Your Honor, they have not provided us with an address for this physician. We had to go to the North Carolina Medical Board and had to Google this provider to find him. He has practiced at multiple locations. We called those locations. They have no record of my client being seen by him."

Olivia calmly approached the bench, provided the judge with the explanation of benefits for Erin's visit, and remarked, "Your honor, the OB/GYN in question is important, given the STD tests that he performed. I would ask the court to allow us to subpoena the records directly."

The judge granted our request and ordered that all of the images for Erin's electronics be turned over to our forensic imaging expert. The judge literally scratched her head when she heard that Erin turned over text messages from December 2015 thru early January 2016.

Cherrie commented that they just wanted to supplement the thousands of pages of documents that they had already turned over. "My client is an open book. She has nothing to hide!"

The judge awarded us $2000 in legal fees for all of the additional work performed to address Erin and Cherrie's noncompliance. Olivia wanted it noted by the judge that we might ask for additional fees related to this motion at another time. The judge agreed to consider revisiting this matter.

Just two days after this hearing, Cherrie turned over the records from the stealthy OB/GYN. Erin supposedly never saw this provider, but magically they were able to produce documents for a visit? It seemed we were finally catching a few breaks, but what's the old saying about counting chickens?

One month before the start of our trial, Olivia received an e-mail from Erin's imaging expert that he had no images from the Galaxy Samsung S4 phone to turn over. He had the phone in his possession, but there was nothing to image. Erin had restored this device to factory settings. In other words, she wiped the phone. This same individual filed an affidavit in November of 2015 that he indeed had imaged this device! Why were we just finding out about this now? Was Erin's previous or current counsel aware of this? In her interrogatories, Olivia specifically asked Erin about wiping this phone. Her answer was an emphatic no. The expert knew about this in November of 2015 but said nothing to us. He did not amend his affidavit. Perhaps Erin and her team thought they had gotten away with it. The depths of her lies and deceit were increasing. We subpoenaed her "expert" for our rapidly approaching trial.

"This is a 'drop the mic' moment," Olivia later commented. "She has an incurable STD that she did not get from you, and she has destroyed evidence."

The emotional highs and lows continued. Just a few short days after we discovered that Erin had wiped her phone, my brother Phil sent a group text to all the siblings regarding our dad. When I was home in May, Dad was not doing well, but Phil informed us that Dad had dramatically declined in just a few short months. He was sleeping sixteen to twenty hours a day, refusing to eat, and was no longer able to care for himself. He once was so meticulous about his appearance and hygiene. The time for my mom to try to continue to manage this, even with her children's support, had ended.

I needed to go home! Katie could join me on this 640-mile trek, a journey I had done solo multiple times over the last two years. This was an excellent opportunity for Katie and me to continue rebuilding our relationship.

I was not sure how Katie would respond to seeing her grandfather in his current state. She had no idea what he had been going through with his dementia. The last time she'd seen him, he was dancing at Cindy and Patrick's wedding. Then again, it seems almost everything had changed over the previous three years!

Arriving in town, we went straight to the hospital. The staff did their best to manage all the visitors our sizeable extended family presented. Dad was in no state for all of the distractions from this many visitors. Our visit was brief, as I could barely stand seeing Dad in such sad shape. His dementia had taken complete hold of him. He was emotionally lost and confused, and just kept pointing at the restraints on his legs, lacking the ability to communicate what he wanted. Heartbreaking! Seeing him rekindled the emotions I experienced when locked up—never restrained, but confused and emotionally lost, with my freedom taken away.

Katie's last visit to Pittsburgh had been in July of 2013 when she was a bridesmaid for my niece Cindy's wedding. Katie quickly picked up where she had left off with her cousins. She was welcomed with open arms by my entire family. As I recall, there was hardly any discussion about my situation with Erin. It was a judgment-free zone, just as it should be! As they had done many times during my trips to Pittsburgh, Jane's sister, Maggie, and her husband, Leith, opened up their cozy little lakefront home and hosted many of us for a delicious meal.

As we prepared to leave town, Katie and I made one last visit to see Dad. I sincerely doubted my father would make it out of the hospital. I placed my forehead on his and said what I thought would be my final words as my tears streamed down his face. I expressed my love and gratitude as Katie stood by my side. I tearfully exited his room, and Katie reached out to hold my hand as we walked out of the hospital. I was so lucky to have Katie's support just then.

Our date in court was only three weeks away, and both Erin and I would be deposed preceding the trial. Erin was very busy leading up to our hearing. She had her annual exam with a brand-new OB/GYN. (Erin obviously wouldn't want to return to her previous OB/GYN, who definitively diagnosed her with herpes 2). She made her way back to the same surgeon who removed her large bowel in February of 2015 to have an "anal fissure" examined.

I was not present at Erin's seven-hour deposition, as Olivia wanted Erin to feel comfortable and uninhibited. I received a copy of her testimony. It must have been exhausting for Olivia.

"It was a challenge to just get a straight answer from Erin about the simplest of questions I asked her," Olivia admitted.

Olivia attempted to focus on Erin's medications, especially her use of Adderall. Erin's deposition began with a review of all the medicines Erin was taking and the rationale behind them. Five out of the ten medications she was taking on a daily basis were written by her psychiatrist (Adderall, Adderall XR, 3 milligrams of clonazepam per day, 450 milligrams of Wellbutrin per day and 500 milligrams per day of Lamictal). Her Lamictal dose was five times higher than what I had been taking for my bipolar disorder. Erin was adamant that she only took Adderall and clonazepam as needed. Her pharmacy claims told a different story.

"I took my Adderall today as I need to concentrate. I started Adderall two years before my first one," Erin remarked quite confidently. Olivia attempted to clarify what she meant by her "first one." Erin was referring to her first stroke-like event in 2011. Therefore, Erin started on her Adderall (behind my back) in 2009.

"Dan knows what I have been on. He was with me at the cardiology appointment after my first one when [the doctor] lowered the dose of my Adderall to 20 milligrams." Olivia pressed her on this fact and continued this line of questioning during our trial. I indeed was with Erin at all of her cardiology appointments, but Adderall was never a topic of discussion. There was no record of Erin filling a prescription for 20 milligrams of Adderall.

Alarmingly, Erin stated she began taking Adderall in 2009, but later in her deposition, she testified that the Clinic suggested that it might be something good to try due to her challenges with cognitive ability and concentration. The Clinic saw her in April and July of 2013. Who recommended it in 2009?

"It has helped me. Trees are greener, and the colors are brighter. I can actually look at you and hear what you are saying."

There was some discussion about Erin's first marriage. "I was married in 1991 but realized after our honeymoon that I made a huge mistake. I never moved in with him. I could not even go to the mall without being questioned as to why I was gone so long. He showed up at my bachelorette party and dragged me off the dance floor. The cops were called. He was so controlling."

So, she was married in March or April of 1991 but dating three men (including me) by June of '91. How much brighter could this red flag have been? During our dating years, Erin informed me that she and Derek had honeymooned in Florida and her father joined them for a few days. Therefore, her relationship was very good with her father right up until her brief marriage fell apart.

Fresh off our discovery that Erin did a factory reset on her phone, Olivia had a list of questions for her regarding this. Erin denied she had wiped her phone, instead vehemently claiming that she put spyware on it.

During this deposition, Erin began her claims of deprivation and poverty. "I know what it is like to be hungry. I would get so excited to receive a care package from my mom that contained toilet paper."

Her insanity was on full display during the deposition as Olivia did her best to get specifics and clarity on her accusations around hacking into e-mails, bank accounts, routers, and medical records.

"He recently went onto the website for my new OB/GYN and looked at my results," Erin claimed. "He had to have heard it through the phone; there is no way he would have known that I was going to a new OB/GYN."

In reality, Erin was still on my insurance, and I was receiving all her claims.

Erin presented some new allegations during her seven hours with Olivia.

"He is intercepting my voicemails. When we were still married, he struck me on my butt that he left welt marks and his handprint (I have a picture of it). He has admitted to doing drugs . . . don't quote me on it but in remission and relapse. He is sexually explicit, but in a secretive and concerning manner, he always wants to have sex."

What Erin had previously filed in the court system contradicted her last allegation:

"During the parties' marriage, the Defendant (Danny) committed several acts of marital misconduct as defined by NCGS 50–16.1A, including but not limited to the following:

The Defendant has withheld love and affection from the Plaintiff and has been emotionally neglecting, rejecting and abusive toward the Plaintiff.

The Defendant refuses to spend time with the Plaintiff."

After reviewing the specifics of Erin's filing, Olivia received this remark from Erin, "There should have been something in there about his sexual appetite and the affair with Mila." I can only imagine how difficult it must have been for Erin to manage this tangled web of lies.

My deposition was a few days later. Similarly, Erin was not present. Mine only lasted three-and-half hours, as my answers were fact-based and concise. Of course, there was a focus on my bipolar diagnosis and my time in Holy Hell. It was clear that they would be alleging that I had an affair with Mila. Their focus was one month of phone calls between Mila and me. There were allegedly 125 phone calls between us during May of 2014. I had worked with Mila for ten to twelve years, and all they scrutinized was one month of phone calls? There was no mention of texts or e-mails between us because there were none. They were grasping at straws. Erin had herpes 2, I was negative, yet I was the one messing around?

I was very clear with Cherrie that I believed Erin had an affair and that she was abusing prescription drugs, in particular, Adderall and clonazepam.

Cherrie's response was, "Her doctor lawfully prescribes these, yet you think she is abusing them? So because you have no knowledge, you think she is hiding them from you."

Then it was time to pivot to the lack of trust in our marriage and my ogling of women. "Was there a time in your marriage when you could not keep your eyes off of a waitress?" She was referring to our honeymoon. I revisited the truth of what had happened during our honeymoon. She then inquired about me taking prescription drugs that did not belong to me. "Was there ever a time(s) that you asked Erin for a few of her clonazepam?" I simply responded no to this question. I had never asked Erin for any of her medications. "Did you ever put rum or some form of alcohol in your cokes after dinner?" Again, the answer was no! I did all I could to maintain a straight face with some of these ridiculous questions.

"Are you aware that we have cleared up Erin's herpes issue?" (Don't even ask how I kept a smirk off my face at this question . . . this new lawyer heals incurable diseases too!) "She does not have herpes. Did Erin ever talk with you about how you speaking with Mila upset her? Did you ever send resumes to employers on Erin's behalf?" This last question aimed at a new computer-hacking ability that enabled me to send incomplete applications and resumes to potential employers on Erin's behalf.

My favorite question was, "Were there times when Erin would go and work out, and you would observe pornography?" I had flashbacks of Erin's two-hour plus March 2015 Y visits where she was nowhere to be found. I was the one working out while Erin was likely participating in pornography.

As we departed from my deposition, Olivia's sense of humor showed as she suggested, "Dan, go home, drink, and watch porn!"

# CHAPTER 21
## *A Sob & Swab Story, Day 1*

Do you solemnly swear that the testimony you are about to give is the
truth, the whole truth, and nothing but the truth, so help you God?
—*Bailiff Petri Hawkins Byrd (*Judge Judy*)*

Day 1: Destruction of Evidence Day

Mid-August 2016 our alimony trial was about to commence. This same
week, our kids began their senior years, one in high school and the other in
college. Even with this saga nearing its end, Katie and Billy had endured
practically their entire high school and college years living our nightmare.
We were all hoping for some semblance of closure.

It was a typical North Carolina August, with both humidity and tem-
peratures well into the 90s. Al and my niece Diane got to Wilmington on
Sunday the fourteenth. I was not entirely aware of the team that Erin had
assembled, but I had a good idea. Communication on the Wizard between
Erin and me had been nonexistent for the last few months.

Sleep was hard to come by the evening before the trial, and it would not be very plentiful over the next several days. I had compartmentalized so much that had happened over the last two years. It all spilled out Sunday evening. The last two years seemed so much longer. Why did this all happen? By the grace of God and the love and support of family and friends, I was able to make it to this point. I was nervous but confident heading into Monday morning.

Al, Diane, and I arrived early to New Hanover County Family Court. Erin's team was present and accounted for. I like to refer to them as Team United We Stand. Erin used that moniker in some of her communications with me. On her team was Mother Doris, Big Bro, Tiffany, and Krystal (eighth-grade friend). The only surprise for me was Krystal. I expected Tiffany to be there based on my "butt-dial" call on July 6, 2015, and my call to her in May of 2016 when Erin had another stroke-like event, but Krystal? What would she have to say about me? Doris, Krystal, Tiffany, and Erin would all have their moment in the sun as they testified against me. We were in the same courtroom with the same judge who presided over my domestic violence hearing and our motion to compel heard six short weeks ago. All told, we would spend the next four days in this courtroom. Of course, other cases would be heard besides our alimony trial. We could not be so lucky as to have the judge's undivided attention, but were granted seventeen hours of the court's time spread over these next four days.

What you are about to read are verbatim excerpts from the seventeen hours of audio recordings from our trial. I have grown quite fond of the words *public record*. I did my best to include only what I felt was pertinent to the storyline of the book.

. . .

The majority of this day centered on our motion *in limine*. At first, I thought it was Latin for "three hundred dollars per hour." *Limine* is Latin for "at the start" or "on the threshold." It is a pre-trial motion. We filed it based on our recent discovery that Erin had wiped her phone. Asking the judge for a negative inference that Erin destroyed evidence, which would have been harmful to her case, we requested that any electronic evidence from this period be suppressed.

Next up, a tediously dry six hours of testimony about the joys of technology. The two opposing forensic imaging experts took turns getting up and down from the witness stand. One redeeming (and entertaining) part of the day occurred when we called Erin and Tiffany to the stand to understand their roles in the destruction of evidence. Erin had multiple visits to her imaging expert, and many of these occurred well before she was court ordered to maintain the integrity of her electronic devices. Her expert testified, "She showed up at my office many times unannounced. She would ask me to look at a phone, or one of her many computers because she was certain that her devices were being hacked. If she did not like the advice I would provide her, she would then consult with AT&T, TWC, or ADT."

Olivia hammered Erin's expert repeatedly regarding his affidavit that he submitted in November of 2015 unequivocally affirming that he had imaged the Samsung Galaxy S4 phone. He responded, "I could have done a better job of managing this whole situation. I did a poor job of transitioning from the role of a consultant for the opposing counsel to legal expert." More than once, he stated that he told Erin not to restore her phone to factory settings.

It was Erin's turn to take the stand. Her answer to Olivia's first question is something that her whole team echoed when each had their turn, "I am not really good with dates."

Olivia asked her about the dates that she used the Galaxy Samsung S4. "At a minimum, was it January 2015 to at least the date of separation? (May 2015)," Olivia probed. "It was that phone that you brought to the domestic violence hearing against Dan and played a voicemail that he left you?"

"Yes, and there was also a text from Dan on that phone. I am ignorant when it comes to technology. I have nothing to hide." (Really?) She finally admitted that she did a factory reset on her phone. "I did a factory reset to get rid of a virus or spyware."

At her deposition, she stated that she did not reset the phone but installed spyware. Olivia was prepared to challenge this. "Your attorney asked you at your deposition if you did a factory reset and you said no! That was less than two weeks ago."

"I was absolutely overwhelmed because you kept asking me about date after date after date," Erin responded. "I was confused. In the afternoons, I get overwhelmed. This is taking over my life. Every e-mail and Google account password I have was changed constantly. I am scared."

On deck was phone friend Tiffany. Billy and Tiffany's son have been good friends since grade school and remain friends today. Erin and I were not close friends with Tiffany and her husband but shared a few dinners together at each other's homes. We rarely connected socially, and if invites were extended, I was not aware. I never had any issue with Tiffany or her husband and was equally involved as Erin in carpooling the boys around until they both started to drive. My involvement in my kids' lives was entirely different from the picture that they attempted to paint.

Tiffany took her solemn oath and sat down.

Olivia began, "How do you know Erin?"

"I met Erin back in 2007. My family moved here from Texas," Tiffany responded. "We became friends through our two boys."

"Did she talk to you about the decline of her marriage?"

"Not in the beginning. Actually, in the beginning, I'd say we were more phone friends. When you first move to a new town, you want to make friends. And it was a little frustrating on my part because I met Erin, got to know her son. Really liked her and thought she was going to be a good friend and it was just not happening. Umm, we were phone friends. Pick up the boys. Drop off the boys. That type of thing. It was just really frustrating. I would invite her places . . . join me with my girlfriends, go out for a drink, go out to dinner or a movie. She always turned me down. It was a little frustrating, but I knew we were friends because of the way she spoke to me on the phone and treated my son. That type of thing. Over the past two to three years, she started opening up to me. Just bits and pieces."

Olivia then focused in on Christmas and New Years of 2015 and whether or not Erin and Tiffany spent any time together.

"I don't recall," was her reply. (Texts revealed they did, both Christmas Eve and Christmas.)

"Did you and Erin text each other?"

"We used to text each other all the time, and now she does not get my texts," said the phone friend.

Olivia confirmed Tiffany's phone number. (Erin destroyed her Galaxy Samsung S4 phone records but turned over text messages from her new phones between December 2015 and January 2016.) Tiffany confirmed that was her number, "It is a Texas phone number."

"Did Erin talk to you about her computer problems?" asked my counselor.

"I witnessed her computer problems," she sighed.

"Did you and Erin discuss wiping any of her electronic devices?"

"Not that I recall," said Tiffany.

Olivia then approached the stand and reviewed several exhibits that contained the following text exchange between Erin and Tiffany as read aloud by Olivia and Tiffany:

Tiffany: "Too many people within that computer in the past months. Wipe it clean and give it away."

Erin: "Yes, I will."

Olivia asked, "Does that refresh your memory about discussing wiping any devices?"

Tiffany stated, "Actually no, but can I read the few texts before it?"

"Absolutely!"

There was some dead air and then Tiffany being quite coy stated, "Umm, I am like Erin when it comes to computers and phones and I am looking at this verbiage 'Yes as long as you not link or share or migrate or use any of the invasive convenience applications.' That is not me talking. Are you kidding [laughingly stated]? I know how to turn on my phone and turn off my phone. I don't recall this. None of this really makes sense to me. I don't recall any of this, and the verbiage is definitely not me."

"So you would say that this text record pulled by a forensic expert off of Erin's phone that has your phone number to it is inaccurate?"

"No, I just don't remember doing it. 'Too many people within that computer within the past months'—I don't know what that is referring to. No, I don't recall it."

"Nothing further, Your Honor!"

Now it was time for a little cross-examination from Cherrie.

"You mentioned something about a butt-dial briefly. What is that about?" she inquired.

"Oh yeah, umm, there are many things that I have witnessed that Erin has been experiencing. One night, 11:30 at night, I got a phone call from Dan and I ignored it. I sent him a text, why were you calling me? His response was, 'Sorry I butt-dialed you.' I responded, 'How could you have butt-dialed me, I don't ever remember you calling me or me calling you.' Then he admitted to lying, saying something about checking the number due to an old boyfriend in Texas. And then he apologizes for lying."

"Did you forward the text to Erin?"

"Yes, I tried to snap, snap it or whatever it is called to Erin. She showed me how to do it, and I sent it to her."

"Do you recall him saying, 'You have no idea about the persecution I have had to deal with for four years,' and then he apologized for lying to you?"

"Yes."

"Then it says it was the first time he has accessed her records?"

"Based on what I have personally experienced, witnessed and felt, no way!" said Tiffany. She went on to state that Erin's issues with electronics were constant and that she felt so bad for her. "There were times when she thought she had spyware on her phone or people were listening. It was a daily conversation and even more recently just trying to contact her can be frustrating."

Cherrie chimed in, "What do you mean by that?"

"I can't send her a text. None of her family or friends can send her a text. I send them, but she just doesn't get them. Other people, like her coworkers, can send her texts, but her mother, friends, and me. She never receives those texts, which is really straaaange! [An audiobook would accurately capture Tiffany's dramatic cadence.]

"Nothing further, Your Honor."

Olivia redirected. "Excellent segue about something else that is really strange. You can remember a butt-dial from July 2015, but you can't remember advising her to wipe her computer?"

"Because it is in my phone," Tiffany laughingly responded.

After Cherrie's overruled objection, Olivia went on to explore how Tiffany's husband made a living. Surprise, surprise . . . he was a tech expert. Tiffany's knowledge, as evidenced by her texts to Erin, goes far beyond her ability to turn her phone off and on. Tiffany's fifteen minutes of fame were not up, as she would return as one of Erin's witnesses.

Just a little sidebar regarding the forty-five texts between Erin and Tiffany from December 22, 2015, to January 5, 2016. All but three of their texts were marked as deleted. Unless you wipe your phone, those texts are recoverable. Erin was under the guidance of different counsel in December of 2015. (As a refresher, they withdrew their representation March 30, 2016.) Perhaps the destruction of evidence coupled with the ADT/TWC audio recordings caused them to withdraw their representation. Next lawyer up!

Our forensic imaging expert confirmed that Erin had wiped her phone on October 4, 2015. Sunday evening to be exact. No effort to back up the phone or preserve the data was made.

"You cannot accidentally wipe a phone," he emphatically stated.

Erin reset her phone two days after the conclusion of our domestic violence hearing when her motion for protection was denied. She did not need the phone anymore, as the voicemail and texts I sent were of no use to her. He also confirmed that she reactivated the Galaxy Samsung S4 (Cherrie referred to it as the Samsung Gallery) on October 11, 2015, two days before she had to turn it over for imaging. The call logs validated that an AT&T employee reactivated it. He also testified that she did not need to reactivate the phone to have it imaged. Therefore, we had no evidence from a phone that she had been using since August 2014 (when she joined our family plan) until August 5, 2015. From the four computers she had imaged, we received fourteen e-mails. Yes, fourteen! Our expert would testify that I had turned over 4,000 e-mails. By the way, there were no texts or e-mails between Mila and me!

The judge ruled, "I agree you are entitled to a negative inference. I want to make it clear that the inference is not going to be that there was illicit sexual conduct, but to me, the inference was that there was something on that phone that was damaging to her case. Although it could be communications about her ability to work, it could be communications with a male colleague or person. It is wide open . . . we are talking about months and months and months of all communication. I am going to give you the inference but, I am just saying, that doesn't mean I am giving you an inference that illicit sexual behavior had occurred, but just that there was something negative on that phone that was damaging to her case."

On the other hand, Your Honor, it *could* have contained months and months and months of communication with the individual or individuals, rounding out her collection of STDs. Know what I am sayin'?

With this small victory in hand, the day marched on. It was now time for opening statements. Given that Erin was the plaintiff in this case, Cherrie went first.

In the interest of brevity, I have only included highlights from Cherrie's filibuster.

"These folks were married back on September 11, 1993," Cherrie said. "At that time, they lived in Pennsylvania where she lived with her family, who are all here today to support her . . . They moved to Kentucky. You will hear evidence that he was traveling three to four nights a week . . . These folks from

Kentucky then moved here to North Carolina, and you will hear evidence that my client had a dog-walking business that did not amount to much. You will hear evidence about the significant amount of money that the defendant makes per year, and my client, when she can work, and that is not very often, makes $8.36 an hour. You are going to hear about the decline in health that has occurred over this period. You will hear the many, many doctors that she has had to go to for her diagnosis of fibromyalgia that was made in 1999. It is a brain issue. It affects your brain, and what you see over the last five years and what you will hear about and what you will observe yourself when Erin testifies is a slow decline over time and how that has affected her . . . You will hear about how Dan will take something, he will take one thing, and he blows it up into his own story. You will hear him talk about his wife the drug abuser. He will get up there, I suspect, and talk with you about how he is in pharmaceutical sales, and he has studied up on this. He has looked at the little thing that goes inside the Adderall packet. He has diagnosed her and has concluded that she is a drug addict. He will tell anyone that will listen to him about this. He will tell her good friend that he called on the phone to make his point that his wife is a drug abuser. People do not want to speak to him. The reality is that Erin has some very serious medical conditions that are being appropriately dealt with through professionals.

"Because this does not fit Dan's mode of what he thinks the reality is, he will dismiss it. She is lawfully prescribed these medications. The evidence will be from her psychiatrist that she takes these medications as prescribed . . . You are also going to hear from another witness that has performed a psychological evaluation on Erin. She will outline in detail the stress that this situation has taken on Erin. It has so adversely affected her that she is really on the downhill slide to the point that it is questionable as to whether or not she can continue to work. It will explain her limited ability to focus and stay on track. Judge, I will tell you that you are going to see this when Erin gets up to testify. She will start talking and will go off and talk about something else. It is challenging for her to focus. I say that not in any way to make her feel embarrassed or to in any way feel shameful for her medical condition, but to give you a preview of even the task of testifying and how that it is difficult for her.

"You will see that she is not a drug addict, as her husband would want you to believe, but she is sick . . . He is also going to want to tell you about how paranoid she is. In his mind, it is a side effect of her Adderall. The reality is that she believes her e-mail has been hacked repetitively, passwords have been changed, and she has been locked out of accounts. She has had to hire expert after expert to help protect her from the defendant that she believes he is doing this to her. Again, it does not fit his reality. His reality is that she has to be paranoid. That is what he is going to tell you. You will hear about how in this marriage he was very controlling. As long as she was under his thumb and everything was okay, then it was all right. When she began to get better and tried to be independent of him, he began accusing her of having affairs. Of being with men . . . When I think the reality is that there was some question, on his end, as to what he may have been doing and you will hear evidence of that.

"You know, he does not have any specifics, just these vague allegations. After he lost a lot of weight and was having serious health issues, Erin found out he was tested for HIV. She sees weight loss and skin coloration. She thinks maybe something is going on. Fearing for her own health, she went and got her own test in December of 2014. She goes back for her examination six months later in June of 2015. She had major bowel surgery. She had her large bowel completely removed in February of 2015 just prior to their separation. It is at the point or at the expense of being gross that everything is kind of going right through her. Literally and figuratively, right through her where she is very raw. She goes in for her 6-month follow-up from all her testing, and she has something that is questionable. She asks the doctor, 'Can you take a look at it?' They do a swab of it. Her doctor's notes will indicate that clearly after the fact they determined that it was a fissure . . . When the test first came back, it shows that she has HSV1, which is mouth herpes. She has that and has always had that. She has had that her whole life. It shows that there were some abnormal cells on HSV2, but when they did the subsequent blood test, it shows negative. She shows this test of this swab to her husband and says, 'Look I now know that you did have an affair and you have given these herpes to me.'

"Which she is calling them herpes when it is an anal fissure . . . He goes and gets a blood test done. Not a test of the body but an actual blood test. His results come back negative. She goes and gets a blood test done, and her results come back negative. Then she gets another round of these tests done to show negative. In his reality, he is going to take that one test to believe that she has had an affair . . . She has never been anything but a good and dutiful wife to him and tried to support him through his emotional situation that he had going on in his breakdown. He twists and turns everything into something that it is not . . .

"I think it is also convenient to try to allege that Erin has had an affair for someone who makes the kind of money he does with a wife who is on the health decline. I think the evidence will show that he has a propensity not to be truthful. That has been a problem in their whole marriage. He worked on these issues through his therapy until the point that his mental health as well deteriorated. He was involuntarily committed in September of 2014 and received a bipolar diagnosis. I just want the court to focus not on all these red herrings that he is going to draw your attention to, because that is just what they are. They are not reality. Focus on the facts of the case, which is Erin, at 48 years old, is in a medical health situation. Her marriage has deteriorated. She is clearly a dependent spouse. Judge, I would submit to you that she is unequivocally not barred from alimony because of illicit sexual behavior in any way. When you look at all the factors, alimony is absolutely appropriate in this case. I am going to ask that at the end of the day you order that and that he pays her attorney's fees."

Olivia's opening statement was not a rambling, disorganized dissertation, but was straightforward and concise.

"Your Honor, the uncontroverted evidence at the end of the day is going to be that the plaintiff [Erin] has sexually transmitted herpes. The one person that you are going to need to listen to is coming tomorrow afternoon. He will be qualified as an expert in infectious disease, in herpes and herpes testing. His expert opinion will be that she has herpes that she contracted in the spring of 2015 before their date of separation. That will be the un-controverted expert opinion. The other part of his opinion will be that the defendant, Dan, does not have sexually transmitted herpes. When you look at the statute for illicit sexual behavior, her sexually transmitted herpes will check that box, and she will be barred. You add that, along with however Your Honor may rule on her spoliation of evidence, which was a phone that she used during that same time period that she wiped. Illicit sexual behavior! She has herpes. It is a complete bar! Thank you, Your Honor."

Time for Erin's team to begin to make their way to the stand. First up, the respected psychiatrist Cherrie referenced in her opening statement.

Erin began seeing this psychiatrist in late October 2013, six short days after Billy was denied a refill on his Adderall during his first year of college. This psychiatrist continues to be in the same practice with a colleague Erin had seen three times in 2011. As evidenced by her medical records, the doctor prescribed whatever Erin requested. What a blessing for Erin . . . since she was running out of the amphetamines she had been filling under Billy and Katie's names.

Nevertheless, under direct examination from Cherrie, she repeated multiple times that Erin is not a drug addict. "There are no red flags at all that she is abusing her medications. I checked the North Carolina controlled substances database this morning. She is not filling prescriptions early and is not being prescribed these medications by other providers. I am ethically obligated to monitor this database. To my knowledge, she does not abuse drugs, and I am a trained and careful observer for that." She also testified that Erin had fibromyalgia, ADD, and generalized anxiety disorder (GAD). "I began seeing Erin in October of 2013 and just continued prescribing what her previous mental health practitioner had been prescribing her for the last ten years. Fibromyalgia is a disorder that causes cognitive dysfunction, sleep disturbance, fatigue, and feelings of anxiety. The Adderall is being prescribed for fatigue and cognitive dysfunction (slowed processing speeds) that comes with her fibromyalgia. The brain fog and fatigue from her condition is why her previous practitioner prescribed it for her." This psychiatrist was not a rheumatologist but had no problem testifying about Erin's fibromyalgia: "Stress exacerbates it, and her disorder tends to worsen. It is degenerative, and the prognosis gets worse over time. She was diagnosed in 1999."

Cherrie questioned her about Erin's slurred speech and if her medical condition could cause this. Her response: "Cognitive impairment with fibromyalgia can seem like the patient is on drugs. The clonazepam that I prescribe for her (3 milligrams) can also cause slurred speech along with sedation." She even weighed in on our marriage: "She is in an emotionally abusive situation. Under constant suspicion and questioned about her medication or what she was doing. I am not an observer or firsthand witness of this. I cannot really quote her, as I do not document those types of comments in my records, as I tend to generalize in my notes. Divorce is stressful." She closed out her direct examination by reading a letter that she had written at Erin's request:

June 9th, 2016

To whom it may concern,

Ms. Erin [Married name] has been in psychiatric treatment with me since October of 2013. Prior to her treatment with me, she was seen by a mental health nurse practitioner [name omitted] for treatment. I have carefully reviewed the medical records from this practitioner. Ms. Erin has an anxiety disorder that is well controlled with medication. I have never diagnosed her with an illness that could impair her ability to parent or participate in a healthy normal manner in relationships. She has no warning signs or symptoms of substance abuse.

Furthermore, she has no history of substance abuse during her lifetime. I monitor her medications closely and carefully. She has never taken more than I have prescribed. I also have access to and have reviewed her controlled substance report on the North Carolina controlled substance database. There are no red flags or inconsistencies on this report. She is responsible and compliant with treatment.

Olivia did an excellent job with all of her cross-examinations. Abby, her paralegal, thoroughly reviewed the stacks of medical records that we subpoenaed. They provided a wealth of ammunition from which Olivia developed her line of questions.

Erin had not seen the mental health nurse practitioner, mentioned by name three times by the witness, for ten years. The facts are that Erin had seen her only five times between April and July of 2013. Did she see Erin for who she really is? Did she ever refuse or even question her prescription requests?

Olivia began her cross-examination of the psychiatrist by asking her to clarify the diagnoses.

"I am a psychiatrist and diagnosed her with generalized anxiety disorder and attention deficit disorder."

Olivia then began to review Erin's medical records. "The diagnosis of ADD or ADHD does not appear in these records until October of 2015 [five months after Erin and I separated]." [Silence followed by verbal stumbling]

"Um. I don't, she does have symptoms of attention deficit disorder. I did not know that I had not officially documented that before 2015, but her symptoms were the same."

"According to the medical records," Olivia continued, "it appears that Adderall was actually suggested to you by Erin." More silence from the doc followed by clarity from Olivia, "Under history of present illness there is one paragraph—"

Olivia was interrupted with, "Well, she did not just try it out of the blue."

Olivia then questioned her as to why she prescribed Adderall and Adderall XR for her. The doc explained her rationale, followed by Olivia quoting from the record that the psychiatrist had documented that Adderall caused Erin's racing heart. Olivia continued, "Are you aware that in the medical records it states that taking Adderall and Adderall XR together were also Erin's suggestion? She specifically requested to be prescribed both in March of 2014. Is that correct?"

More silence from the plaintiff's witness.

"Under history of present illness second sentence—"

"Yes, I see it. That is what I documented, but that is not an unusual strategy especially if she had been prescribed that in the past. The doses of her Adderall are not unusually high or concerning." Her responses were becoming agitated.

"Did Erin inform you that her cardiologist recommended more than three years ago that she reduce her dose of Adderall to under 20 milligrams?"

"I don't know if she told me that."

"Has Erin informed you of her transient ischemic attack that occurred in May of 2016?"

"Yes," said the witness.

"Can Adderall increase a person's risk of a stroke?"

"If Adderall increases a person's blood pressure significantly, then it can increase the risk of stroke."

Olivia kept swinging. "Does Adderall have the potential to increase anxiety and paranoia?"

"Yes. For some patients," was her sharp response.

"You have testified about Erin's stressors, the status of her relationships and that she has not had an affair," stated Olivia.

"To my knowledge," stated the witness.

"You see Erin for eighty minutes in a year?"

"Yes."

"In your notes, on April 5, 2016, you indicated that her illness does not cause impairment, her orientation is good, and her thought process is good. When you testified today that she is taking the medications as prescribed, that is based on her self-report. Is that accurate?"

"Right," says the doc.

Olivia closed by addressing the eloquent letter that the psychiatrist read aloud during her direct examination. "That letter was not part of your medical record, was it?"

"I wrote that after the medical records were turned over."

Olivia asked, "That letter was written simply for this litigation. Is that correct?"

"Yes!"

"Nothing further, Your Honor."

Strategically, we decided not to pursue Erin's drug diversion utilizing our children to supplement her supply of amphetamines. I distinctly remember Olivia saying to me, "Family Law Judges don't care about drug addicts. We have had drug abusers, pedophiles, and child abusers awarded alimony by the Family Courts. Our focus must be on the destruction of evidence and the fact that she has herpes and you do not."

We closed out Day 1 with a few more of Erin's witnesses. First up in a line of family and friends was Erin's eighth-grade friend, Krystal. Olivia and Abby got a kick out of the beach dress she wore into court. "Is she headed to the beach when she leaves here?" chuckled Olivia. Given that Krystal was probably going to kick sand in my face, I said she was appropriately dressed. Krystal is Katie's godmother, or at least she had been. Erin and I attended her first wedding many years ago. Now she was on her second marriage. Her first husband was a very nice man, but Krystal decided she no longer loved him. That decision occurred after she started getting some looks that were nonexistent in high school. Krystal had started running, lost weight, grew her hair out, dyed it blonde, and had her breasts enlarged. Her soon-to-be-ex paid for the physical enhancements. Erin shared this with me when we were still in love. Both Erin and Krystal had some oats left to sow. You reap what you sow, "ladies."

Krystal testified that she had not seen Erin in about a year and a half. She saw her when Erin made a trip to Pittsburgh to assist Doris. "When I first saw her, it was absolutely not the same Erin I had known. She seemed fragile, overwhelmed, and at times just scared. She was somebody I did not recognize. I was aware of their marital discord. Dan being very controlling, the phone stuff, and other incidences. Personally, I have just never experienced anyone like him. Somebody who was worried about every aspect of her day and what she was doing."

Her testimony continued by her recounting a phone call Erin made to me as they were heading out for a drink following dinner with Doris. "I believe she called Dan. He got into this conversation, and he was upset. As we were driving down the street, I can hear him on the phone. He was accusing her of driving by an old boyfriend's house that was near my house. These accusations are so bizarre. That is a boyfriend from high school. Then at the end, I heard him say, 'Fine, have a good time.' Then I heard a click. He hung up on her. Erin stated to me, 'See, he controls everything I do.' I was like, 'Erin he is 10 hours away. We are not doing anything wrong.' When we got to where we were going, I ordered a drink and Erin was just broken. She stated that she could not stay. I took her back to her mom's. I have never seen someone so worked up like that for an evening out." Now the tears begin to flow. "As I pulled away, I could not help but think, what happened to this friend of mine? Why would someone do this to someone? He has this thing about these men that she has known since we were young."

Excellent question, Krystal! Why would someone do this to someone he or she supposedly loves?

Cherrie pursued this by inquiring about other stories about men I accused Erin of having a thing for. Krystal thoughtfully obliged. "I do recall an incident back in Louisville when Katie was twelve that Dan accused Erin of having a thing for a gym instructor."

We moved to Wilmington when Katie was almost three years old. If Katie were 12, it would have been 2010, and it was then that I believe Erin was finding her way socially outside of our marriage. Perhaps it was a gym instructor, neighbor, car salesman or pizza guy. Krystal would reach back to 1991 to share a story about a pizza deliveryman I accused Erin of being interested in. "I remember when they first started dating and we were at Erin's mom's house. We ordered a pizza and Dan accused Erin of flirting with the pizza delivery guy. He said, 'Oh geez, Erin, why don't you ask him to stay.' I was like, oh my gosh! Really? Erin was a girl that was vivacious and went out. Now, I don't think she does that. She is so controlled."

"Can you describe the Erin you once knew and whom you see today?"

"She was beautiful, outgoing, ambitious, spirited, and always up for a fun time. I don't see that anymore." [For the love of Pete, Krystal, that was when you were in high school!] "The stress from her illness and all these things that are happening to her are deteriorating her. I believe she was in a controlled marriage."

In full disclosure, there was a phone call between Erin and me when she was with Krystal. I was cold to her but did not accuse her of driving by an old boyfriend's house. The call was very brief. I was not wild about the idea of her hanging out with Krystal in a bar, as Krystal was working the circuit following her divorce. I was wrong and should not have judged her. I apologized to Erin when she returned home and explained that I did not like what Krystal had done to her family and first husband. Erin would later try to rationalize, "Krystal made a mistake with her first husband." Little did I know that Erin was working the circuit as well!

Olivia's cross-examination lasted less than two minutes. Krystal testified that she speaks to Erin every three months and sees her about every year to year and a half. "You and your former significant other never socialized with Erin and Dan, did you?" inquired Olivia.

"No."

"You have never really spoken with Dan have you?"

"I have spoken with Dan. I have been at their house in Kentucky. I just saw him and Erin at the Sunset Grill in Pittsburgh, Pennsylvania."

Olivia refreshed Krystal's memory that it was three years ago. Erin and I met her and her second husband there for a few drinks. We were in Pittsburgh for Cindy and Patrick's wedding. I was amazed that Krystal could recall a pizza story dating back to 1991, but could not remember when we met at the Sunset Grill.

Olivia wrapped up her cross-examination with, "All your source of information has come from Erin. Correct?"

"Yes," said the revisionist friend.

Erin's new financial planner closed out the long day. Erin had met him at a conference for abused women. He was the person looking me up on LinkedIn as I sat waiting for her bowel surgery to conclude in February of 2015. He testified that without alimony, she would be broke in two years. She was $128,000 in debt, and her earning potential was not great. I will say no more about his tedious testimony. This character had the audacity to put me on his mailing list! For a while, I was receiving mailings from his office regarding their services . . . incredible!

# CHAPTER 22
## *A Sob & Swab Story, Day 2*

A liar should have a good memory. —*Quintilian*

### Day 2: Destroy Danny Day

Day 2 was all about Erin's witnesses taking the stand and expressing their love, respect, and admiration for me. Not! Strongly encouraged to display my best poker face, Abby reminded me, "The judge will be watching you and your reaction to every comment that is made about you." Olivia chimed in, "The testimony of family and friends usually does not carry much weight with the judge, but they are going to bash the hell out of you." It was also my day to take the stand for the first time.

Danny-bashing would not begin until mid-morning, so Al, Diane, and I had a chance to grab breakfast. Despite zero appetite, I forced myself to eat a little something.

A familiar nemesis took the stand first—Erin's therapist, the same counselor who had testified against me at my domestic violence hearing. I silently lamented, "Not her again!" She had objected to the subpoena, but the judge ordered her to testify.

Following a boilerplate overview of her credentials, she began. "I have been treating Erin since 2013 or 2014 for an adjustment disorder due to marital issues and ongoing separation."

Let the record show that Erin's first visit to this caregiver was actually on September 12, 2014 (the day before Erin called the cops on me). "When she first came to see me, she was concerned about her marriage and her husband's erratic behavior. By her description, he had been a controlling and abusive husband. It had escalated recently, and she was scared for her safety. She was not sure what was happening and what was going to happen next. She was also concerned about her daughter's safety. She had heightened anxiety about the break-up of the marriage. Erin was a stay-at-home mom. She had raised two children, and her primary concern was about how this would affect her children. She was concerned about her future and her ability to support herself."

Cherrie pivoted the direct examination toward the impact that Erin's May 2016 TIA (transient ischemic attack) had on her. Olivia objected to the term TIA as the witness was not qualified to make that statement.

Cherrie then referred to it as a medical event. "Her moods were different. Her anger more pronounced and her ability to follow conversations. She would switch subjects quickly. She was tired. Worn out! At times, it was hard for me to understand what she was saying. I was concerned that there was some cognitive damage from this medical event."

"So you referred her for a cognitive evaluation?" asked Cherrie.

"I did."

Her testimony continued with her opinion that Erin was not abusing drugs but that her symptoms were due to her brain event. "She has fibromyalgia, has had three or four TIAs, neuropathy, attention deficit disorder, and anxiety."

Time to paint the picture of my craziness. "Have you referred Erin to anyone else?" asked Cherrie.

"I referred her to a center for abused women when she first came to see me and then again at Christmas-time in 2014." (This was the first I had heard of these referrals.)

Cherrie requested additional rationale as to why she made these referrals. "I made a firmer request that she go around Christmas-time when it seemed like her home environment was dangerous and I was concerned for her safety."

"What did she report to you that made you believe that her home life may be dangerous?" Cherrie prodded.

"Her husband had been leaving the house and going up the street. She was concerned that he might be taking drugs. He was smoking more cigarettes. He was pacing. He was angry faster over things that did not use to make him angry. He was suspicious of her actions and where she was going. He was monitoring her. Things escalated one evening where she needed to barricade herself in her bedroom with her animals and her daughter. She called her mother and attempted to process what to do next. I believe the police were called that evening.

"There were other times that she had to stay at a hotel for safety reasons. I encouraged her to do that. It is better to be safe. The defendant had been admitted to a mental hospital, and there were some concerns about what was happening."

"Involuntarily committed. Do you know?" asked Cherrie.

"That is my understanding." Liars should indeed have good memories. She testified about a time that I showed up at her office in the fall of 2015 and announced that I would be joining Erin in the session. In actuality, in the fall of 2015, we had already separated, and I did not force my way into an appointment. In the fall of 2014, I joined Erin for an appointment after I was released from Holy Hell because according to Erin, her therapist also believed that I was cheating on her. Erin made the arrangements.

"It was very surprising to me," she testified. "It was clear to me that Erin did not have a choice but to allow Dan to join her. She was steamrolled over. Erin did not do much discussion during that session."

"How did Erin physically appear to you during that session?"

"She was closed off, quiet, pulled back, and alert. Hyper-vigilant! Erin told me that he always lied. He told lies about small silly things. Dan would lie and tell her that he was going to the hardware store or something. She would go out to run an errand, and he would be at the gas station down the street standing outside pacing and smoking cigarettes. When she would ask him about it later, he would deny it and swore he was not there and told her it was her imagination."

In a very sympathetic tone, Cherrie asked, "Is this difficult for Erin to reconcile?"

"Yes, it was tough for her to understand why this was happening and wondering whether or not he was hiding something. She was concerned that due to his extensive travel and charges on credit cards that there were other women involved in his life. She was concerned about some of their intimate sexual interactions and some of his preferences and what that might mean regarding his true choices and activities outside of their marriage."

"Has Erin ever talked to you about having any sort of affair?"

"Absolutely not! As a matter of fact, she stated that she could not imagine even being with a man, dating a man, meeting men. She was pretty much done. She was going to move in with her mother and have a nice quiet life with her animals and her mom and hopefully grandbabies."

Cherrie closed out her direct examination by relaying the story of the smack on Erin's backside and that she had seen pictures in session. Her testimony would not have been complete without revisiting the claims that I was cyberstalking and physically stalking Erin.

"There has been a lot of discussion in session about cyberstalking, physical stalking, and a new doorbell being put in the old house. Was there a camera in it? Was there not a camera in it? Someone had come into the crawl space and tried to enter the house. She had come home, and the garage door would be open."

"Did Erin discuss with you whom she believes is doing all of this?"

"She believes that either Dan is doing this himself or he hired someone to do it, or one of his family members was assisting him in doing it. She often spoke of Dan's erratic behavior. There were times when he would come in and be happy, then angry and volatile. If she did not do things just the way he wanted, he would be angry. He would withdraw from her and give her the silent treatment. A few days later would be clingy and be shadowing her. She would not be able to go and do what she needed to do in the community. I was concerned that Erin's stuff was being tracked and monitored."

The only truth in her entire testimony was that my cigarette consumption had increased! Erin's fear of me did not prevent her from sexually assaulting me in bed December 30, 2014, suggesting that evening, as she sat in the tub, "Do you want to have a night?"

Then it was Olivia's turn to cross-examine.

"Your primary source of information has been Erin. Is that correct?"

"Yes. Correct."

"Do you know Dr. Ann Birch?" asked Olivia.

"I do."

"What is her role with this family?" Olivia inquired.

"I believe that she has started seeing Katie."

"Isn't it accurate that Dr. Birch has reached out to you in the last two weeks?"

"Correct."

"With regards to the conversation she had, was she reaching out to you with concerns she had?"

"Not concerns she had. No."

"Concerns that the minor child had about her mother?"

"Yes."

"Your discussion here is about many things that Erin feels. Correct?"

"Correct."

Olivia then revisited the testimony the therapist had given at the domestic violence hearing. "At that time, according to your testimony, you had no idea that Erin was on Adderall. Did you?"

"I believe I said something that I did not have my notes in front of me that I had a list of her medications in my chart. I think that may be where I was coming from."

"The question was is she taking Adderall, and your response was you were not aware of that. In fact, you were not aware that she has two different prescriptions for Adderall. Accurate?"

"Correct," was her reply.

"Are you aware of the fact that during your sixty to sixty-four sessions with her that her Adderall dose had been increasing?"

"No, that is not the role that I play."

"Have you ever had a conversation with her psychiatrist?"

"No, but I have seen a letter from her."

"The letter that she prepared in anticipation of litigation?"

"Correct."

"You have testified that Erin has fibromyalgia. You haven't diagnosed her with that, have you?"

"I am not a medical doctor, no."

"Again, that is her self-report to you. Correct?"

"Correct."

Olivia then pressed her on the date that I forced my way into Erin's appointment. "You let him into the session. Correct?"

"Correct."

"You did not stop the session, pick up the phone, and call anybody because you were concerned about Erin's safety. Did you?"

"No."

"You did not tell Dan to leave and that it would have to be rescheduled. Did you?"

"I asked Erin if it was okay if he came into the session and she said, 'I did not know that we were going to do this, but he is here. Yes, he may come in.'"

Olivia ramped it up a little. "I am asking about your concerns. You just testified about all kinds of concerns that you have about him. My question is, as a professional, if this happens outside of your protocol, why do you allow him in the session?"

"Because the client was comfortable having him come in, and I monitored him once he was in to see if he was oriented to space and time," was the retort.

"You testified about garage doors being open, cameras in doorbells, crawl spaces being accessed. In your professional training, could those also be signs of paranoia?"

"It could be."

"Are you aware that one of the side effects of Adderall is paranoia?"

"Yes."

Herpes time! "I have read your notes, and in your notes, there is extensive documentation about a time when Erin came in and told you she had herpes and you processed that with her. Do you recall that?"

"I do."

"What I find interesting . . . Has Erin told you that Dan does not have herpes?"

"She has told me that through the process of what I call the herpes saga is that my understanding is that neither one of them has herpes at this time."

"Would it shock you that nowhere in your extensive notes does it mention that Erin came back in and told you that she does not have herpes?"

"It wouldn't shock me, no."

"Nothing further, Your Honor."

Re-direct from Cherrie. "How did Dan appear in that session with you?"

"He was agitated. Hyper-alert."

Olivia objected, "She has no frame of reference as she had only met Danny once. Perhaps he is always hyper-alert."

The therapist continued. "He had pressured speech and tangential thoughts inconsistent with the goals of the session."

"Is it unusual that you did not document that Erin had told you she does not have herpes?"

"No. My records are not written normally for court."

Cherrie asked about the notes in her medical record regarding how Erin felt about the herpes diagnosis.

"She was upset because of the medical diagnosis and how that could affect her and what that meant. Erin was embarrassed and wondered about the social stigma. She was also concerned about Dan sharing this with the children to change how they viewed her. She was also heartbroken to think that if she had herpes, then he stepped outside of the marriage."

Re-cross from Olivia. "You just testified to a concern about Dan telling the children. Is that what you just testified to?"

"Yes."

"Read with me your notes here six lines down in the notes section. Your process with your client was that it was not a good idea to tell the children that Dad gave Mom an STD."

"Correct."

"Did you have that discussion with Erin?"

"I had that discussion in response to her concern that Dan would tell them, because his behavior was erratic and she was concerned that he would do that."

"Did Erin process with you telling the children? Because she told the children. Correct?"

"I don't know about that."

"You don't know if she told the children?"

"No."

"You don't think that would be clinically significant to find out whether or not she told the children? That their Father had given her an STD?"

"No, I don't think that is my role to question and follow up."

"Would you have advised her to do that?"

"We talked about the pros and cons of doing that and that it was her choice."

"Nothing further, Your Honor."

Then, oh joy, Tiffany was back! Time to revisit the July 6, 2015, "butt-dial" and the phone call I made to her in May of 2016. She could not remember the date of the butt-dial but did remark that she believed that I was out of the house at that point.

"I believe they were separated because I was over her house a lot. I would go and sit with her."

Cherrie proceeded, "Were there other times that he contacted you?"

"May 19 of this year when Erin had her mini-stroke. I contacted her children to let them know. I guess he heard through Katie. He called me and asked one question about Erin. I was shocked he contacted me. Then he started ranting about her drug use. I was like, oh my God!" [Heavy sigh from Tiff]

"What was he saying?" asked Cherrie.

"She did not have a stroke. It is her drug use, her drug abuse. Her doctors should know this. He was ranting to the point that I stopped listening and was getting a little irritated. I said he was full of shit and this call is ending. Then I hung up. Then he sent me a text, 'Thank you for talking to me. I will talk to my children from now on about Erin.' He was like Jekyll & Hyde."

"Was he making it clear to you that he believes she was a drug addict?" asked Cherrie.

"He really wants me to believe she is a drug addict."

"Do you believe that?"

"Oh gosh no! I have been around her so much the last two to three years I think I would know." She too would try to paint the picture that I prevented Erin from having a social life. "I am not a phone person. I often leave my phone in the car or at home. Erin's phone would drive me crazy. Ding, ding, ding. Text, text text. I just ignored it because it is not my business, but eventually down the road, she opened up to me. She would be like, 'Oh Dan. Sorry it is Dan.'"

No dates or timelines were provided for the alleged texts that I barraged poor Erin with. It simply never happened. She testified that Erin and Katie stayed with her because Katie was so afraid. However, once Katie moved in with me, she admitted Erin forced her to go to Tiffany's house. All of this played out after I had moved out of the home.

Perhaps Tiffany was in the crawl space of our home. I know I never saw her while I still lived there. Olivia wasted no breath cross-examining her.

Before our lunch recess on Day 2, it was time for the Team Captain to make an appearance. Doris, who at this point needs no introduction, took the stand. Now in her mid-70s, the last few years appeared to have taken their toll. Erin and her mom not only shared the same middle name, Marie, but they were now rocking matching hairstyles. Her direct examination from Cherrie was extensive.

Following her introduction and swearing in, she needed a few minutes to compose herself. Cherrie opened with, "It is difficult for you to be here?"

Doris's response was harsh for me to stomach, as it was baseless and without merit. "It is difficult to hear these allegations against my daughter when I know a completely different person. She was raised to be a strong, feisty, intelligent, and independent woman. I have seen that destroyed, and I take issue, serious issue, with that. Between the fibromyalgia that she suffers, which is certainly out of her control, to the emotional, verbal, and mental abuse that I have witnessed against my daughter to bring her to the point that she is today. In my opinion, she was manipulated, lied to, and abused."

Olivia interrupted Doris's monologue. "Objection. Is there going to be a question?"

Cherrie resumed. "What you are talking about is why it is difficult for you to be here today?"

"Absolutely, and the toll it has taken on my daughter because of someone else! When she first met Dan, she was vibrant. She had a few knocks in her life. She pulled herself up by the bootstraps, continued her education, and got an associate's degree. She then pursued her Bachelor of Science degree and graduated from the University of Louisville magna cum laude, and she is reduced to what you see today!"

Doris continued, "Erin's behavior was not the same around family when Dan arrived. I started to develop some concerns about Dan early on in their relationship. Feelings that were confirmed by a photographer that I worked with. He was at my home to take some pictures of Erin for a painting he wanted to do, and there was a knock at the door. It was Dan. Erin did not know he was coming, nor did I. He showed up unannounced and followed the photographer from room to room. My colleague confirmed for me the next day how uncomfortable this made him feel."

Doris attempted to drive this theme home further by sharing a "story" about a 1997 family reunion when I had Erin and Katie on lockdown in her Florida room when all the other family was gathered outside.

"Erin had always been close to our family. She grew up in a single-parent family, and her extended family was beneficial in that situation. Erin was always close to the family and in particular one cousin, who was similar in age to Erin. By this time, they are all grown up and have children of their own, and we had a great big family reunion. I was busy with all the food preparation, and it was only after everyone ate and we were all sitting around, and I noticed that Erin was nowhere to be found. Her husband and daughter were nowhere to be found! She was usually always within the family and very happy. Very glad to be with all these people.

"I went to look for her. We have a Florida room. All alone in that room was Dan, Erin, and Katie on Erin's lap. Dan had his arm around Erin and one hand on her knee. I remember it specifically. I said, 'Why don't you come and join the family? We are having such fun!' We are a family that laughs! Always laughs! Dan stated that they 'would be out in a minute.' Eventually, they joined us, but Erin's behavior was not the same as it had been before Dan. She was guarded and went out of her way to avoid her cousin Ricky who she had previously been very close to."

I do get it! Blood is thicker than water, but the complete fabrications were challenging to sit through. Doris's stories were about when Erin and I first started dating in 1991 and family reunions from 1997. Seriously?

As a side note, when I first started dating Erin, her story was quite different from Mom's version. Erin informed me that she had indeed been very close to her cousin Ricky, but their relationship had changed because of an alleged incident at his now-wife's bachelorette party. According to Erin, Ricky's fiancé was being inappropriate with another man. Erin allegedly discussed this with her aunt and Ricky's sister and was told to let it go.

Doris was an excellent cook. Her specialty was Italian cuisine, especially spaghetti sauce and homemade pasta. I am sure she cooked for the reunion, but a lot of the food was compliments of her niece's husband who owned a catering business. I too remember this reunion very distinctly, and it was a great time. I spent no time in Doris's Florida room but interacted all day with Erin's grandmother and all of her cousins!

Doris proceeded to discuss our transitions from Pittsburgh to Louisville and ultimately our move to North Carolina. "It was hard for Erin to leave Pittsburgh, but she was going to support her husband." Doris tearfully described her daughter's challenges with fibromyalgia. "A lesser woman would not have been able to raise their children with all that she was dealing with. Erin would make dinner, pack lunches, assist with homework, and then collapse from exhaustion."

Yes, the theme was that she did it all. Doris consistently used phrases like "her children." She could not remember the year that Katie was born or when we moved to North Carolina (somewhere between 2003, 2005, or 2010 was her answer) but was adamant that between 2005 and 2010, I traveled Monday through Thursday while Erin raised her children. In a backhanded way, Doris did recognize my support of Erin during her illnesses. "I will say that Dan was there for her. However, I now realize that when Erin was ill, Dan could be in control of EVERYTHING! The doctors, the house, the bills. Everything! Which in my opinion is an indication of who Dan is!"

During the majority of Doris's direct examination, I did not make eye contact, as I was busy taking notes. I was also feverishly scribbling notes to hand to Olivia and Abby for cross-examination purposes. However, I was intently focused on her as she discussed our illustrious beach trip.

"It was not my place to interfere in their marriage. I have told both of my children this. I suggested that they try to fix their marriage together and that it could have been something that happened in his childhood or hers!" (You nailed it, Doris! It was something that happened in your daughter's childhood and not mine.) Doris continued, "You have to acknowledge that you have a problem so that you can begin to address the issue."

Cherrie then inquired about Doris threatening to kill me. "Did you really want to kill Dan?"

"Physically kill him? No." Doris then stated that Erin considered leaving the marriage in December of 2014. "She finally had the courage to give up the lifestyle that she had been living and leave an abusive marriage, and now she is living below the poverty level. My daughter cannot afford to buy food"—Doris broke down at this point—"gas for her car and cannot afford all of the medications she needs. She is happy to receive care packages from me that include toilet paper, peanut butter, paper towels, and dog food. She needs nutritious meals. Nutrition is so important to someone with fibro-myalgia, and she cannot afford to eat at times. I was sent a picture of her refrigerator, and it infuriated me."

Well played, Erin! Then again, you have had many years to hone your craft and have fooled so many. Unfortunately, that long list of people in-cludes my two beautiful children.

As Doris's direct examination began to wind down, there was testimony about me smacking Erin on the butt and about her view that I had always lied. "Dan does not know how to tell the truth."

Of course, there were no examples or specifics provided when Cherrie pressed her. Just baseless open-ended statements. The "pot" sat on the stand calling the "kettle" black.

Doris provided specifics on all of the financial support she was providing

Erin. "I have worked for over forty years, and I am now retired. We have gone through three mediation sessions to avoid what we are going through today. My daughter is living in poverty, and even though I am on a fixed income, I have had no choice but to support her." Doris testified to giving Erin a $40,000 loan, $800 per month to live on, money for expert testimony, and rent! She added that she has had to cash in some of her retirement funds.

Doris closed with this, "He is moving into a beautiful, brand-new townhome, and she is living under the poverty line."

Truth be told, in less than a year's time, Erin had received over $52,000 from me in various forms. The federal poverty level for an individual in 2016 was $11,800. The math does not add up. Erin had been living in a 2,300-square-foot home since February of 2016 that Mom was paying for while I was residing in a 1,000-square-foot apartment.

The tears quickly dried, and Doris's demeanor dramatically changed during cross-examination. As Olivia approached, Doris moved up to the edge of her seat. I was at full attention with my eyes locked in on her. All the while, I did my best to show little to no emotion.

Olivia began her cross-examination by running down the list of the support that I was providing Erin, Katie, and Billy. "You are aware that Dan pays for Erin's rent? Correct?"

"Yes."

"He pays for her car, car insurance, and health insurance? Correct?"

Doris angrily responded, "Yes, but he won't be paying her health insurance forever."

"He gives her $750.00 per month. Correct?"

Doris's anger intensified, and she questioned Olivia, "What was that amount?"

Olivia repeated, "$750.00 per month."

Doris responded with a sarcastic thank you. I was giving Erin $2,250 a month, but her counsel called $1,500 her rent to minimize what I was giving her.

Olivia transitioned to the support I was providing our kids. "Through-out this time, you have not spoken of your grandchildren, Billy and Katie. Their support is important. Correct?"

"Of course," stated Doris.

"Their financial support is important. Would you agree?"

"Yes," stated their grandmother.

"Katie no longer lives with Erin. Do you think it is appropriate that Erin has made no financial provisions to care for Katie? Are you aware of any money that Erin has given for the support of her daughter?"

"She has given small amounts when she is able, and it probably comes from me," snapped Doris.

"She doesn't pay Dan any support that you are aware of?"

Doris interrupted Olivia and yelled her response, "Why should she give any support to Dan? He makes a lot of money!"

Olivia took back control with, "If you would let me finish. My question was are you aware of any payments she has given Dan for support of their children? Are you aware of any money that Erin has paid for Katie's private school tuition? Are you aware of any money that she has given Dan for either of the vehicles that Katie and Billy drive? Are you aware of any money that she has given to support Billy's college expenses?"

Doris's only response to these questions was, "I am not aware."

Olivia then turned her attention to the beach trip in 2014. "Let's talk about the beach trip in June of 2014 when you threatened to kill Dan. I think you commented that you would not physically kill him. Right?"

"Of course not," replied my soon-to-be ex-mother-in-law.

"But you would spend about $40,000 in attorney's fees for your daugh-ter. Correct?"

A long drawn out yes was Doris's reply.

Olivia revisited Doris's testimony about the family reunion incident and the Florida room. She focused in on the fact that it could not have been in 1997 as Katie was born in 1998.

"Katie was definitely there as we have photographs. Oh, my mistake, I must have had the date wrong."

"Isn't it true that Dan personally met with you to ask for Erin's hand in marriage?"

"Oh, he did," Doris bitterly spat.

"Didn't you tell him at that time that Erin was a very complex and complicated individual?"

"I did."

"You love your daughter?"

"Of course!"

"Would it be fair to say that you strongly dislike Dan?"

"I dislike the actions that Dan is taking against my daughter."

"According to your testimony today, you have disliked him for two decades."

"I dislike the actions that he was taking against my daughter for two decades."

Olivia continued, "But the entire time she was financially supported. Correct?"

"This is true," admitted Doris.

"Your two grandchildren are successful individuals. Correct?"

"Somewhat. And she chose to not, the very difficult choice, not to live the lifestyle and be free of the emotional and verbal abuse which has caused her to live below the poverty line now," a tearful Doris sobbed.

"You testified that Dan was supportive during her illnesses. Correct?"

"Yes. I do not deny that in the least."

"You have testified at times that Dan was controlling of Erin, but isn't it true that Erin went down to the Clinic in Florida not once, but twice and Dan did not go with her?"

"Well, he was working," stated Doris sheepishly.

"And taking care of Katie. Correct?"

"I do not recall how that worked, to tell you the truth."

"But she went down on out-of-state trips on her own," added Olivia.

"But as I said, during those out-of-state trips, Dan was in total control of everything. Not Erin at the Clinic, but total control of the life that he was living with Katie and the children."

"He was responsible for the household while she was gone. Is that a fair statement?" inquired Olivia.

"That is a fair statement."

Olivia attempted to clarify the financial support Doris provided Erin. "Would you be surprised that Erin testified at her deposition that your financial support was an advance on her inheritance?"

Doris verbally stumbled but recovered, "I clarified to her that if I dropped dead today the monies that I leave my children will be first split in half and then she will repay to my son the $40,000 that I spent."

"Nothing further, Your Honor!"

Under re-direct, Cherrie did some quick math focusing in on the $750.00 per month and ignored the other $1,500 I was giving her per month. "Dan gives Erin $750 per month. Correct?"

"That is correct," Doris loudly remarked.

"That is $9,000 per year. Has your daughter had to make some difficult choices because of this?"

Doris responded, "Due to her latest medical situation, her fibromyalgia, and her limited finances, she has at times had to choose between her medications and food. Nutrition is ultra-important to someone with her condition, and she can't afford to eat nutritionally." Doris also testified to the fact that in addition to the $40,000, she had paid $5,000 for private investigators. Their services included sweeping the house for "bugs" and, on two occasions, sitting at the house while Erin was not home. You know, just in case I showed up!

Olivia conducted a brief re-cross examination, inquiring about where Erin is now living and who is paying for that home. Doris testified that she was paying for the lease and the security deposit.

Doris stepped down off the stand and approached her daughter, and they shared a sweet long tearful embrace. In the twenty-five years I had known this woman, I never had a cross word with her even when she threatened to kill me. I loved and respected her for who I believed she was. When I asked for her daughter's hand in marriage, there was not a single concern raised. I can still picture the broad smile on her face when she quite happily agreed to me marrying her daughter. Behind that smile may have been relief that her next "victim" had arrived to take her daughter off her hands. Included in the Third Gift is my newfound ability to see people for who they truly are.

Al, Diane, and I returned early from our lunch recess, and as we re-entered the courtroom, Olivia approached me and inquired, "Do you have thirty dollars on you? I'll explain later." I cracked a smile, wondering why she could not just take it out of the big bucket of money I had been refilling repeatedly. I do not carry much cash on me, so Al once again obliged by fronting the money. Olivia then handed it to Abby who hurriedly left the courtroom and courthouse.

Olivia explained that Abby was on her way to the New Hanover County Sheriff's Department across the street. "We need to get Erin's regular OB/GYN under subpoena for tomorrow." As it turned out, Cherrie had lied to Abby and Olivia about the fact that they could not get him served to appear. "Yes, we had him under subpoena to testify on Erin's behalf, but we could not get him served," were Cherrie's exact words. Upon checking the court records, Abby discovered that he had been served papers to appear on behalf of the plaintiff and her counsel. They were not going to put him on the stand after all!

The court would resume a little after 2 p.m. The next witness to take the stand for Erin was a PhD in clinical psychology. She was as green as the frames around her lenses, having received her PhD in clinical psychology two years prior. She had met with Erin based on a referral from Erin's therapist, just five days before our trial began, spending a total of 50 minutes with her.

The purpose of the referral was to assess Erin's executive functioning through a battery of standardized tests. Executive functioning looks at an individual's ability to plan, organize, and focus. There was a lot of back and forth between Olivia, Cherrie, and the judge regarding this witness being tendered as an expert in neuropsychological testing. Cherrie wanted her recognized as an expert. Olivia did an excellent job of challenging her credentials. Including her time in school and clinical practice, she had administered and interpreted the tests that she performed on Erin only three times. She had never testified in court as an expert in neuropsychological testing, but the judge ultimately allowed her to be tendered as an expert witness.

She stated from the bench, "I agree that she has conducted and interpreted these tests on a limited basis, but I am not sure how much more training she could get. I think she has had as much training as she could have in this area, so I am going to allow you to tender her as an expert in neuropsychological testing."

With all due respect, Your Honor, perhaps a few more years under her belt should have been required!

They were trying to establish that Erin's declining cognitive function would impair her ability to work. Under direct examination, the psychologist testified that the extent of her review of Erin's records was 2013 evaluation by the Clinic and a letter from Erin's therapist.

"One of the tests I conducted was a Psychiatric Diagnostic Screening Questionnaire. It is a self-report tool and Erin selected all of the measures that would indicate that she had major depression, post-traumatic stress disorder, and generalized anxiety disorder. The second test I conducted was to look at her cognitive function. She scored in the mild range of impairment."

Cherrie asked, "Can you explain what that means to the judge?"

"Sure. The results scale is average, low average, mild, and borderline. Erin scored in the mild range of impairment. Borderline is just above mental retardation. She did have difficulty with memory, language, and orientation. Her processing speed is only better than 6 percent of people in her age range.

She has shown processing speed declines, and immediate recall has declined."

"Can depression affect your processing speed?" Cherrie asked.

"Yes, it can."

Quite surprisingly, Cherrie asked, "Can extended or long-term drug abuse produce these same types of results?"

PhD responded, "Long-term drug abuse can impact cognitive functioning."

Cherrie dug a little deeper, "How many years constitutes long-term drug abuse?"

"It would depend on the type of drug and how much was used, but at least a minimum of 8 to 10 years."

As Cherrie's direct examination was winding down, she asked, "Based on your findings, do you believe that Erin can live independently?"

So my soon-to-be-ex-wife, who has two degrees and graduated with high honors, is now cognitively just above mental retardation and may not be able to live alone? Then again, she had been abusing many drugs for at least seven years now.

Olivia began her cross-examination challenging the length of time the psychologist spent with Erin.

PhD replied, "The clinical interview lasted for fifty minutes, and the testing was about an hour." She only met with Erin once.

Olivia proceeded, "What experience do you have in normalizing test results when people are in specific situations? For example, as I understand the dates, she took this test about five days ago?"

"Yes."

"So would you say that coming up on litigation is a very stressful event for most individuals?"

"Yes."

"Would you agree that stress is going to play an impact or have a role in how somebody responds to testing?"

"It can."

"I am unclear as to what records of Erin's you reviewed."

PhD responded, "I reviewed her psychological evaluation from the Clinic in 2013."

"Did you have an opportunity to speak with anybody at the Clinic?"

"No."

Olivia pressed forward, "Did you examine Erin's neurological records? Psychiatric records dating back two years? Would it be a concern to you if Erin had access to those documents and did not provide them to you to complete your evaluation? Could that potentially change the results of your evaluation?"

"Yes. More information could potentially change the results." Additionally, she testified to the fact that she never spoke to Erin's therapist. "I received her letter, and she probably would have told me the same thing." The heat was getting to this young and inexperienced professional. She was wide-eyed, and the look on her face screamed, "What the hell did I get myself into?"

Olivia began to put the hammer down. "I understand that the testing is what the testing is, but I think your testimony was that, 'the testing is just one part and that it has to have a translation into everyday life.' Correct?"

"Yes"

"And so, you did not interview any collaterals. Correct?"

"Yes"

"So all you have is some test results. Correct?"

"Yes, and a collateral report."

"A two-paragraph letter from her therapist whom she has seen for almost two years now?"

PhD remarked, "I cannot recall how long."

"In those fifty minutes with Erin, did she talk to you about her job?"

"Yes."

"Did you read her deposition testimony?"

"No!"

Olivia then laid out all that Erin testified to during her deposition regarding her job responsibilities. "Are you aware that she manages individuals with autism, assists them with budgeting, administering medication and driving around these individuals?"

PhD's answers to all of those questions were, "No, I am not aware of her responsibilities."

"Did she share with you that part of her job responsibilities includes documenting all of her interactions with these individuals?"

"No."

"Those responsibilities as she describes them seem quite different from the test results you talked about. Would you say that is fair?"

"Different. How?"

"Different in that you indicated she had memory issues and recall issues, but she can administer medication to someone and handle budgeting issues which in general would require some level of memory. Correct?"

The good doctor replied, "Yes."

Guided by Abby and her attention to detail, Olivia started to dive into the PhD's own report. "And so, you state in here that part of this could have been due to her TIA. Correct?"

"Yes."

"You have not seen any medical records that have diagnosed her with having a TIA, have you?"

"No, this was based on her self-report."

Olivia followed up with, "Same with her fibromyalgia. That was based on self-report?"

"Yes."

Olivia then focused on the statement that she had made about long-term drug abuse and its impact on cognitive functioning. "You didn't drug test her, did you? You did not ask her to bring in her full medication list, did you?"

"No."

"So she self-reported her medication to you?"

"Yes."

"How much Adderall did she report she was taking?"

The response occurred after a long silence, "I did not get a specific amount."

Olivia followed with, "Did you ask her if she had taken Adderall in the last couple of hours when she came in for her appointment?"

"No."

"Would that not be significant if Adderall is meant to help her focus to know whether or not she had taken that medication prior to performing all those tests?"

The direct response was a quick yes.

Olivia then stated, "Based on your report, her delayed recall is above average."

"Yes."

Under re-direct, Cherrie had opened the door regarding the Clinic records documenting Erin's fibromyalgia diagnosis going back 14 years. Of course, this is what Erin reported to them on her first visit in April of 2013.

Olivia, during her re-cross, approached the bench and reviewed the Clinic records. "In your report, you stated that you relied on the Clinic records for her diagnosis of fibromyalgia. Is that accurate?"

"Yes, and her self-report."

"In the Clinic records, and if you will look at that because I am going to read the last two sentences of that paragraph, it says, 'regarding the question of fibromyalgia she was seen by this doctor who was unable to confirm the diagnosis of fibromyalgia or any autoimmune disease. If she does have fibromyalgia, he felt it was very mild. He felt there was no evidence of systematic inflammation or active autoimmune disease in any event, fortunately.' Her Clinic records do not diagnose her with fibromyalgia. So is it fair to say that you were relying on her self-report that she had been diagnosed?"

Surprisingly the PhD's response was, "I did not have access to this report! The only evaluation I got was the neuropsychological report from 2013."

"Are you aware that she went to the Clinic two times in 2013?"

"No."

"So this is the first time that you have been made aware that you weren't given all of the Clinic records?"

"Yes."

"Nothing further, Your Honor!"

This witness could not have been happier to get off the stand. Erin's troubling state of mind was illuminated, and her entire team was present to hear the fact that she does not have fibromyalgia or autoimmune disease. How would Doris process the fact that the only person with something more profound going on was her own flesh and blood?

I had the privilege of closing out the day by taking the hot seat.

After a few quick opening questions about how Erin and I met and when we were married, Cherrie spent a fair amount of time on my financial affidavit, tax returns, and pay stubs. She wanted to highlight my employment, compensation, and all that my organization provides for me.

She transitioned to my townhome purchase. It did not take Cherrie long to begin to highlight all that I offer for Billy and Katie, by reviewing my financial affidavit line by line. "You are currently supporting Katie more than double what you are providing Erin. Is that a fair statement?"

I simply responded, "I don't believe that is a fair statement."

Olivia asked for a short recess. As I made my way to the men's room, Abby pulled me into a conference room. She sharply snapped, "You look like a dick up there!"

Olivia then joined her sentiment and offered additional guidance, "You need to relax and slow her down. Sit back in your chair and before you respond to her questions, count to five on your fingers."

Their coaching was on target. As I listened to the audio recordings post-trial, I saw I was a dick! My tone was curt. Without question, the events of the day negatively affected my disposition.

As the direct examination resumed, my tone was significantly improved, and I effectively slowed her pace of questioning. I was deliberate and measured in my responses. The line of questioning continued to center around my financials and Katie's checking account. She scrutinized line-by-line deposits and transactions in Katie's account. She was staying on the path that my support was more significant for Katie than Erin. In all actuality, many of the deposits were ATM cash deposits from Katie's babysitting.

Cherrie would eventually move away from the financials and focus in on a letter I wrote Erin on September 5, 2014, the evening of Erin's first attorney visit. I was doing all I could to hold onto our marriage of almost twenty-one years. It was also ten days before my time in Holy Hell. I share that to provide proper context for my state of mind at the time.

"Why were you writing this letter to her?"

"I don't recall what transpired on that day or what day of the week that may have been, but I was expressing my feelings for Erin."

Cherrie then inquired about another letter I wrote to Erin in December of 2014. "In here you said, 'I do understand that you never trusted me and that has caused things to spin out of control.' You referenced an HIV test at the bottom of the page. What is that about?"

I simply explained the rationale for the HIV test.

She asked me to read from the letter, "I thought that we were making progress other than the two stupid lies and the insecurities and flashbacks we both have had."

Cherrie pressed on. "There have been problems with your untruthfulness. Is that a fair statement?"

After a bit of a delay, I responded, "I would say that is semi-accurate."

"How is it inaccurate?"

"It is inaccurate in the sense that I have been painted as an individual that can't be trusted and that I am a pathological liar is simply not accurate."

"It is something that Erin has taken issue with during your marriage. Correct?"

"I would say that she took issue with it early in the marriage and beginning in the spring of 2014."

Of course, the direct examination would not have been complete without my bipolar diagnosis resurfacing and the alleged drug use in my medical records from Holy Hell. I attempted to provide appropriate clarity and the efforts I made to give Erin closure on this.

"You have a friend named Mila," remarked Cherrie.

I stated, "I would like to clarify that she is a professional colleague."

"You don't consider her a friend?"

"Perhaps, but my introduction to her was as a professional colleague."

Cherrie sarcastically asked, "Where does your professional colleague live?"

I answered her with her city and state.

"How often do you talk to your professional friend, I mean your professional contact?"

"I have not spoken with her all that consistently since she left the organization in the late summer or fall of 2014."

"Before that time frame, how often were you speaking with her?" inquired Cherrie.

"It depends on what we had going at work."

Cherrie directed me to an exhibit of my May 2014 phone records. "Would it surprise you if there were 125 phone calls back and forth between you and Mila during that time frame?"

"No, it would not surprise me. I do not know if that number is correct based on what you have highlighted, but it would not be surprising. I do not work out of an office, and when I am not traveling, I work from home. It is impossible to recall what was going on in May of 2014, but we were involved in many projects together and developed contracts for the company together. My relationship was nothing but appropriate."

"Do you recall if you called her your friend when we had our deposition?"

"I do recall I called her that."

"If you look at the time stamps of some of these calls, there are some that are very late at night. Are they not?"

"Which, in particular, are you talking about?"

"Did you ever speak to her late in the evening?"

I responded, "As we discussed during my deposition, perhaps on one or two occasions."

Cherrie asks, "Did that become a sore spot with Erin?"

"No. I do not recall Erin ever coming to me and having an issue with a conversation with Mila. We used to exchange Christmas cards. Matter of fact, when I was in the hospital after they took my phone, shoelaces, and everything else, I had to alert my boss to the fact that I was going to be out of work for a few days. I had a new boss, and had not yet committed her number to memory, so I gave Erin Mila's phone number. Erin and Mila were texting back and forth with each other."

"You had Mila's number committed to memory, but not your boss?"

"I had known Mila for fourteen or fifteen years. I had no problem giving my wife Mila's number."

The direct examination of me, for this day, would end with Cherrie focusing in on phone calls I had made to ADT. She was trying to establish that I violated our mediated agreement by calling them on September 15, 2015, to change the billing address on the account. She also wanted to play my phone call to them from September 30, 2015, but was not prepared with the right equipment to do so. That call occurred two days before my domestic violence hearing. I called them to get prepared. Yes, I was less than flattering of Erin as I told the ADT representative that she was fucking crazy. I was also amped up having just learned that Katie might testify against me in court.

As I prepared to leave the court, Abby and Olivia gave me my home-work assignment. They asked that I spend some time listening to the call to ADT from September 30 to be prepared to defend myself. I was asked to revisit hundreds of pages of bank statements and financial documents for additional questions that might arise under direct examination.

Al, Diane, and I made our way to my car with my homework in hand. It was equally as hot and humid outside as it had been in the courtroom that day. The temperature was in the high 90s. Along with many other cars exiting downtown Wilmington, we made our way toward highway seventeen moving at about sixty to sixty-five miles per hour. It was about three miles outside of downtown when a car rapidly approached. The woman in the car next to us rolled down her window and yelled, "Your papers!"

All I could say was, "Shit!"

I had left my Samsonite leather portfolio on the top of my car, and the papers were blowing all over both sides of the street. Quickly, we pulled over and decided to divide and conquer. Al and Diane took one side of the road, and I took the other. Sweat was pouring off all of us as we walked two to three miles down either side of the street collecting financial documents and pharmacy and medical claims documents. Fortunately, the speed of the vehicles pushed the papers to the sides of the road. I needed to find the portfolio to determine how far back it had fallen off the car.

As I was picking up papers, a rusted-out van full of African American men rolled up on me. The passenger rolled down the window manually and yelled, "Pick up those papers, white boy, before I hit you with the okey-doke!" I looked up at the sky and busted out laughing.

Unbelievably, the Samsonite portfolio was intact after being run over by hundreds of cars. My notes from the day, complete with tire marks and wrinkles, were still legible. That portfolio is still in use today.

*The sun will come up tomorrow,* I thought, *and it will be our turn with our medical witnesses!*

# CHAPTER 23
## *A Sob & Swab Story, Day 3*

The O.J. Simpson case, they had no understanding of that
DNA evidence, and didn't want to. —*Joseph Wambaugh*

### Day 3: DNA Day

It was another mid-morning start for our alimony trial. Hard to understand why the court system doesn't begin its day at 8 a.m. It could potentially
bring another $75,000 in annual revenue for the attorneys (250 hours at
$300 per hour). Something for you family law counselors to lobby for. It may
also alleviate the backlog in this broken system we taxpayers are funding.

Both sides had done their best to accommodate the experts' schedules,
and today was no different. The continuance of my direct examination was
bumped so that Olivia could put both Erin's regular OB/GYN and our
STD expert on the stand. I was more than happy to give up my seat for these
two witnesses. This was going to be good!

Here is where the "Swab" part of our "Swab Story" begins. Apologies
in advance, dear readers, but the following testimony's graphic nature is
necessary to highlight the strength of the evidence.

. . .

Following the customary review of the witnesses' credentials, Olivia began her direct examination, referring the regular OB/GYN to Erin's medical records. He confirmed that Erin had been a patient since 2004. "On June 16, 2015, you treated Erin as a follow-up to some testing she had done?" asked Olivia.

"Correct."

Olivia continued, "She came in with the following complaint: white clusters around her rectum and itching for about a week. Is that accurate?"

"That is accurate," he confirmed.

"Did you conduct a physical exam?"

"I conducted a limited physical exam of just that area. I saw two raised ulcerated lesions at the 11 o'clock and 1 o'clock positions on the rectal sphincter."

Olivia then asked, "Is this a classic presentation of sexually transmitted herpes?"

The OB/GYN responded, "Ulcerations are typically first thought to be HSV (herpes) lesions until proven otherwise."

"Based on your visual inspection you believed that she had herpes. Correct?"

"I believed it was worth testing. I never make a definitive decision just based on visual inspection."

Olivia pressed, "But at that point you suspected?"

"Absolutely!" the witness confidently said.

"You prescribed her valacyclovir, or Valtrex?"

"Correct. I treat empirically. If a patient were to have HSV 2 (herpes) and to leave the office without any treatment that would be cruel and unusual punishment."

"You swabbed that area? Was it that specimen that was tested?"

"Correct. The results of that test confirmed my suspicion that she had herpes simplex virus number 2."

Olivia addressed the refill that he had written for an additional thirty days of valacyclovir that Erin filled on July 6, 2015. "According to your notes, on July 6, Erin called your office again. Correct?"

"Yes, that is correct."

"The notes state that she called because she had reported that she had been doing well on Valtrex. Correct?"

"That is what the note says."

"At that time, you wrote another prescription for Valtrex?"

"Correct."

"Nothing further, Your Honor."

Even though Cherrie had subpoenaed this witness, but did not want to put him on the stand, she still had the prerogative to cross-examine him. After Olivia's direct examination, this now made sense. During Olivia's direct examination, Cherrie had sat stoically, arms crossed.

Now she began her cross-examination with an assumptive question, "It is true that if you have herpes, it can lie dormant in your body for a long period of time?"

"Correct," he responded.

Cherrie continued, "There is no way to know—"

Olivia cut her off. "Objection, Your Honor. He is testifying as a fact witness for me. I have not qualified him as an expert. If she wants to qualify him as an expert, she can. He is testifying about things that I would deem as expert opinions regarding herpes."

Cherrie began a line of questioning to have him tendered as an expert. "Judge, I would seek to have the witness tendered as an expert in sexually transmitted diseases. Specifically, herpes."

Olivia then took on the witness for further clarity around his "expertise." Ultimately, Olivia did not object to the witness being tendered as an expert.

Cherrie continued, "Is there any test that can be done to determine when somebody contracted the virus?"

"No, not definitively. Unfortunately."

"Erin told you from your notes here that the Valtrex did not help. Do you recall her talking with you about that?"

He responded, "Yes, she called the office, but I never spoke with her about that."

"It says that the patient has seen her primary care physician and stated the Valtrex did not help."

The witness stated, "That was two months after the initial diagnosis and she left the message with my nurse"

Cherrie then pivoted to getting clarity around the swab and blood tests performed to diagnose herpes.

The recently tendered expert responded, "The PCR test (swab test) that was originally done on Erin looks for the DNA virus in the lesion. It is very sensitive. It is nearly 100 percent. The lab that I utilize states that their false positive rate is 1.7 percent. So it is highly sensitive. If you have it, you have it. The blood test that you are speaking of is utilized to detect antibodies that developed as a result of the virus. At twelve weeks, only 70 percent of all patients infected with the virus would test positive for the virus as a result of the development of antibodies. The diagnostic standard is to find the DNA of the virus in an active lesion."

Cherrie then attempted to go down the path that the lesions were an anal fissure that resulted from her bowel surgery in February of 2015. "You are aware that Erin had her large bowel removed a couple of months prior. Correct?"

"Correct."

"Do you recall Erin telling you that she had an anal fissure?"

"Correct, and I spoke directly with her surgeon about the anal fissure. The anal fissure was in a different location than her ulcerations. Her surgeon informed me that her anal fissure was at the 6 o'clock position and, as the notes that I have written confirm, her ulcerations were at the 11 o'clock and 1 o'clock position."

*Tick tock, Erin!*

"Did Erin talk with you about her concerns as to whether or not her husband had herpes?"

"She was getting STD testing over concerns for STD exposure. I cannot recall if it was specifically related to her husband or not, and I do not write those things down," said the doctor.

"Has she come to you before with problems with yeast infections?"

"She has had problems with chronic vaginitis. Correct."

"So if someone has never had a swab of any lesion, you can't say definitively from the blood work whether he or she has herpes or not?"

"Correct. To diagnose definitively that someone has the virus, you need to find the virus. You would have to swab the area when you have an active lesion."

You won't have any lesions if you don't have the virus, Cherrie. Unless of course, you become infected by your spouse who was significantly less than faithful in her marriage.

Under re-direct, Olivia confirmed again that what Erin's OB/GYN saw was a herpes lesion and not an anal fissure. Her own OB/GYN stated, "She tested positive for herpes 2."

During her re-cross examination, Cherrie inquired about non-sexual ways herpes transmission could occur.

The witness responded, "The vast majority of herpes transmission is sexual contact."

"Are there other ways?" asked Cherrie.

"Yes, you can get the virus on your hand from contact with an open lesion and place it on something else. That is way down the list!"

"But it's possible?"

"It's possible, but that doesn't happen."

Olivia then called our expert to the stand. Without question, a national expert. Olivia received no objection from Cherrie when she tendered this witness as an expert.

Olivia began, "What documents have you reviewed of Erin's as part of your work on this case?"

"I have reviewed her OB/GYN clinical visit records, her primary care provider records, and the records from her colorectal surgeon. All the records submitted to court I have reviewed. I have reviewed them several times."

Olivia asked, "Have you reviewed all her herpes testing records?"

"Yes, I have."

"Did you receive any records from Danny?"

"I did. I reviewed his herpes testing records."

Olivia continued, "Based on these documents, were you able to form an expert opinion about whether Erin has sexually transmitted herpes?"

"I was able to form an opinion as to whether or not she has genital herpes due to HSV2 (herpes simplex virus 2). Yes."

"And does she?" asked Olivia.

"She does."

"Did she contract genital herpes from Dan?"

Our expert stated, "No. Also, the basis for that is the fact that he has no history of genital herpes. His HSV2 antibody test was negative, and we use that as the definitive screening test. So, with him having no history and a negative test, he does not have genital herpes due to HSV2."

Olivia asked, "HSV2 is a sexually transmitted disease. Correct?"

"Almost exclusively. There are a few exceptions. Most of those are a neonatal transmission from mother to infant, but regarding adults, it is almost exclusively an STD."

"Were you able to form an opinion about whether Erin had an incident herpes infection?"

"By definition, we would consider incident infection someone who has the presence of a virus detected through culture or PCR (swab). Which she did have and the lack of presence of antibodies, which she did not have."

"Can this disease be transmitted by coming in contact with a toilet seat?"

After a slight chuckle, the doc responded, "No. It requires intimate contact of the genital region."

Olivia then had our witness read aloud the North Carolina Alimony Statute. "You are aware that we are here on an alimony trial." Our expert read the state's definition of illicit sexual behavior.

"Is there any way to acquire the virus that would not be considered sexual intercourse or a sexual act as defined by that statute?"

"It would be extremely rare so that I would say, no." Our expert then provided his explanation of the tests utilized to diagnose herpes. "When you have someone that has a positive swab test, then you can confidently say that a person has the herpes infection."

Olivia lasered in on when Erin contracted genital herpes. Our expert stated, "Knowing that she had a positive swab test she probably would have been infected one to eight weeks before the swab test, possibly as much as twelve weeks but no longer than that."

Olivia clarified, "So if she had the swab test in June, what time period, in your expert opinion, do you think she acquired the virus?"

"If we put all that together we are looking at somewhere around April or May of 2015. But not before that." (We were together three nights in a row in April!)

As Olivia ended her direct examination, she confirmed his testimony and addressed the concept of dormancy raised by Erin's OB/GYN. "Your expert opinion is that Erin has sexually transmitted herpes. Is that accurate?"

"That is correct."

Olivia rolled on. "She did not contract it from Dan. Is that accurate?"

"Correct."

"She contracted it somewhere in the April or May 2015 timeframe. Correct?"

The response was, "April or May or as early as a week before seeing her OB/GYN."

"What can you tell us about the dormancy argument? That I have had this virus for twenty or twenty-five years?" Olivia asked.

Our expert remarked, "I wouldn't disagree with his description, but our view of herpes has changed in that it is not a dormant or latent virus. It is chronically shedding, and reactivation is the norm. Most people don't recognize outbreaks. On average, people will have six outbreaks during the first year that they contract it and four each year after."

"In this case, you testified in your expert opinion that she has incident herpes which would not qualify her to be a dormancy argument or dormancy case."

"Right. Based on my opinion in looking at the lab tests."

"Nothing further, Your Honor."

Because of the first two days of our trial, I was becoming uncomfortably familiar with folks taking the stand and lying about my character and me. When I took Erin's hand in marriage, I never imagined that we would end up in a courtroom discussing genital herpes, and who gave it to whom, but the final straw was the stories about my genitalia.

Cherrie began her cross-examination discussing male genitalia. "If a male is infected with herpes how would his genital area present? Would it have red marks on it?"

Our witness stated, "Typically again with most people they don't recognize anything, and they don't have necessarily lesions. So, if you are having an outbreak, sure you can have ulcerations, vesicles, lesions, blisters or nothing."

"Is it possible also to have white bumps?"

That question caused our expert to pause as the look on his face said it all. He responded, "No, not white bumps. It would be an ulcer, blister or a pustule."

"Have you ever physically examined Dan?"

"No, I have not."

"The only thing you have reviewed is his one blood test that showed a negative as well as Erin's negative blood test."

"Correct."

Cherrie then revisited the testimony regarding the dates that Erin could have contracted the virus. Our expert confirmed that it could have been as late as June 9, 2015. We separated May 18, 2015.

Recall that Erin had invited me to our home on the evening of June 9 upon my return from Nashville. The house was locked up, and I did not attempt to enter it. Maybe she had already had a visitor keeping her company that evening.

Cherrie was potentially laying some groundwork that Erin contracted it after we had separated. If that were the case, then under the law, Erin would not be barred from receiving alimony. It was a very narrow window of twenty-two days from the date of our separation (May 18) through June 9, 2015.

The cross-examination continued with Cherrie reviewing Erin's negative blood test in August of 2015 and her second swab test in June of 2016. Our expert acknowledged those results.

"So is it possible that Dan could have an open lesion that he gave to Erin during a window of time in April and May but if he has never had it swabbed you would never know definitively if he has herpes. Correct?"

The response was, "You would have to suppose that he got an incident infection as well in the window period and then transmitted the virus to her during a window period in which she didn't get infected. Given the timeline and the testimony the probability of that is incredibly low."

Cherrie proceeded with, "You are aware that Erin had major bowel surgery in February?"

"Yes."

"Presumably, if you are removing your large bowel that kind of area is exposed as part of that. Is that a fair statement?"

A quizzical look appeared on our witness's face, followed by the response, "No. Not regarding the transmission of HSV2."

"Just in general. That if you are having surgery in that area. My understanding is that you reviewed her surgeon's file?"

"I did."

"You saw that she had pretty major surgery and that area, in general, would have been exposed as part of that surgery?"

Our expert, "That area in reference to . . .?"

Cherrie responded, "The vaginal and anal area."

The quizzical look was magnified. "I don't see where the colonic surgery is related to the vagina regarding the surgical procedure or the area."

Cherrie pressed on. "What I am asking specifically is you said 'albeit small, there are times when you can have active shedding on your hand, and if you touched your vaginal area you could infect.' Is that correct?"

The quizzical look evolved into that of annoyance.

Cherrie was not a big fan of silence, so she continued, "Is that a misstatement of your testimony?"

Our expert, "No, it is not a misstatement of my testimony. You can have transmission, but it has to be sexually transmitted. You have to have transmission to the genital area that by definition would be sexual because you would have touching of the genital area. Regarding nosocomial (originating in a hospital) transmission to the genital area, I have never heard of that. Not in surgery ever!"

You read that correctly. Cherrie was suggesting that perhaps Erin got herpes from the sterile and gloved hand of her surgeon!

"If Erin were to have another blood test now and if she were still negative, what impact would that have in your opinion that this is an incident?"

The witness responded, "By definition, she would still fit the definition of incident disease, but that would also suggest that she may be someone who does not process antibodies properly. With the test that she had, 98 percent of folks with HSV2 will seroconvert (develop antibodies). That is the diagnostic test that is performed. Immunosuppressive therapy may further delay the time for developing antibodies." (Erin had been taking an immunosuppressive agent for years for her "illness.") "By definition, she had to get it from somewhere, and it didn't come from him, being his test is negative."

Cherrie asked, "Being his blood test?"

Our expert, "His blood test was negative. The blood test is the definitive test outside of incident infection."

"But the only way you would know the incident infection is if Dan went to the doctor complaining of these and then they would do a swab. Correct?"

"No. His blood test would be sufficient. A swab test as I mentioned would not rule it out. If you are concerned about having it, the definitive test is repeated blood tests."

Olivia re-directed to ratify the period that Erin contracted the herpes 2 virus. She asked, "Just to confirm, the time in which Erin contracted the virus was March thru May of 2015?"

"Yes."

Our experts' time on the stand ended with Cherrie clarifying that it could have been as late as June 9 that Erin contracted it. She then asked the judge for a short recess.

Erin sprang from her chair, took a few quick steps back to her "team," and implored them not to believe what they heard!

After a brief conversation with Olivia during the recess, our medical experts were released. As Erin's OB/GYN departed, he commented to Olivia, "I have known that she was crazy for years!" Other professionals would share those sentiments, but nobody did a thing to get her help. Ann Birch, Katie's therapist, shared her concerns as well about Erin with Cherrie a few weeks before our trial.

It was back to the stand for me. Fortunately, my time there was brief. Cherrie revisited my truthfulness in our marriage, my support of both Billy and Katie, and whether or not I was legally mandated by our settlement agreement to support Billy, and of course, my phone calls to ADT. I admitted to not using very flattering terms when discussing Erin with the ADT representative. I was peppered once again about paying a $23.40 bill to ADT and changing the phone number and address on the account.

"At the time, you were not living in the home. Where in the mediated settlement does it state it was your responsibility?"

I calmly responded that it did not state that Erin was responsible either, so somebody had to pay the bill.

She then asked to play the recording from the call I made on September 30, 2015.

Olivia objected, "There were over ten hours of recorded calls to ADT and my client only made four of them. The plaintiff made the large majority."

The judge did not allow the call to be heard. Cherrie stated, "I would like the Court to hear his tone."

The judge responded, "He already admitted to making the call, changing the address and phone number. His tone is not relevant. It's ADT."

What is it with twenty-three dollars? At my domestic violence hearing, it was alleged that I bought twenty-three-dollars-worth of men's underwear with Erin's Kohl's card, and now I am being crucified for paying a twenty-three-dollar home security bill.

Olivia seized the opportunity to cross-examine me, enabling us to highlight an additional 401K loan I had taken out well before our date of separation to pay Erin's initial legal fees. Olivia's further questioning enabled me to discuss my healthcare issues that began in the spring of 2014: my rapid and significant weight loss, liver enzyme issues, white blood cell count, and mental health issues.

Finally, I was able to share my side of the story regarding my eventual journey to Holy Hell, which included my involuntary commitment by our family practitioner in less than two minutes with his back turned to me. Olivia did a great job of presenting the fact that Erin had already secured an attorney in September of 2014.

Olivia asked, "Have you ever had a series of health scares like this in your life?"

I responded, "No. Never."

"So when you had these health scares, Erin was busy hiring an attorney?"

"Right."

"Those letters that Miss Barr had you testify to indicate that you still loved Erin and were fighting for your marriage. Correct?"

"Correct."

"She, in turn, had started planning for your divorce. Correct?"

"Correct."

"Did you become aware at some point that she had the forethought to execute a power of attorney over your IRA?"

I shared the details of how I became aware of this in July of 2015. Indeed, it was my signature, but the rest of the handwriting on the document was Erin's.

Olivia inquired, "Do you recall signing this document?"

"I do not."

Olivia continued, "When was this signed?"

Quite emotionally, I responded, "September 24, 2014, the day after my release from Holy Hell." I noticed from the stand that Erin looked back at her "team" and shrugged her shoulders.

Olivia then turned her attention to the phone calls with Mila. "Did you have an opportunity, after direct examination with Miss Barr, to review the one month of phone calls that were introduced yesterday from AT&T?"

"I did."

"Is it fair to say that you called Mila close to 100 times in May of 2014?"

I stated, "It is accurate."

Olivia, "How many of those calls occurred after five p.m.?"

"Two."

"Did you have an affair with Mila?"

"I absolutely did not!"

Olivia pushed forward. "When did you first learn that Erin had any issue with Mila?"

I chuckled a bit before my response. "Probably as recently as three or four months preceding our trial."

"So this was not an ongoing allegation about Mila during your marriage?"

"Absolutely not."

Cherrie attempted to undo what Olivia had laid out under her cross-examination. She revisited the power of attorney for the IRA. "This is not a notarized document. That is your signature on there. Correct?"

"Yes ma'am," I said.

"Do you believe that Erin signed this?"

I responded, "I don't know. I do not recall signing the document."

"You were asked on cross-examination if during your health scare Erin was hiring an attorney."

I muttered, "Uh-huh."

Cherrie started spinning it. "During that time Erin was locking herself in a bedroom with her daughter to get away from you. Wasn't she?"

I did my very best to maintain my composure as she had been pushing my buttons for the last day and a half. "That is not an accurate statement."

"What is your understanding of what happened?"

I calmly replied, "Erin, our daughter, and the dogs, as I was informed yesterday were never corralled in a bedroom and locked away. It is simply not accurate because it never happened. Was there an occasion when Katie was in her room, and Erin was in the guest room? Yes!"

"During that time you were drinking when you were told not to drink."

Following a slight pause, I responded, "Actually, that is not accurate either because the incident with Erin in the guest room and Katie in her room, occurred in July of 2014, and I was not under the care of a psychiatrist until September 9, 2014."

Cherrie continued, "Describe to me what occurred during your drinking episode."

I stated, "That was in July of 2014, a typical weekend for Erin and me. We had been in therapy and were counseled to communicate with one another when something bothered either of us. If I raised an issue with Erin, I would be dismissed, get a raised hand from her, or be told 'that everything is hurtful to me,' or she would ignore me. That played out the weekend of July 2014. My coping mechanism was to keep myself busy. I kept myself busy that day. I have apologized many times to Katie for the drinking episode, and I recognize that it was not the proper way to cope with our situation.

"I have owned that situation with Erin and with our daughter. I sat on the back porch at eight o'clock at night and was drinking a few beers. I was out on there until 9:30. I never entered the guest room where Erin was, but I did go into Katie's room to address some text messages she had been sending me about smoking and drinking. I stood by the side of the bed, never put a hand on her but did state, 'You can stop texting me at any time.' I took a shower and went to bed. It was 9:30."

Cherrie kept pursuing the fear angle. "You heard Tiffany testify that Erin came over to her house and spent the night because she was afraid."

I reiterated, "That is inaccurate as well."

"Nothing further, Your Honor."

Cherrie called Erin to the stand next.

Cherrie had Erin begin by slowly running down the list of medications she was taking.

"These are all lawfully prescribed?" Cherrie asked.

"Absolutely!" Erin emphatically replied.

Not surprisingly, Cherrie's pace of questioning was quite different with Erin. She was very deliberate and questioned her as if she were a child. Cherrie slowly asked Erin about her medical issues.

"What if any medical issues do you have?"

Erin slurred her response. "I have fibromyalgia and neuropathy. Neuropathy affects my speech and balance. My retrieval process is difficult. There are times when words come out, and it sounds like I have three tongues. That has gotten worse."

"What other medical issues do you have?"

"I have thyroid and cardiac issues."

In a motherly and sympathetic way, Cherrie asked, "Have you had any surgeries recently?"

Sounding almost intoxicated Erin stated, "I have had many surgeries and recently had my large bowel removed." Erin acted as if she could not remember when the surgery was. "Don't hold me to it, but it was a couple of months before we separated."

"So maybe it was February of 2015?"

"You know how I am with dates. So yes, it was around that time."

"So other than the fibromyalgia, neuropathy and bowel removal, what if any other medical issues do you suffer from?"

Erin hesitated as she looked to Tiffany for guidance on how to respond.

The judge admonished Tiffany from the bench. "If you are going to talk to her, you will be asked to step outside. I will have the bailiff remove you from the courtroom.

Tiffany's response was classic. "I was talking to myself, Your Honor."

Erin responded, "I have cardiovascular issues. I have stage 2 hypertension. Dan was with me. My cardiologist said that I am constantly dehydrated. If I don't drink triple or double what you guys drink, I start having stroke-like symptoms, and I will slur my words. I get tired and disoriented."

"How often does that happen that you don't have enough liquids and get disoriented?"

"If I am not drinking enough liquids," Erin replied, "it will happen. I always have something with me. I had a tilt table test and a cardiac catheterization, and it showed that I don't have enough volume going into my heart. I am dehydrated most of the time. My cardiologist said I would not last one day in the desert."

Cherrie continued her line of questioning around Erin's TIAs (transient ischemic attacks). Erin struggled to remember what a TIA was, so she referred to it as a mini-stroke. She then described what happened with her last episode, with no issue remembering the exact date that it occurred. As Cherrie promised in her opening statement, Erin was all over the board with her responses. Her testimony, although an act, was painful to watch.

Cherrie attempted to have Erin recount all of her hospitalizations for this condition.

Olivia interrupted. "Objection. I want to make clear that she keeps calling it a TIA. I am fine with her saying that is what she believes, but the medical records do not indicate that it was a TIA. I want to make sure that it is her testimony and not a medical diagnosis that she has had a TIA."

The judge weighed in. "She can call it whatever she wants, but she is not qualified to give an opinion of what it was."

I think you can get the picture of the foundation that they were trying to lay.

Al and Diane, my eyes and ears in the back of the courtroom, noticed that Erin had brought plenty of fluids with her such as Gatorade, water, pineapple juice, and Hi-C drink boxes. She immersed herself fully into playing this character with a lifetime to rehearse.

The direct examination trudged on with a review of our various moves over the years and their impact on Erin.

Cherrie asked, "What effect did the move to Kentucky have on you?"

Erin looked at her mom and tearfully stated, "I missed my mom. That was hard. Don't get me wrong, I loved Louisville but missed my mom."

Cherrie then focused on Erin's employment during our marriage, specifically her pet-sitting business and volunteer efforts.

"Was your health affecting your ability to work?"

"Objection, Your Honor," said Olivia. "She is leading the witness."

Cherrie shifted to Erin's financial affidavit, highlighting her gross income of $217 per month. "Tell me about the place you currently reside?"

"It is a nice neighborhood. I am just glad I have a roof over my head. It is infested with massive bugs right now," Erin laughingly admitted.

Cherrie asked, "How long is your lease?"

"I am getting out of it. I want a smaller place so I can afford . . . I am not even living right now."

Cherrie proceeded, "How is your life different now that you are separated?"

Fighting back the tears Erin stated, "I know what it is like to be hungry." The tears begin to flow, "I know what it is like to have bread for breakfast, lunch, and dinner. I got a care package from my mom and was so excited to have toilet paper and paper towels. I am doing the best I can right now. So hopefully, after this, I will be able to get a better job where I won't have to be hungry anymore."

Cherrie's gentle direct examination continued, focusing on Erin's lack of insurance following our divorce. "Do you have any idea what your cost will be to obtain health insurance?"

Erin, very child-like, responds, "Yes. My approximate costs will be $560 per month."

"How often do you have to go to the doctor? How much do your prescriptions cost per month?"

Erin chuckled. "I go often. Right now, my prescriptions cost nothing, but I will have to start all over again."

"Do you have any idea how much your deductible will be?"

"$5,000."

Cherrie continued to paint the sad picture Erin faced. She focused on her standard of living during the marriage compared to her new reality. "Do you have Internet? Do you have a housekeeper? Do you spend less on your animals now than you did during your marriage? Have you been on vacation lately?"

As lunch recess approached, Cherrie reviewed the debt Erin incurred because of our legal journey. She raised the issue of Erin requesting a new Social Security number because I had compromised the integrity of it.

Erin stated, "Dan had been using my Social Security number for purchases."

No proof, just more hearsay.

Erin's finale was a dramatic recollection of my swatting her on the rear.

Cherrie asked, "Did you hear some testimony from your mom about an incident when you were hit on the rear?"

"Yes."

"Can you tell the court about your recollection of being hit on the rear?"

"It was before we were separated and we weren't getting along, and he came home from work."

"Who is he?"

"Dan. I had pajama pants on, and he was standing there. At the time, we weren't talking. I walked by, and I got a slap on my butt, and it sounded like a ball, no a bat hitting a ball."

"Who slapped you?"

"Dan."

"Did he say anything when he slapped you?"

"He said he was just kidding."

"Do you think he was kidding?"

"No. Not with that power. No."

Cherrie laughed. "Did you go look at it?"

"Yes. It hurt like . . . yes."

"What did Dan say when he did this?"

"He said he was just kidding around."

"When you looked at your rear what did you see?"

"A welt and a handprint." Erin closed out the morning by sharing her side of the story regarding my drinking episode. "My daughter and I were afraid of him and his behavior. His behavior scared me. Katie did come into my room and laid on my shoulder. She wanted to leave."

No surprise, the story Katie revealed to me was remarkably different. "Mom told me that you were drunk, and it was not safe. I was told to go into my room and lock the door!"

When we returned from lunch, we saw our infamous family practitioner in the hallway. Cherrie had subpoenaed him, but although he had a brief visit with Cherrie, he never testified. He had nothing damning to say about me, as he had long since backpedaled on his bipolar diagnosis, recording in my medical record that it was anxiety. He had already done enough damage to our family.

Team United We Stand began to dwindle in size as Krystal and Big Bro left. They would not return to the courtroom, because they had flights to catch to return to Pittsburgh. On the other hand, Al had already spoken with Jane about changing flight arrangements for him and Diane. Al was adamant, saying, "I am not leaving him."

The afternoon session began with Cherrie's continued direct examination of Erin.

How would they combat the testimony given by our medical experts? Erin must have refueled on her electrolytes, as she was a completely different person. Well coached, focused, and her responses were straightforward and not delayed as they had been previously. Her alleged cognitive impairment seemed to disappear. Anger and denial were on full display.

Cherrie began, "Erin at any time have you had an affair?"

"Absolutely not," Erin angrily responded.

Cherrie followed, "Any time post-separation, have you been with anyone else?"

Erin protested, "I have been with one person for the last twenty-eight years!"

"And who is that?"

Erin looked directly at me, pointed her finger and proclaimed, "Danny."

Once again, the math does not add up. We met in 1991 and it was now August of 2016. In the last twenty-eight years, she would have been with her first husband, two other boyfriends (that I was aware of), and me.

"Do you have any explanation as to how you have an HSV2 positive test?" inquired her counsel.

"I had a swab, and he did not," stated Erin.

"When was the last time that you were intimate with your husband, if you recall?"

Quickly Erin replied, "I think it was about March. Right, before we separated."

Somehow, she forgot about our three nights together in April of 2015. In fairness, it was probably difficult to keep straight when she was with her husband versus other interests outside of our marriage.

Erin went on to proclaim that the herpes lesions were an anal fissure. "Not to be a gross, but I have diarrhea all the time. So it gets extremely sensitive and red down there."

Cherrie asked, "You have heard your OB/GYN testify that you have vaginitis. Has that been an ongoing problem for you?"

"Well, I am not on any hormones, so my lining is thin. Because I have fibromyalgia it is very prevalent for vaginitis. Absolutely! Yes," Erin answered.

Olivia leaned over, covered the microphone, and whispered, "Anger seems to improve her cognitive function."

Cherrie then moved away from discussing genitalia to discussing cheer competitions. You can't make this stuff up. I went on a trip to Punta Cana, but Erin could not afford to go to Katie's cheer competition because I would not give her money to do so. "I asked Dan for money, and he would not contribute. I cannot tell you how difficult it was when I got a phone call from my daughter that I was the only mother not there to hug her," Erin stated as she wiped back her tears.

"Did you hear Dan testify about you not mentioning Mila as a concern? Is that your recollection?" asked Cherrie.

Erin chuckled her response. "Absolutely not! He knows that. It has always been an issue. She would even call on a Saturday. I found his Blackberry, and they were at a meeting and texting each other back and forth. 'How boring is this?' 'Oh you are so funny.'"

"When did you discuss with Dan your objections to Mila?"

"Oh God, way before he was admitted to Holy Hell."

"Did Mila call you?"

"Yes. She called when Dan was in the hospital. I felt it was very odd. It has always been a problem, and he has always denied it."

Then it became all about me ogling other women. Mila never called on a Saturday or called Erin when I was in the hospital. Erin only called her after I gave her Mila's number. The Blackberry she found had not been operational for years.

She had no recourse. She had been caught and had to do her best to spin her way out of it. Rectal lesions and DNA evidence are hard to ignore.

Erin ranted, "There were trust problems from the beginning. He will admit it. I think that is one of the main reasons why we split."

"Other than the trust issue, were there other reasons why you split?"

"We went to counselor after counselor. We went to the deacon, and he said, 'Sometimes Humpty Dumpty falls off the wall, and he just doesn't get back together.' He and his wife separated, and he said it was the best thing they ever did.

"In the meantime, I am trying to help him [Dan] with his diagnosis. I went to his psychiatrist for his first visit, and I know what his doctor said. Dan would not own it. I am trying to be there and trying to help him but some days, yes, he has bipolar, and some days he says he doesn't. I was trying. I can't help or support somebody if they don't own it," Erin emphatically stated as she slapped the witness stand.

She continued, "Not only that, it was a trust issue and . . . then when I got that result, I think 'I got ya!' All along, I knew he was cheating on me. I know it. I know it to this day."

Cherrie drilled down. "What result are you talking about?"

"When I went and got that swab."

Coy Cherrie asked, "Who do you think gave you HSV?"

She pointed at me and proclaimed, "I have been faithful to this man since the day I met him, and he knows that deep down inside. I did not give him herpes. I don't have herpes, and if I have it, you have it! I had the swab. You did not!"

Author's note: Our deacon separated for a short period and reconciled with his wife. He had a trust issue with her. There was never any discussion about Humpty Dumpty. He did feel that a separation would be good for us, but we should not divide assets or involve attorneys. He provided this advice in April 2015. Less than a month later, I was exiled from my home.

"Erin, going back to what you were saying about his diagnosis and the fact that he would not own it. What diagnosis are you talking about?"

Erin replied, "Bipolar! I would tell him that we don't have to call it that. I can stand on top of a mountain and say that I have anxiety issues. I own it. We don't have to call it bipolar. We can call it a watermelon. We can call it a lemon. Whatever you want to do. He was not taking medicine the way he should, and he was drinking on it. Things just started to explode! When I was in the hospital, my daughter had an escape route. I still loved him and was willing to do whatever I could to help him. But basically, I can't help somebody when I can't trust him. Everything that comes out of his mouth is a lie. Even the things that I read from his deposition, I was thinking, 'You have got to be kidding me!'"

Erin continued on her rant interspersed with a few questions from Cherrie about the evening she called the cops on me (two days before I was involuntarily committed).

"I had Katie's clothes in the back of my trunk. I had my clothes and a toothbrush because I ran out of the house when my mom was on the phone. I had no shoes on. I had to go to Walgreens and ask the manager if I could at least get a pair of socks," Erin tearfully stated.

Cherrie turned her attention to Erin's visits to the Clinic. As it turns out, Erin's team did not get complete records. They received abstracts.

Olivia did an excellent job of communicating what was missing. "The only thing I would say is that there are things noted in here . . . For example, there is a rheumatology report, and it is not included. There are specific references in the abstract that says they are referring to another report, but it is not included in here." Important if you allegedly have fibromyalgia or an autoimmune disease, since the rheumatologist is the main doctor who treats them. There was dead air on the recording as Cherrie scrambled through the Clinic file. She was all about being in the courtroom but was not very big on preparation. She relied on her staff for the prep work. She was not as buttoned up as she should be.

"Erin, while I am finishing up the rest of the papers here, I am going to ask you a couple of questions. Do you have the means to pay for counsel?"

"No."

"How have you been able to pay for your counsel?"

"Mom."

"Did Dan pay a portion of your prior attorney's fees?"

"He says that but honestly, I am not going to say he is lying but I don't remember. I don't." They were asking for attorney's fees, and Cherrie was introducing her affidavit for the judge to consider. Yes, I did indeed take out a loan in November of 2014 to pay for Erin's legal fees. Yes, I hoped we were still in love! Yes, I was a dumb SOB!

Cherrie closed out her direct examination of Erin by revisiting the $23.40 ADT bill. Following her question, Erin admitted, "I was responsible for the ADT bill. An attorney gave it to me during mediation. I had to call and change the account into my name."

"At this time, I have nothing further, Your Honor."

I tip my cap to you, Erin. It was one hell of a performance. I can't own what I don't have. I don't have bipolar, so I won't embrace it. My nine days in Happy Town (Holy Hell) helped me realize that. So, thank you for that experience. I gave you the best I could, but I can't provide you with what I don't have. I don't have herpes 1 or 2, so I could not have bestowed those upon you. I am sorry! You got it somewhere else. You must have a pretty good idea who the generous individual is.

Olivia had plenty to work with during her cross-examination.

She began, "Do you have the final neuropsychological report in front of you? Exhibit 6A? Can I approach, Your Honor? While I am here, I am going to read a portion of this. Correct me if I am reading any of it wrong. 'Erin presents with mild cognitive inefficiencies that reflect mildly slowed processing speeds and mild difficulty with organization and complex problem-solving particularly under time pressure. Nonetheless, she has many cognitive strengths including visual-spatial skills, reasoning skills that don't include time pressure and memory. In particular, memory is superior for material that is repeated.' Did I read that accurately?"

Erin replied, "Yeah you read that accurately. That is when I just started to get my symptoms." Olivia then began to further expose Erin's pathological nature, honing in on the fact that Erin did not disclose her repeat test for HSV2, conducted by her new OB/GYN two months before our trial. She had another swab test done that was negative, but at that time, she did not have any active lesions. "You never disclosed in here that your new OB/GYN tested you. Did you?"

"I had just had it."

"You are right,' Olivia agreed. "You had just had it four days earlier before submitting your sworn answers. You did not mention that test, did you?"

"I have no idea."

"I will give you time if you want to read it. The only way that I discovered this new OB/GYN was at your deposition, correct?"

(I also provided Olivia with the explanation of benefits from this visit, since Erin was still on my insurance plan).

There was silence from Erin followed by Olivia, "You need to answer the question."

"I will, but I am looking at Cherrie."

Cherrie said, "I can't answer for you, Erin."

"All I know," Erin replied, "is that we followed protocol and the right channels."

Olivia said, "You conveniently did not mention this test in your sworn answers."

Olivia then focused on Erin's Adderall dosage. Liars get frustrated when they get caught, and Erin's frustration began to show.

She testified during her deposition that she was only taking 20 milligrams of Adderall and only taking it as needed. Olivia read directly from Erin's deposition to corroborate what she was challenging Erin on.

Frustrated, Erin replied, "I don't have my bottle with me. It was 20 milligrams, and now it is 30."

Olivia continued to press her. "You also testified at your deposition that your cardiologist advised you to be on 20 milligrams. Correct?"

"No, it was 30 milligrams, and he told me to drop. At the time, I was on 60 milligrams, and he told me to drop. Dan was there."

Not true. Adderall was never mentioned in my presence, and I made many trips with her to see the cardiologist.

Olivia said, "I understand that your testimony may be different today, but at your deposition, you testified to taking 20 milligrams."

Erin replied, "I don't even think they make 20 milligrams!"

Olivia continued, "Were you surprised when your psychiatrist testified that she had never heard that your cardiologist wanted you to drop down to 20 milligrams? You had never told her that he wanted you to be on 20 milligrams."

"She knows. She has a list of all of my medications. I don't even know if I was seeing that psychiatrist back then. I have no idea."

"You also testified at your deposition that you only take Adderall as needed. You refill it virtually every thirty to thirty-five days. Therefore, you are not taking it as needed. You are taking it every day."

"If I need it, I take it."

Olivia then highlighted Erin's job responsibilities at the time of our trial. She was making the point that it requires memory and cognitive skills to fulfill her job responsibilities. Olivia challenged Erin on the last time she saw her rheumatologist. "Typically, fibromyalgia is treated by a rheumatologist. Correct?"

"Correct."

Olivia leaned in. "You are not currently under the care of a rheumatologist, are you?"

"Yes, I am."

"When was the last time you saw your rheumatologist?"

"It has been a while. However, I see specialists for my symptoms. I do have an appointment." Erin had seen her only once in the last six years. It was one of the other revelations I made as I "dug deep" into her medical claims.

Olivia was just warming up, and Erin's composure was gone. "You had testified . . . Let me see if I get it correct. As best as I can remember, you know what it is 'like to be hungry' . . ."

Erin cut her off and responded, "Yes, I do!"

Olivia continued, "You have had bread for breakfast." Then with a little edge and a spring in her step, Olivia quipped, "Let's look at your bank statements. Your Honor, may I approach? Let's look through these because I have highlighted them."

Olivia slowly and deliberately reviewed eleven months of bank statements, highlighting Erin's deposits. My eyes and ears in the back of the courtroom later informed me that during this discussion, Doris scrambled to find her purse and checkbook in an attempt to reconcile the amounts she was hearing.

Doris had received pictures of an empty refrigerator from her daughter. Her daughter, her best friend, had financially played her. The bank statements would reveal that in an eleven-month period, Erin made deposits totaling $53,590.

Doris's testimony was ringing in my ears, "She finally had the courage to leave an abusive marriage and is now living below the poverty line."

Erin had fairly little to say other than, "You have no idea what my bills are. I need time to process this."

Olivia brought it home with the following, "All of those deposits into your account, and Dan is paying for your car payment. Correct?"

Erin muttered, "That is correct."

Olivia then highlighted for both the court, and especially for Erin, the significant sum of money she had already received from my retirement as part of our property settlement.

Olivia then drove home all of the financial support that I had provided Erin and the kids. She hammered Erin on the fact that she had not offered me any support for Katie, as she was still a minor and no longer living with her.

Then she tackled the herpes testing records and results. "You heard testimony this morning from two herpes experts," Olivia began, "your own OB/GYN since 2004 and our expert. Correct?"

"Yes, I heard them."

"You heard both of their expert opinions that you have sexually transmitted herpes."

"There are loopholes, but I heard their testimony. Yes."

"You heard two experts, but you fail to believe that you have HSV2?"

"I don't know if Dan has . . . he has never been swabbed. So . . ."

With a curious tone in her voice, Olivia asked, "My question is you. Are you still in denial that you have herpes?"

"Yes. However, if he has it, if I have it, then he has it."

"Are you aware that when Dan went in for his blood test with your family doctor, that he was physically checked out?"

"Was he swabbed?"

"No, but I know that you were!"

Moving on, Olivia addressed Erin's education and the two degrees that she has. Additionally, she went back to the deposition to highlight that in 2009 and 2010 Erin was working almost full time with her pet-sitting business and had even hired two employees. She focused on the hours that Erin was spending as a volunteer, including her role as a head volunteer that coordinated the program.

Olivia began to close out her cross-examination by addressing Erin's medical issues. In particular, she focused on her neurology records.

"In your neurology records, this is a visit from June 28 of 2016. Correct?"

"Yep. That was a follow-up visit after I had my TIA. I know it doesn't say it here, but my mom was there."

"So I am looking under the paragraph 'history of present illness.' It says she feels, and she is you, feels that her strength has returned to normal. She does continue to notice some slurred speech especially if fatigued or dehydrated. So on June 28, according to your self-report, your strength had returned to normal. That is what it says there, correct?"

Erin slurred, "That is what it says there. Yes. However, it is not back to normal. I went to PT [physical therapy]."

"Let's now turn to the mental status section. I am going to read that. 'Patient is alert. The patient is oriented to time place and person. Patient has normal attention and concentration. Patient's knowledge is intact for four well-known facts. Patient has intact, recent memory and normal remote memory. Patient has intact language.'"

"Yep, that was after . . . my mom was there with me."

"Let's look at your visit for May 27, 2016." [seven days after her fourth 'TIA.'] "I want to review the mental status exam on that visit. 'Patient is alert. The patient is oriented to time, place, and person. Patient has normal attention and concentration. Patient's knowledge is intact for four well-known facts. Patient has intact, recent memory and normal remote memory. Patient has intact language.'"

Erin mumbled her response. "I guess everybody has their interpretation."

Olivia did not relent. "The May 27 visit notes also reflect that 'symptoms are not suggestive of TIA. Symptoms have improved overall, though she continues to have some left-sided weakness and cognitive complaints.'" Olivia emphasized, "'Symptoms are not suggestive of TIA.'" Then, "Nothing further, Your Honor."

Cherrie conducted an unremarkable re-direct, with no evidence in Erin's medical records to refute Olivia's direct examination.

On Day 3, after calling eight witnesses to the stand on their behalf, the plaintiff's side rested. The majority of their witnesses were family and friends. There was no evidence to refute the fact that Erin had contracted sexually transmitted herpes. No experts were called or evidence presented to validate her diagnosis of fibromyalgia. Her records showed that she did not have fibromyalgia and she never had a TIA.

Dancing with the Devil is expensive and exhausting.

# CHAPTER 24
## *A Sob & Swab Story, Day 4*

Ah, yes, divorce . . . from the Latin word meaning to rip out a man's
genitals through his wallet. —*Robin Williams*

Day 4: Danny's Day

Fortunately, this would not be a full day. No parade of liars taking the
stand, none of my eighth-grade friends or family testifying on my behalf.
Our focus was not on character assassination but two simple facts: Erin's
infidelity resulted in her contracting herpes 2, and she deliberately destroyed
evidence. We had already called our two medical experts to the stand, so I
was the last man standing.

Team United We Stand continued to dwindle, and Tiffany was a
no-show for Day 4. Faithful as always, Al and Diane were present and
accounted for on Day 4.

Mental exhaustion and the comfort of knowing my own attorney would
be conducting the direct examination caused me to be more relaxed on the
stand. Olivia began by reviewing the history between Erin and me dating
back to our first meeting. I discussed our various moves and the joint deci-

sions we made. I reiterated her comment, "If we had stayed in Pittsburgh, we would have ended up divorced."

Additionally, I presented detailed examples of all of the support that I had provided Erin for her education and interests, quite contrary to the picture painted the previous few days.

Olivia dove into our exhibits, beginning with the non-abandonment agreement that I signed on May 18, 2015. Olivia asked, "At the time that you signed this document did you think that you and Erin were going to separate?"

Of course, my response was an emphatic no, and I proceeded to share the events as they occurred in May of 2015. "Erin came downstairs from Katie's room and remarked, 'I finally see the look of belief in her eyes. She no longer believes that I am a liar.'

Since the spring of 2014, Erin had manipulated our daughter, convincing her that she, Erin, would be there to protect her from me. We met with our deacon in April of 2014 and had some conversation about possibly separating, but Erin and I never revisited that discussion. There was no discussion about Humpty Dumpty. I laid out my timeline of living out of hotels from May 18, 2015, until August 13, 2015.

Olivia then had me describe our marital home that Erin was living in during this period, and I related that all the while, I continued to show up at our residence to stay ahead of practically all of the yard work and maintenance.

"At what time do you think that your marriage started to go downhill?"

"The spring of 2014."

"You say that definitively. How do you know for certain that was the moment your marriage started going downhill?"

Without hesitation, I responded, "Because I specifically recall a couple of events. We have already discussed the beach trip, but I would be happy to revisit that. The concept of my ogling and disrespecting women took a break for sixteen or seventeen years, but was resurrected by Erin in the spring of 2014. Then there was our illustrious beach trip to Topsail Island in the summer of 2014."

As I shared my side of the story of this incredible trip, I looked directly at Doris. She did not return the favor, lowering her head. Then I closed out the story. "In hindsight, I probably should not have been as respectful to Erin's mom at the time, but I stood there and took it." Becoming emotional, I said, "On the beach trip, people had no idea of what was going on behind the scenes. Every morning as we would wake up to get ready to head to the beach, I would be confronted with Erin's comment, 'If you are not happy in the relationship, get out!' It was also constantly about my phone. I have explained to her 400 times about my two e-mail accounts on my work phone, a work phone that was never password protected. People wonder why I may have been a little moody on that trip. That is when the concept of not being able to trust me was born. It was also when the verbal, mental, and emotional abuse began, centered around 'One lie is enough. Openness, honesty, and transparency.' It wasn't just Erin. Whatever Erin was telling her mother, I was getting it from both sides."

"Did you notice any behavioral changes in Erin at that time?"

"Yes. I started to notice some changes before that. We have talked a lot about her fibromyalgia and in my mind, I thought there was a connection. I would see some cognitive impairment, anger, and hostility."

Olivia's line of questioning enabled me to address my bipolar diagnosis, my time in Holy Hell, and post–Holy Hell therapy, including medications I was taking. "I have not taken Lamictal (100 milligrams vs. 500 milligrams for Erin) since October of 2015, and this was under the advisement of my psychiatrist and therapist."

At last, it was my turn to provide clarity on my HIV test. Cherrie had done an excellent job of spinning that my HIV test was the cause of Erin's concerns and the rationale for her STD testing, including her analysis in June of 2015, when she tested positive for herpes 2.

Olivia said, "Erin made a great deal in her testimony about her HIV testing. Did that cause any issues between you and Erin?"

"Oh, it sure did!"

"What did you tell Erin regarding the HIV test?"

"What I told her was that I had not consented. I was not aware that it had occurred until I received my results. Subsequently, I received an e-mail from our family practitioner providing clarity on why he tested me for HIV. He also apologized for the lack of communication around consent."

Laughingly, Cherrie objected, "I am sorry it is delayed, but, motion to strike what his family practitioner had to say or what he sent in an e-mail." The judge overruled her.

Olivia continued, "Is this an e-mail that is part of your family practitioner medical records?"

"It is. Correct."

Naturally, Cherrie needed some time as she did not recall the e-mail being part of the record. "I am sorry, Your Honor, I just don't recall this e-mail being part of the file, so I object to it being entered."

Olivia clarified. "These are his records from the family practitioner." Then she inquired, "This was an e-mail that you sent in an attempt to defend yourself with Erin. Correct?"

"Correct."

"I have pulled an excerpt from those records. Can you read those four lines at the bottom of the excerpt for us?"

Gladly, I obliged. "'I called patient and reviewed why I tested him for HIV, hepatitis B, and hepatitis C. He was tested due to weight loss, chronically elevated white blood cells, and liver enzymes. His wife was concerned as to why these tests were done. I apologized for any miscommunication. He said he appreciated my call and would convey the information to his wife.'"

"You said this was in response to the e-mail that you had sent him?"

"That is correct."

Olivia fast-forwarded to our first mediation on July 7, 2015. "As Erin testified and I think her phrase was 'she got ya,' she had the herpes test going into mediation. What was your intention going into mediation?"

I fought back the emotion. "First of all, I still loved Erin that morning. My intention going in was similar to my intentions when I first met with you. If you recall, I inquired with you if there was a way to do this other than mediation. I was hoping to work out an arrangement where I could take some money out of our slush fund to find a suitable place to live versus a hotel. I also asked our mediator, Robin Wright, about the possibility of building marital counseling into our agreement. I still loved Erin but agreed with the idea that we probably needed some time apart. Foolishly, I was hoping that we could work things out."

"Had you had an affair on your wife? Did you give her sexually transmitted herpes?"

"No."

Olivia then reviewed my herpes test results for the Court. "How did they conduct this test? Was it a blood test or a swab?"

"I was tested for herpes 1, herpes 2, and a complete panel of all STDs. They were all blood draws."

"Did your family practitioner do a physical examination of you at this time?"

"He physically examined my genitals."

"Had you ever gone to the doctor previously about an STD?"

"No. Never."

"At that moment did you think that Erin had an affair?"

Emphatically I responded, "I knew that she had an affair!"

Olivia did a great job of providing a platform for me to discuss the financial impact that all of this has had on me. Additionally, I verbalized for the court all of the obligations that we have with Billy and Katie, including what we had historically provided them during our marriage. We made it clear that there had been little to no support of our children from Erin in the last few years.

"You have paid for therapy for Katie. Correct?"

"That is correct. You will also see in the exhibit that I have also paid for intake visits for both Erin and me so that Katie could receive therapy."

"Were you court ordered to do that?"

"No."

"Why did you cover Erin's visits?"

"It was the right thing to do, and I wanted Katie to be able to get therapy. Ann Birch and her staff were quite clear that unless they met with both Erin and me (individually), then they could not provide therapy to Katie."

As my direct with was winding down, Olivia wanted to revisit the phone fiasco. "What is your recollection of what phone she was using in the last five months before you separated? The January to May 2015 period?"

"The Galaxy Samsung S4 phone. She had the phone since August of 2014 when she joined the family plan with AT&T with Billy and I. So from August of 2014 until August 5, 2015, she had the Galaxy Samsung S4."

"Did you ever have any, what now appear to be odd, conversations with Erin during the spring of 2015 about that phone?

"We did. Late May or June, Erin commented, 'Dan, because you are the primary account holder you would have access to any of my texts and phone calls at any time.' My response back to her was, 'Erin, that is great, but I have never looked.' On another occasion, she came out to the yard with a password she created for our account. She handed it to me, and I threw it out. All of this was a couple of months before we separated."

I then provided my side of the story concerning the two phone calls to Tiffany. The call on July 5, 2015 and May 19, 2016.

Olivia asked, "Did you tell Tiffany that you had butt-dialed her on July 6, 2015?"

"I did."

"Tiffany also testified about a call that you made in May of 2016."

"That is correct. It was May 19, 2016."

"Tell the Court why you remember that day so specifically and why you called Tiffany?"

"I remember that date so specifically because Erin had another . . . let's call it a cerebrovascular event. I simply called her out of concern. What folks don't realize is that the only two people who have lived this are Erin and me. I have been there for Erin with all of her medical challenges and the other two incidents that she has had. She never revealed her use of certain medications to any of her other doctors outside of her psychiatrist. I was simply concerned for the mother of our children."

Olivia continued, "Tiffany testified that you were ranting at her. Is that accurate?"

"No. That is not accurate."

"Tiffany also testified that there were many times that Erin stayed at hotels because she was afraid of you. Is that true?"

"It is not accurate."

"Do you remember any time in the last year and a half of the marriage that Erin did stay in a hotel?"

"Yes. She stayed at the Springhill Suites on June 20, 2015, which was Father's Day, and July 3, 2015. We had mutually agreed to it. When she got to the hotel on June 20, she commented, in a conversation we had, 'Oh, poor Dan! It is nice being at a hotel. It isn't so bad!'"

"So those were after the date of separation?"

"Yes."

"Was there any time before the date of separation that you are aware of, that Erin stayed at a hotel and did not come home because she was scared of you?"

I had become pretty good with dates due to my little diary. (Thanks, Al.) I immediately responded, "September 13, 2014."

"Is that the evening that we had heard a great deal of testimony about when she called the police?"

"That is correct."

"Nothing further, Your Honor."

Yippee, one more visit with Cherrie. Under cross-examination, she did her best to cloud the picture concerning the division of the 401K and pension. I appreciated her attempt but was able to provide high specificity on the equal division of these assets. I damn near laughed when she posed this question: "Erin would bring you things to the hotel when you were staying there after you moved out. Correct?"

I chuckled, "That is not correct." (Not even my arsenic-laced protein powder.)

"That is not correct?"

I repeated, "That is not correct. What I had with me at the hotel I picked up from our home."

"Your herpes test that was admitted into evidence was a blood test. Correct?"

"That is correct. With a genital exam."

"The results were a blood test. Correct?"

"That is correct."

"Was it your testimony earlier today that you could not get credit from Sears for a washer and dryer?"

"That is correct. Sears denied the request."

"Did they give you any indication as to why?"

I gladly replied, "Yes. Due to the overutilization of credit cards and too many credit inquiries in the last twelve months. Quite frankly, I was overextended."

"Erin was nineteen when she dated someone who now lives in Texas. Right?"

Following a brief laugh, I responded, "That is correct, but a couple of years ago following lunch at a Cheesecake Factory, Erin commented to me—"

"Your Honor, I am going to object it is non-responsive. He answered my question."

The judge replied, "Overruled."

I continued, "So we came out after having lunch and Erin says, 'You know things haven't been going so well, so I looked up my ex-boyfriend on Facebook.' This ex-boyfriend lives in Texas."

"Erin obtained her associates degree before your marriage. Is that correct?"

I looked directly at Doris as I responded, "That is correct, but I picked up her remaining tuition from that education and paid for it."

Doris appeared somewhat puzzled.

Cherrie then attempted to highlight my lavish apartment. "The apartment lease you are paying is $1,550 per month, and it was just for you at the time of the lease?"

"That is correct. However, it was for a nine-month lease, and I rented a two-bedroom apartment just in case our daughter needed a place to land." Again, I directed my response at Doris who simply lowered her head.

"But that is what you chose to move into, and you thought $1,550 was reasonable to pay?"

I was keeping my emotions in check as I could see right through her agenda. Get me rattled one last time for the judge.

I calmly responded, "It was the only option I had. I spent many weekends when I was living out of the hotel looking at apartment complexes. I had folks helping me on Craigslist suggesting a home for $700 a month with free Wi-Fi, a master bedroom, so forth and so on. I show up at the residence, and I would have been living with four or five other people." Tearing up at this point, I continued, "I came out of that home and called Erin, and I said, 'I can't do this.' Erin's response to me was, 'I am so sorry you had that experience, Dan.'"

"All I am asking is that apartment for $1,550 per month is what you chose to move into for just you."

"That is correct. Again, I had done my research, and it was the most reasonable place I could find. It is 1,000 square feet."

"Nothing further, Your Honor."

Cherrie then put Erin back on the stand as a rebuttal witness to address my testimony about her ex-boyfriend.

"You just heard Dan testify about your ex-boyfriend in Texas. Tell the court about that!"

I swear Erin was putting on her best act to sound impaired or just pitiful as she slurred, "I dated him about nineteen or twenty years ago. Um, we were at the Cheesecake Factory and were talking about Facebook, and I said 'I did look up my ex-boyfriend.' However, I never friended him or spoke with him. Dan called his office and talked to his secretary and wanted to see if they had a website so he could get a picture of him."

"So Erin. Did you ever friend him or e-mail him? Did you ever call him or have any communication with him?"

Erin slurred, "No. That is what Facebook is all about. Right. Although I am not on it anymore." Who knows, maybe her impairment was real . . .

I did indeed call her ex-boyfriend's office in Texas and spoke to his assistant, looking for a website. I should have done a lot more than that to try to figure out what Erin was doing behind my back.

"Nothing further, Your Honor."

Being the attorney for the defendant in this case, Olivia would present her closing argument first. Before this commenced, I received more coaching from Olivia and Abby to continue to remain stoic and maintain my composure as Cherrie went through her closing argument. At this point, I was emotionally numb and too exhausted to care. I just wanted out of the courtroom.

Olivia began, "I am going to spend a majority of my time talking about alimony. That is the substance of why we are here. Our defense has been illicit sexual behavior. As Your Honor knows, it is a complete bar, and we stop there. Typically, when we talk about illicit sexual behavior, we are talking about opportunity and inclination. We don't usually have DNA evidence. We don't have expert testimony that identifies a time during the marriage. We have that here. I forecast that in my opening. I stated that our expert's testimony would be crucial.

"Interestingly enough, the plaintiff's own OB/GYN's testimony was also crucial. The plaintiff's counsel tendered that witness as an expert. Initially, the burden of proof, as I deem it, is more likely than not based on the evidence that you will review. Erin, in June of 2015, went to her OB/GYN complaining about white clusters around her rectum and itching for about a week. He testified to that, and his medical records support it. Erin took the witness stand, and she never contradicted his testimony. Her OB/GYN, plaintiff's expert in herpes, testified that it was a textbook presentation for genital herpes. Plaintiff has alleged that it was an anal fissure. Their expert, her OB/GYN, testified that it was not. It was in a different location than what he saw. He swabbed the lesion. Our expert in herpes, herpes testing, and sexually transmitted disease and her OB/GYN, an expert in herpes, said, 'PCR testing [DNA test by swab] is the gold standard for determining if someone has genital herpes.' Both experts agree that was the case. A swab for genetic material sensitive and specific to the herpes HSV2 strain doesn't mix up HSV1 and HSV2. It identifies HSV2. It was there! She was positive, and there is no dispute about that. One thing that I think Your Honor can take judicial notice of is that her OB/GYN was under subpoena by plaintiff. I had to get him under subpoena. I intended to have him testify as a fact witness. It was the plaintiff's counsel that proffered him as a herpes expert.

"She has sexually transmitted genital herpes. Both experts have aligned that it was a recent herpes infection. The period for acquiring the virus would have been as early as February of 2015 and as late as the first week of June. The first week of June would have been two weeks post-separation. He gave that range. She never disclosed her June 2016 swab test to us. She lied in her interrogatories. A specific question on June 29, 2016: 'Identify all of your STD tests,' she did not. She had just been tested a few days earlier. She went in and asked for the test. The only way I found out about it was at her deposition. I would submit to Your Honor that the plaintiff is an entirely unreliable source of information. The undisputed scientific evidence, DNA evidence that is good enough for a criminal court, is that the plaintiff has herpes. Plaintiff has a recent infection of herpes. Plaintiff acquired herpes before the date of separation.

"So let's turn to the defendant. He does not have herpes. Expert in testing said he does not have herpes. His opinion was that Erin had a recent infection. The counter to that, and what I expect Ms. Barr to argue, is that

Dan has had herpes for years and he finally just gave it to her in the last couple of months of the marriage. Well, that gets blown out of the water when our expert said that 'the probability is very low that they somehow both got an incident infection at the same time.' If it were a long-standing infection with my client, it would have shown up in the blood test. Our expert talked about that. The uncontroverted expert testimony is that she has a recent infection and there is about a ten-to-twelve-week window that you look at. So at best, being generous, one to two of those weeks was after separation. I understand that plaintiff's counsel is going to want to focus on those two weeks. I ask you to look back at the standard, Your Honor. Is it more likely than not? She has genital herpes—it is no dispute. We have talked about when again; Ms. Barr is going to want you to look at this remote period. It is just not a reasonable position to take for Your Honor. He testified it was in the spring of 2015. So, we know that she has genital herpes and know that he does not have genital herpes. We know she acquired it in the spring. So we go this question, which candidly, Your Honor, I don't think I have to answer. But it is, who? Who gave it to her? How did she get it? I'd like to know . . . however, she wiped her phone. Moreover, that is where the inference comes in. I know Your Honor can apply that inference however you want. However, the natural inclination is to take the inference on the phone that she was using during the time in which she contracted herpes. The phone that she wiped just a few days before going into her experts' office to get it imaged. The phone that she wiped that she never disclosed until we ferreted it out. Not once, not twice, when she answered her interrogatories did she ever say, 'Yeah, I did that." Nor was there any evidence to cure. She had a backup. Both imaging experts identified that. No effort was made to recover it. So I think, Your Honor, the natural, logical conclusion there is that when she wiped that phone, she was hiding evidence that was damning to her. That evidence had to do with that spring of 2015 and whom she may have been in contact with. It is fascinating that you add in the evidence that she reactivated the phone right before taking it to her expert. Why would you do that? If you thought the phone had spyware, why would you then reactivate it? Well, she reactivated it because she wanted to make it look like it was an active phone. She probably thought she had gotten away with it until the last couple of weeks. I would certainly like to know the how, but I don't because I don't have the phone. It is not my client's fault. That is the plaintiff's fault. That is the most natural inference to make given the other evidence that we have. We are asking that you deny attorney's fees and you deny alimony. It is a bar under illicit sexual behavior.

"I was reading through this last night, and I was thinking about it, and it came to me. I don't know if the plaintiff wants to take the position that this is somehow the *virginal conception of her genital herpes*. However, the scientific evidence does not support it. Her statement was, 'I don't have it, and if I don't have it, he does.' Well, her self-serving statements mean nothing and should carry no weight with this court. However, that is the only way that you can somehow explain the chain of events that we have.

"I want to talk about her earning capacity briefly. She is currently working and earning between $8 and $9 per hour. She had been offered a job at $13 per hour. I understand that there was much testimony about cognitive issues and her ability to work. I would submit to Your Honor that there is a clear disconnect between plaintiff's conception of her medical issues and what the medical records show. I would ask that you examine that in the medical records. Also, examine the plaintiff's testimony. It was amazing to me after lunch yesterday she was coherent. She could recall dates. All of a sudden when she wanted to get up there and defend herself, she was spot on. She can work, and she can work full time!

"One thing I want to mention briefly is a couple of witnesses they had. In looking at the big picture, we have what I label as the 'friends and family.' We have her mom, her phone friend, and her eighth-grade friend who has not had much contact with her. They all bring their version of revisionist history. Your Honor sees these folks all the time and can deal with that. Let's get down to a few others. Her therapist admitted that the plaintiff's behavior could be characterized as paranoia. She admitted that it could be a side effect of Adderall. Her therapist was fully capable of regurgitating everything that Erin had self-reported to her. The PhD that testified about the neuropsychological testing should not carry much weight. There is no merit to her report. She did not have all the records that she said would have been relevant. These were in the plaintiff's custody. Her testing was flawed. She admitted that she should have asked about Adderall and when it was taken in relation to the plaintiff taking the tests. She didn't, and she admitted that was relevant. Let's talk about her psychiatrist, a fact witness. Her entire testimony centered on her seeing the plaintiff for eighty minutes a year. Your Honor has had a lot more than eighty minutes with the plaintiff so far this week. Her records are in evidence, and I would ask that Your Honor review them. The records consistently show that her thought process was good and her orientation was linear. Interestingly enough, 'the illness does not cause impairment.' I think it is interesting that when you are here making a medical argument about your client's capacity, no one of merit came to testify in expertise. They only had one fact witness, her psychiatrist, who sees her eighty minutes a year. Consider whom they chose to call considering the issues.

"The only way that we discovered that her phone had been wiped was just a couple of weeks before our motion to compel hearing. Almost a year ago, the phone was wiped. I would ask for the balance of attorney's fees related to our motion to compel. I am asking for an additional $1,800.

"I just want to come back to one issue because I think that it is good enough for the criminal court that DNA evidence works, and it is just so significant." Olivia turned to face Erin and stated very loudly, *"Erin Married Name has genital herpes!"* Two experts, one being her own, all said she has got it. There is no credible evidence to the contrary. When did she contract it? Again, expert testimony was that it was the spring of 2015. Who gave it to her? I don't know. I guess she shouldn't have wiped her phone. So I would ask that you apply the inference to answer that question.

"This isn't the virginal conception of genital herpes so I would ask that you deny her alimony request. Award us child support and award us the outstanding attorney's fees and expert fees associated with our motion to compel.

"Thank you, Your Honor."

Olivia's use of the phrase, "virginal conception" did elicit a smile from the judge.

Bring us home, Cherrie.

"I first want to address this whole situation with herpes. I said it in my opening, and I want to repeat it, when you talk about apples and apples and oranges and oranges. Erin was not aware that her husband had an HIV test done. When she heard about that in December of 2014, she was rightfully upset. 'Why are they doing an STD test on my husband?' She went to her doctor and had her own HIV test done. She had a 6-month follow-up test. She was showing up for her follow-up and said, 'By the way, I am having some itching problems.' Not uncommon as Erin has had some problems like that before. There was a swab done. She had it done. It was positive. She takes it and waits until mediation. She slaps it down and says, 'I got ya! I know you have had an affair. I have suspected this for a long time.' Lord knows he has had lots of opportunity and inclinations. She says, 'You have this, and you gave this to me.' You heard her say this many times over, 'If I have it, you have it. You gave it to me. I have not been with anyone.' She has been unequivocal about this. She has not been with anyone in the last twenty-four years." (Erin said twenty-eight, but oh well!) "So she has this positive test, and Dan has had a blood test. I am not going to stand here and argue about the first test she had. It was a positive test. I heard her OB/GYN say that there is no way to know for sure when you get herpes. You could have it, and it can lie dormant for many years. He has never had a swab done ever! She has. If you give credibility to the testimony of their expert that it was a recent infection, there was his testimony that it could have been in April, May, or as late as June 9, 2015. That is twenty-three days after their date of separation. So, if you find that she has herpes you certainly as equally could find that it occurred after the date of separation. Why would someone want to believe that his or her spouse has committed illicit sexual behavior? Dan has many reasons to believe that she committed illicit sexual behavior. He has thousands of reasons per year. He knows that it is a complete bar. You have no other evidence that points to illicit sexual behavior on her part. The only evidence that he can put forth of any time that she went to a hotel or was away from the house was the one night that he was admittedly drinking against doctor's orders. My client testified that she was locking herself in a bedroom and he keeps trying to come in despite her trying to push her dresser in front of the door. She calls the police and leaves. She went that one time to a hotel for the night. She went to her friend's house on other occasions to get away. You would think that if he truly believed that she was having an affair, he would have paraded all that evidence in here, but he didn't. To the contrary, you have repetitive concerns on Erin's behalf of him being unfaithful. You have heard tons of evidence on this. I would ask that you would award alimony in this case.

"Erin has nothing to hide. She was diagnosed with fibromyalgia in 1999. Her psychiatrist treats the cognitive symptoms of fibromyalgia. The slow processing, poor memory, and brain fog as I think she called it. She treats it with Adderall, which is regularly used in the treatment of it. There were no red flags at all concerning Erin's use. While she was not aware of the cardiologist's specific recommendation, because Ms. Esquire wants to poke holes in every little thing, she regularly takes her blood pressure. I want to address too how Erin's illness manifests itself. Olivia hit on something, and I think it is important. Regarding timing, Erin had to start her testimony right before lunch. She had been sitting here all morning without snacks and had nothing more than a bottle of water. She did not want to drink too much to avoid having to go to the bathroom too frequently. Her speech was markedly different before lunch and then after lunch. She had difficulty finding words and explaining herself. She was not focused on what she needed to do. After lunch, she was so much better. Well, she was, because she had eaten, which is important. She had fluids, which are important. Because not only do you have the fibromyalgia, you have several other medical conditions that my client is confronting . . . She has cardiovascular issues. She has had TIAs in the past, which are like the central tremors, and she has medications for that. She has problems with her stage 2 hypertension, which deals with her water retention. She has to drink Gatorade. Also, as you heard her testify to, 'If she were in the desert she would die in a day.' Other people may live a week, all because of her hydration issues.

"She has lots of medical issues. Her husband was supportive of her as she was dealing with all of her medical issues in their marriage. In 2009, based on everyone's testimony, is when things got markedly bad where she had that huge TIA and things started to decline. She went to see doctor, after doctor, after doctor and then ended up at the Clinic. You have those records. I would ask you to review those records. They are unequivocally clear that her cognition was beginning to decline. Now on some of these tests, she is borderline. Borderline was the lowest that you could have right before a diagnosis of mental retardation. This decline is expected as part of the diagnosis and this disease. I don't know that it is going to get any better. Her capabilities are going to be limited in the future. It might not be realistic for Erin ever to work full time. As difficult as it is, her mother got up there and testified, 'I see what my daughter has been reduced to.'

"Erin's imaging expert testified to that fact that she was not computer savvy and did not understand how this stuff works. I realize that Your Honor has already made a ruling on the negative inference, but I don't think that you can jump to that she was in some way trying to hide an affair that she was having. I think in many ways, she was just very naïve about it. She was terrified. He testified that he saw enough that was suspicious that he continued to review things. You heard her girlfriends testify that in the very rare instance that they could get Erin out of the house, they witnessed her phone blowing up with texts and calls from Dan. Lying and trust with Dan have been a problem since the inception. As far as communications go with another woman, you have into evidence the calls with Mila. One hundred and twenty-five calls in a month's time. I think any wife would be upset about that. When I asked him how he characterized Mila, he called her a professional contact; I believe that is what he called her. The same professional contact, whom he referred to as his friend in his deposition, is calling his wife when he is in Holy Hell. This woman is calling his wife! There has been testimony about his sneaky behavior.

"There is a significant discrepancy between their incomes. While she did receive money from his IRA, you heard our financial expert testify that she would have to cash out a significant portion to liquidate her debts and that within two years it would be gone without any help. You have a twenty-two-year marriage. You have a spouse who was a homemaker. She moved not one, but two states with her husband to support his job. She took care of the kids while he was traveling three to four nights a week. She did it at the expense of her career. While she did receive her Bachelor's degree a month before her daughter was born, she has never used it other than for volunteer work up until recently. I want to address a couple of issues. Dan moved out and moved into an apartment. It was just for him. He was paying $1,550 per month for his apartment. Erin is living in a $1,500 rental home that is infested with bugs right now. I don't think it is unreasonable for her to be living the way he was when he moved out. Dan is getting ready to move out of his apartment into the beautiful new townhome that has been under construction since January. He is going to the Caribbean, golfing, and out to dinner with friends. I would submit to you that he is doing nothing different than when he was married.

"Meanwhile, my client is excited when she gets a care package from her mother with toilet paper. Dan wanted to talk with you about his obligations to his son, Billy. I certainly understand a parent's moral responsibility to want to support their children. I get that! You can't do it at the expense of what I would submit to you is your legal obligation to help your spouse. If you look at what he is paying Billy and Katie, it is more than what he is paying Erin. There are some months when he is putting more money into Katie's account than Erin's. Erin has had to make some hard choices in not getting medications filled. They both have an extreme amount of debt related to attorney's fees."

The judge alerted Cherrie to the fact that she had three minutes remaining from her allocated time for the week. Wrap it up!

"I realize that this has been a long trial. I certainly appreciate Your Honor's patience in listening to all this, but it is one of these situations that it is a very long marriage. The health of my client is such that it is a grim outlook if she doesn't have alimony. So I would ask that you award my client alimony for the next seventeen years and attorney's fees. Thank you."

Cherrie hoped to get Erin to the retirement age of sixty-five with an outlandish amount of alimony!

The judge commented, "I am not going to decide on the fly. I am going to take it under advisement." She then called Cherrie and Olivia into her chambers for, at least from my sense, thirty excruciating minutes. Olivia emerged from the judge's chambers and pulled me into a conference room. The discussion that occurred in chambers is not public record. Without sharing specifics, I was encouraged to learn that Erin's comment about knowing what it is like to be hungry did not resonate with the judge.

Most deflating was that it would be four or five months before the judge would render her decision.

Olivia shared, "The judge is allotted only two administrative days per month to review her cases. Her caseload is quite substantial. Let's just put all of this on a shelf for about eight weeks and then sit down with Zoe Davis just in case."

With that, I hugged Olivia and Abby and thanked them for all that they had done for me. It was now well over two years since this began and there was no light at the end of the tunnel!

# CHAPTER 25
## *The Ruling*

The remedy for speech that is false is speech that is true. This is the ordinary course in a free society. The response to the unreasoned is the rational; to the uninformed, the enlightened; to the straight-out lie, the simple truth.
—*Supreme Court Justice Anthony Kennedy*

Communication between Erin and me was limited to text, e-mail, and in case of emergency, phone calls. In less than a half hour after leaving the court, as Al, Diane, and I sat down to eat some lunch, her first text arrived. I did not respond or retain it. It was another verbal assault about what this process has done to our kids and of course, it was my entire fault! It would be just the beginning of a string of texts that I was disciplined enough to ignore (for a while). One contained a picture of her new driver's license bearing her maiden name. She must have been proud to shed her married name so quickly. Good for her, and I can't say I was unhappy for the name change. Much later, Katie would share with me that while she still lived with Mom, Erin hinted that Katie change her last name as well. I shook my head, remembering a line Erin shot me about my hopeful reconciliation with Katie, "I don't see that coming to fruition anytime soon."

I spent very little time beginning to process the trial. I had to get back to my full-time job and prepare to move Katie and me out of our apartment. Factually speaking, Erin's rental home was more significant than my townhome. In spite of what she testified to, as Cherrie alluded to her in her closing argument, Erin's house was infested with bugs, but only in her mind! Her infestation issue would be the subject of multiple texts that Billy, Katie, and I received. The more colorful texts she sent our son. Billy sent me one with pictures of blood running down her back and arms from Erin cutting bugs out of herself. She described disinfecting her cuts with the Grey Goose that Big Bro had left behind from his visit. In typical college student fashion, Billy remarked, "Dad, I am not sure why she is wasting good vodka." He wasn't insensitive, but we had all reached our limit with the drama and needed to laugh. Erin would text me pictures of bowls, cleaning bottles and pots and pans that she placed over her vents to keep out the bugs. She also insinuated that Billy and I conspired and had the bugs placed in his room. Via text, Erin wrote, "They appear to be coming from Billy's room. I wonder how they got there."

The imagined bug infestation along with Erin's "neuropathy" is another side effect of her amphetamine abuse. Our expert, who reviewed all of her medical records, believed that she was suffering from delusional parasitosis among other mental health issues. It is a delusional disorder where an individual incorrectly perceives that they are infested with bugs or insects. As sad as it was to see what my now ex-wife had become, I had to move on from trying to help her. As Erin angrily accused me in court, "I can't help somebody if they don't own it."

At the end of September, I visited Erin's rental home. Due to the "bugs," she was moving out and into an apartment without appropriate storage for some of Billy's possessions. I probably shouldn't have, but I went alone. I wanted to see her. I figured it would be my opportunity to say goodbye. Regardless of what she had done to our family, I did not have any anger or hatred toward her. Rather, sadness and empathy. Upon my arrival, Erin was gloved up in the garage, and she was going through boxes. The gloves were a precaution against the bugs. I was civil to her, but there was no response in kind.

"You look skinny, and your belt is gay. You look like a faggot," Erin snapped.

I laughed it off. My therapist, Kasey, continued to be spot on in her assessment of Erin. Kasey had opined, "Erin is socially stunted. It is clear that she has not grown beyond her teenage years. It is usually the case with borderline personality disorder."

I was there for about thirty minutes. I collected Billy's possessions, gave Erin a long hug, and kissed her on the cheek. As I walked away, I turned around and said, "You see how nice I am?"

She replied, "Today you are."

As I returned home and unloaded some of the boxes Erin had given me, I was more than surprised. In one box was the Father's Day letter that Katie had written when she was eight years old! No human can be entirely devoid of a conscience. The letter that "did not exist" and that "she did not have" showed up! I very happily want to share that letter with you.

My dad and why he rocks!!!!!

My Dad has always been there for his family. He had carried me from when I was a baby to helping celebrate my First Communion. My Dad is definitely in the top 1000 best Dad's in the world. He gives me advice and a hug when he has missed me and because he loves me. He grills me my favorite foods when I want a whole rack of ribs or a foot long hotdog. I remember that one time when I was choking when my Mom recently got out of a painful medical treatment and my Dad was on the phone he came and helped and it came out happily. My Dad might smoke, but he is trying to quit because our family wants it for the best. He keeps most of my secrets and loves my Mom so much. He agrees with my Mom when she is sleep talking very very nutty. My Dad has done a lot like making my bed and making money for our family.

Happy Birthday, Dad!!!

Thanks for being my Dad!!!!

XO Love Katie

With all sincerity, thank you, Erin, for not destroying this letter. It fit perfectly in the empty, pink matted frame that you had initially given me. It has been hanging on my bedroom wall ever since returning to its rightful place.

For clarity's sake, my birthday is within a few days of Father's Day.

Erin's brief moment of kindness would not last long, as the assaults began again. According to Erin, Tiffany's husband and Big Bro wanted to kick my ass. Of course, I considered the source of information. Allegedly, Tiffany's husband was not pleased that I was telling everybody that Erin had herpes. Big Bro's issue was that I was pond scum and not a real man!

Erin alerted me, "You better not go near his neck of the woods!"

A few of Erin's aunts even utilized social media to lash out at Katie for the decision she made to move in with me. One of the aunts, probably seventy-four years old, had not seen Katie in over ten years. Katie handled her own business concerning the messages she had received. On one occasion, Tiffany was the channel by which Billy and Katie received a text from Mom as I supposedly blocked Erin from their phones. She had to keep the story going that I was messing with her electronics.

The message read: "Hey, guys your mom asked me to fwd message it was blocked on her end." Erin's message follows:

"Okay, thank you for being honest. If you and Katie want to get together for lunch or something, let me know. I do love you both and like I told Katie, I am always here when you are ready.

"I just am just so disappointed how both you and Katie have judged me and not once asked my side of the story, because there is one. I realize that you don't like to talk about divorce, but Billy you and Katie are adults and adults have to discuss pretty difficult subjects at times. That's the way life is. You are being told so many lies about me and take it from one who knows, it is very convincing the way things are presented.

"I did not cheat on your father, nor do I take drugs and for the herpes issue, my 2nd test was negative. However, you probably didn't know that. My last comment to you and Katie is, I DID NOT LIE! You know my character, that is just not me, and you know that deep down in your heart. Your father spent $200,000 on this trial and paid specialists to say what he/counsel wanted him to say, and I requested to stop this trial four times. We are in the financial state that we are in because of this!

"All I know is I went and told the absolute truth on that stand each and every day. My attorney said to me if I got on the stand and said after the date we were legally separated I had an affair it and that would make it legal. Therefore, alimony would definitely be awarded. Do you know what I said? I will forgo all alimony if it takes me to get up on that stand and lie. So, I did not! That speaks volumes!

"I love you and Katie sooooooo much, and there is plenty of information you both are unaware of. However, it should stay that way. I hope it doesn't take ten years of wasted time like it did with my Dad and me to recover our relationship. Billy, if you recall, you were responsible for reuniting us, and we had the best five years before he passed. You gave us a gift."

The continued hypocrisy and sense of entitlement irritated the hell out of me. Doris would preach to them, via text, about the need to "find the courage to have open and honest communication with Mom. Communication is the key. There were two people responsible for the demise of this marriage, and you have a relationship with one and why not the other? Your mom cries herself to sleep way too often because she loves you both so much and does not understand why she is being treated this way."

After eight weeks of "putting it on the shelf," it was time to explore my legal options in case the judge's ruling was not what we had hoped. Olivia and I met with Zoe Davis, an appellate attorney, to explore our potential path forward. I briefly met Zoe at the courthouse during our trial. After the enlightening two-hour session with Zoe, I inquired, "What do I owe you for your time?"

Her generous response was, "Nothing! I don't like what she has done to you." Zoe is one of many kindhearted and gracious people that had stepped forward when I needed it the most.

Given that I had missed the majority of Katie's junior year in high school, I became far more involved in some of the functions at her school. Although their football team was not very good, it was nice to be able to attend her games and to reconnect with some of the families that had once viewed me quite differently. My intention was not to clear the air or to prove my stability to anyone. I had grown in that area and did not care what people thought of me. I was just happy to be there for Katie.

Erin must have believed differently. She was working the phones with some of the parents at Katie's school. Unfortunately, one of Katie's friends was on the receiving end of one of her calls. This young girl had the same first name as one of the parents and received the call by mistake.

As she answered the call, Erin immediately launched into, "You can't believe everything that was said in court. Dan paid a lot of money for his experts to say what his—"

The confused girl cut Erin off and informed her that she had the wrong person.

One evening, after returning home from one of Katie's games, I discovered that somebody had been at my home. The back patio furniture had been thrown all over the place, and my doormat tossed into the woods. I was pissed, so I called Erin, only to be told, "Now you get to experience what it is like to live in fear."

Perhaps Tiffany happened to be in the neighborhood or maybe it was one of her buddies from a major car dealership in the area. Shortly after our trial ended, the hang-up phone calls began from the sales department at a prominent car dealership. I attempted to return their call twice as I was curious as to why they might be calling.

The receptionist asked me, "Did they leave a message? Are you in the market for a new car? I am sorry, sir, but there is no way to tell which line those calls may have come from in our sales department."

I stopped returning the phone calls, but after they exceeded a dozen in number, I met with the general manager. Occasionally, it comes in handy to have two attorneys on retainer. I made him aware of the situation between Erin and me and the fact that somebody in his sales department or dealership was harassing me with hang-up phone calls.

I directly stated, "If the calls don't stop, we will get a court order to obtain your phone records."

The calls ended. Imagine that.

As I counted the days until a potential ruling from the judge, I was relieved that the legal work and their accompanying fees had slowed down. I immersed myself in my job, traveling extensively between work and multiple trips to Pittsburgh. My father's health continued its rapid decline. Miraculously, he survived a hospital stay and had been a resident in a dementia unit since August. I planned to stay put in North Carolina for Thanksgiving and invite a couple of friends to join the kids and me. I invited JG and Mary. They graciously declined, since Mary's sister was coming to town and they had asked Erin over. Ever the victim, Erin had informed Mary that she would be alone for Thanksgiving. Sincerely, I was happy that she had a place to go. At least she would not be in a bowling alley as I had been the previous year. Billy, Katie, and I headed to Pittsburgh. For me, it was a dream come true, the first time in a long time, I had both of my kids with me to celebrate a holiday. Of course, we visited my dad and seized the opportunity to get some pictures of Billy and Katie with their grandfather. It would be the last time that all three of us would see my father alive. God does work in mysterious ways.

Regrettably, I was not with my dad when he passed. He died just a few days into 2017. As I painfully listened to his labored breathing through the phone, I said my goodbyes and gave my thanks to him for all that he had done for me. As difficult as it was, I took comfort in the fact that he was now at peace. He had suffered enough with this awful disease. Reduced to 105 pounds, this once strapping man had not been able to communicate for some time and had stopped eating. He would no longer have to wander around the dementia unit, looking out of the locked door, frantically trying to get out. He could now rest his mind without desperate frustration, unable to verbalize his thoughts. Despite also losing his gift with the written word, I am thankful his ability to communicate with such ease and impact left its mark on me. We laid him to rest in the middle of a classic winter storm.

Dad, lights do turn out, but they give way to eternal light. As kids, we heard that phrase from him many times, as we would leave every light on in the house. With a smile on his face, he would state, "Lights do turn out!" All who knew you miss you. Thank you for sitting on my shoulder as I have written this book. At times, as I have struggled to find the perfect words, you guided me. Revisions to this book occurred with a smile on my face recalling your famous phrase, "No, no, no! You don't want to say it like that!"

Rest in peace, my good man!

While at the funeral home, I received a few e-mails from Olivia regarding the judge's ruling. Our mess had been intertwined in our lives for the last three years, so why should a funeral get in the way? The judge had previously scheduled rendering her ruling on January 13. I wasn't holding my breath, as I had already experienced dates being pushed out in our overloaded system. The same held true here and the judge would now rule on January 31, 2017.

Erin and I were not required to attend the ruling. I traveled to Tampa, Florida, on the thirtieth for work and was relieved to be getting out of town. As you can imagine, that evening did not provide me much sleep. I tossed and turned to wait for it to be the thirty-first, with the hope that this nightmare would end!

Olivia informed me that they would be meeting with the judge at 9 a.m. I was to expect a call from her at approximately 10:30 a.m. I made my way to my room at about 10:00 a.m., as I wanted some time alone. The phone rang at precisely 10:30 a.m., from a private number. I knew it was Olivia!

I took a few deep breaths and did my best to steady my hands as I answered the phone. "Good morning Olivia, how are you?" I inquired.

"Shitty!" was her response. After that comment, I had difficulty focusing on what she had to say next. She proceeded to tell me that the Honorable Judge had awarded Erin alimony.

Emotions of shock and bewilderment quickly gave way to anger, and I unleashed on her. I dumped a big bucket of fucks on her.

"What the fuck, Olivia. How could this have happened? I have spent all this money for nothing. We are no farther ahead than when we started!"

Without question, anybody that was residing on the tenth floor of the Marriott heard every word. Olivia's stunning news continued as she shared some of the judge's findings. The result was that I would be paying Erin about half of my paycheck for the next nine years!

I don't recall much of the rest of the conversation other than Olivia stating, "I will send over the PDF that contains the judge's findings."

I had to sit down before I fell over. With my head in my hands, I sat for about twenty minutes devastated and overcome with disbelief. Repeatedly, my mind screamed, "This bitch got away with it! She has been out screwing around on me for years, and I am the one that gets nailed? How in the hell am I going to be able to fulfill all of the obligations to Katie and Billy?"

My first call was to none other than Al, once again interrupting his time at work. I contemplated leaving my conference and going home, as I wanted to be with Katie. Al convinced me otherwise, and I stayed put. Somehow, I quickly refocused and started building a budget in Excel. I knew damn well that there would be no cooperation from Erin concerning our obligations with our kids. Both Erin and Doris's testimony made it very clear that it was all about Erin. Olivia's statement to Doris while she was on the stand summed it up. "You have not spoken of your grandchildren."

I received text messages from both Katie and Billy inquiring about the outcome. They, too, desperately wanted it to end. I responded to them, "It is not good news. Unfortunately, I don't think we are done yet. I love you both with all I have to give and will call you tonight."

In short order, Olivia's e-mail arrived containing the judge's findings. In my reply, I took the opportunity to apologize for my tirade and my language. The shock, disbelief, and bewilderment that I experienced during my call with Olivia only escalated as I attempted to process the ruling. The emotions were more significant than when Erin accused me of giving her herpes 2, as there was no gift or blessing in this ruling! The court's findings are known as "findings of fact" (FOF).

The most significant FOFs are as follows:

(As a refresher, the plaintiff is Erin, and I am the defendant.)

*FOF #19* Prior to the start of the hearing, the Defendant made a motion *in limine* regarding certain electronic devices and ESI (electronically stored information). Plaintiff did a factory reset on her phone in violation of a spoliation letter. The Court is considering the fact that the Plaintiff "wiped" her phone as evidence that there was damaging evidence in her phone. This inference alone will not be the basis for the finding of marital misconduct.

*FOF # 43* There is no reason why the Plaintiff cannot continue her dog sitting business. Plaintiff is able to care for her own pets regularly, and medical issues should not affect her ability to pet sit or walk animals. Plaintiff has had fibromyalgia since 1999 and most of her medical issues before she closed the business in January 2016.

*FOF #47* Plaintiff stated in the November 2015 Consent Order that she could earn $1,300 per month from her pet business. Although this Order was non-prejudicial, the Court finds that she can earn at least $1,300 per month. This amount is only minimally higher than what the Plaintiff would earn making minimum wage and be working full time.

*FOF #52* As a result of the parties' separation and divorce, Plaintiff suffers from an adjustment disorder coupled with stress. Plaintiff has also been diagnosed with fibromyalgia (in 1999), neuropathy, generalized anxiety, ADHD and she has had at least one TIA on May 19, 2016. .

*FOF #54* Plaintiff informed her therapist that Defendant was controlling, exhibiting erratic behavior and that he lied to her often.

*FOF #55* Plaintiff sees a psychiatrist. Her psychiatrist has reviewed N.C. Controlled Substance Database and does not believe Plaintiff is abusing controlled substances.

*FOF #56* As a result of her symptoms, the Plaintiff is prescribed several medications including clonazepam, Lamictal, Wellbutrin, Neurontin, and Adderall.

*FOF #61* Since the TIA, Plaintiff has difficulty following conversations, her anger is more pronounced, and she has some cognitive delays. Defendant believes this is due to substance abuse by the Plaintiff.

*FOF #74* In December of 2014, Defendant was given a blood test for HIV, hepatitis, and other sexually transmitted diseases due to significant weight loss and other medical issues he was experiencing. These test results were all negative.

*FOF #75* In June 2015, Plaintiff had two lesions in her rectal area. Plaintiff tested positive for HSV2 (herpes 2) antibodies after a swab of the area (PCR test) on June 16, 2015.

*FOF #77* In July 2015, the Defendant took a blood test for HSV2 that was negative.

*FOF #80* Dr. "STD Expert," was accepted as an expert in HSV1 and HSV2 testing and diagnosis, and in "incident" HSV2 infections. This individual believes Plaintiff has herpes (HSV2) and that her infection in June of 2015 was an "incident" or newly acquired infection. Further testimony was that the Plaintiff got the herpes infection in April or May 2015, but it is possible she got the virus in early June 2015.

*FOF #81* Plaintiff denied having sex with anyone in June 2015.

*FOF #82* Based on this information, the Court finds that the Plaintiff has the HSV2 virus. It is not possible to tell when the Plaintiff obtained the virus, but she has genital herpes due to HSV2.

*FOF #83* Defendant has no history of HSV, and he did not test positive for the antibodies in July 2015. It is possible that Defendant also has the virus but no antibodies yet.

*FOF #84* Both parties deny having an affair during the marriage.

*FOF #85* Plaintiff did a factory reset on her phone in violation of a spoliation letter. There is a negative inference that there was something negative on her phone that the Plaintiff did not want the Defendant to have for this litigation, but the Court cannot find that the Plaintiff committed illicit sexual behavior during the marriage and she is not barred from seeking alimony.

*FOF #86* The Court cannot find Defendant committed illicit sexual behavior during the marriage based on the evidence presented.

Erin will receive half of my paycheck for the next nine years! At the time, I did not count the blessing that it *could* have been for the seventeen years that Ms. Barr asked for in her closing. We were awarded almost $1,900 in legal fees for the extra expenses attached to our motion to compel when Erin and her legal team were withholding evidence and discovery. Erin would have to pay me back child support and a whopping $140.00 per month in child support until June 2017. Adding insult to injury, the judge stated in her ruling that Erin could pay the legal fees and child support over a 24-month period via deductions from the alimony that I would send every two weeks.

As you may imagine, I was not able to comprehend or digest the ruling even after reading it multiple times. I had to step away! Oh yeah, I had a day job. I returned to my conference at 1 p.m. As I entered the room and sat down, my phone rang. Erin was trying to call me! I did not take the call, and there was no voicemail.

Let the victory parade begin for Team United We Stand!

Later that evening, I spoke with both Billy and Katie and was very open and transparent about the ruling and the road ahead. Katie was beside herself. As Katie sobbed, she said, "Dad, I feel like this is my fault."

I reminded her, "None of this is your fault. You did me a favor by getting me out of a very abusive marriage. I loved your mom for who I thought she was. All I would ask is that you continue to make good choices."

Katie relayed a bit of the conversation she had with Erin. Erin told her, "The judge found that I did not cheat on your father and I am not doing drugs."

Katie must have been less responsive than Erin hoped, because the next gem she hurled at Katie was, "You don't want any of my money? I have been persecuted for two years and have done nothing wrong. I will not let you ruin this happy moment for me. There are so many people that believe in me and have stood by me, and they are happy for me!"

As I spoke with Jane, she was the first to echo the sentiment offered by many others, "Erin can't buy what you have with the money you will be providing her. You have your kids in your life, and she does not!"

Upon my return to Wilmington, it would be time to evaluate my options more seriously. My name and character were going to be defamed in a public record.

I had my laces tied tight and was willing to keep dancin' with the devil!

# CHAPTER 26
## *One More Song*

It is your character, and your character alone,
that will make your life happy or unhappy. —*John McCain*

For me, the decision to continue to fight was an easy one. Yes, I had already spent a ton of money looking for the truth and seeking justice, but this was my name, my reputation, my character. Not to mention, the judge failed to uphold the law. I did not have herpes nor any STD, ever. I was "nothing but faithful" to Erin. I was committed to pursuing this next step to, at the very least, regain some measure of my dignity.

Returning to Wilmington late Friday evening, my first priority Monday morning was to be retested. I did not consult with Olivia or Zoe regarding this, but was frankly surprised they did not suggest it. A comment Robin Wright made during our first arbitration kept echoing in my head, "There is no justice in the justice system!" There is no common sense either! If the judge had questions about my test or me not having antibodies yet, then why didn't she order me to get another test? The burden of proving my innocence was on me.

My new family practitioner retested me. I had long since moved on from the doc that had been our family physician for years. Once again, I counted the days until the results came in. It was 19 months since my previous negative test, yet I was still anxious. My first test occurred 73 days after my last potential exposure ("One more night," per Erin, April 25, 2015) and the thought crossed my mind that perhaps I had not yet developed antibodies. Every twist and turn throughout this mess convinced me anything was possible. Whatever reassurance our expert provided in October of 2015 that I did not have herpes 2 was long gone.

While in Tampa, I had scheduled a meeting with Zoe to revisit my options. During our initial meeting, she presented the idea of a Rule 59 or Rule 60 motion. These motions were an option before moving forward with an appeal. I prepared for that meeting by reviewing both possibilities and developing my list of questions for her. I was encouraged by the potential of a Rule 59 motion. In brief, a Rule 59 motion is the means by which you can ask the court for a new trial or modification to the order from the judge's decision. Olivia met with Zoe separately and reported to me via e-mail, "Based on my conversation with Zoe, Rule 59 is not an option as it would simply allow the judge to correct her mistakes. We both believe that you should appeal this ruling."

By the time I met with Zoe, I would have my second set of negative results. I had new evidence that dismissed the judge's belief that perhaps antibodies were still a possibility! I had become very familiar with the Rule 59 motion, and the first question that I posed to Zoe was, "My interpretation of the motion is that it provides a vehicle to ask the court to consider new evidence. Is this accurate?"

Surprisingly, Zoe responded, "What new evidence do you have?"

"Did Olivia not inform you of my second negative test results? It has been nineteen months since my last negative test, and I don't have antibodies for herpes 2!"

"New evidence would provide us with a valid reason to file a Rule 59 motion," she replied. I felt a sense of relief knowing that we had a path forward before filing an appeal.

Be your own advocate!

Before I pulled out of her parking lot, I received an e-mail that Zoe sent to Olivia regarding our plan. We had ten days to file this motion once the final alimony order was entered. Unfortunately, the filing of the alimony order was Cherrie's responsibility, and she would continue with more of her games, delaying the filing of the order.

She challenged Olivia on the judge's ruling as to when I was to begin paying alimony to Erin. Via e-mail, Cherrie took the stance with Olivia that, "You asked the judge to allow payments to begin in February of 2017, and she said no. I will request the audio recording of the hearing."

On April 18, 2017, eight months after the conclusion of our trial, the final alimony order was entered. Two days later, we filed our Rule 59 motion. By the end of the month, Cherrie had taken the bushel full of money she received from Doris and Erin and gone home. She filed her own motion withdrawing her representation of Erin. In case you are keeping count, this would be Erin's third attorney to withdraw their representation.

The essence of our eight-page motion is captured as follows:

"Pursuant to NCR Civ. P. 59(a) (4), a ground for amending or altering a judgment includes: 'Newly discovered evidence material for the party making the motion which he could not, with the reasonable diligence, have discovered and produced at the trial.' Pursuant to NCR Civ. P. 59(a) (7), a ground for amending or altering a judgment includes: 'Insufficiency of the evidence to justify the verdict or that the verdict is contrary to law." Rule 59(a)(8) further permits a Rule 59 motion to correct errors in law' occurring at trial. In this matter, Defendant respectfully submits this Court's verdict and resulting alimony award is not justified by the evidence, particularly in lieu of newly discovered evidence under Rule 59(a)(4), is contrary to law under Rule 59(a)(7), and constitutes an error of law under Rule 59(a)(8) on the basis: On February 8, 2017, Defendant received the results of a blood test from blood drawn on February 6, 2017, post date of the August 2016 alimony trial, which definitively establishes that Defendant does not possess the antibodies for herpes simplex virus 2 and therefore does not have the herpes simplex virus 2. Consequently, Defendant could not have infected Plaintiff with the herpes virus; Plaintiff must have contracted the disease from a third party during the parties' marriage before their date of separation."

This motion was scheduled to be heard September 6, 2017. We made sure that the filing included Erin's maiden name, as I wanted the public record to be accurate.

Meanwhile, I attempted to do my best to shield Billy and Katie from the continued legal proceedings. Billy's college and Katie's high school graduations were rapidly approaching. Erin kept her estrangement from our kids. She would be moving twelve hours away to southwest Florida where she had secured a part-time job. Erin could not possibly face all of the former friends whom she had deceived. This was particularly true with all the folks at Katie's school.

Erin completely vanished from Katie's senior year. While Billy and Katie seemed a bit relieved that Erin was moving out of state, they felt rejected.

When Katie received the news, she said, "When you were not in my life, you did not move twelve hours away and leave me."

I was sad and speechless . . . no consoling, fatherly words came to me.

Billy graduated in early May with a job already in hand. Another opportunity for me to remind Billy and Katie that in spite of all that they'd gone through, blessings abounded.

Without hesitation, Al and Jane traveled down to help celebrate. Their continued support for our kids and me was just amazing. Jane flew in from a business trip to California.

Erin and Doris attended Billy's graduation, held in a 20,000-seat arena; I was hoping to avoid them. No such luck! As we entered the building, there were Erin and Doris in the handicap-accessible area.

I quickly moved past them and headed to a seat. Jane seized the opportunity to scare the shit out of Erin. She walked up behind her, rubbed her back, and congratulated her on Billy's accomplishment. Erin damn near hit the ceiling of the arena.

Following the ceremony, there was another brief interaction in an over-flowing lobby. Erin's anger was on full display as she rolled Doris by our party. Al quietly greeted them with, "Hello, ladies."

Through clenched teeth, Erin fired back, "Yep!"

Is it possible some of her ire stemmed from our Rule 59 motion? Since our filing a few short weeks ago, she would have to retain another new attorney!

Two days later, we enjoyed Katie's baccalaureate ceremony, but Mom and Grandma were not in attendance, busy making their way down I-95 to sunny F-L-A. They had no problem trying to make Katie feel guilty about excluding them.

The happy memories Katie posted on Facebook elicited the following text from Doris, "I saw your beautiful pictures. Perhaps someday you can explain why Mom and I were not included in this very special time in your life."

Admittedly, I loved the directness and brevity of Katie's response, "Because she moved to Florida. That is why!"

Erin would later claim that Katie did not invite her. Katie graduated a few weeks later, again without Mom or Grandma present. Katie presented the rose provided to the moms by the graduates, to me. It sits on my dresser with other sentimental reminders of our kids.

Diane, who grew very close to Katie, made the long trip from Pittsburgh to be part of the day. Big G, little g, and their daughter, Miley, also celebrated with us and helped round out our new family.

If there was ever a need for a best friend to step up, it was at this time in Katie's life. Emma's family continued to provide so much love and support to all of us, but especially Katie. Kay stepped up on many occasions, filling every void Erin's absence created. She offered guidance and comfort to Katie, who was deeply hurt by Erin's graduation no-show. Kay and her husband, James, opened their home for a beautiful, shared graduation party. So many folks who attended recognized Katie's accomplishments.

For me, it was nice to reconnect with former neighbors that I had not seen in a few years. There were no open conversations about our situation, but Diane was privy to a comment from Emma's cousins that spoke volumes. "We were led to believe that he was the crazy one. We all see things quite differently now!"

On the one hand, I wanted the summer to fly by so that we could get to September 6. On the other hand, I knew that it would mean that Katie would be gone again. I never could have imagined our bond would grow stronger after she came back into my life, and I dreaded the thought of her being so far away. Billy was in Charlotte, and now, on top of everything else, I would have to deal with the emotions of being an empty nester.

Although the months moved quickly, we made the most of them. As the summer neared its end, we attended my niece's wedding and then headed to New Hampshire's Lake Winnipesaukee for a "Family & Friends 2" vacation—another emotional milestone for me, as I had both Billy and Katie with me. It had now been over three years since I had been on vacation with both of them!

Our last vacation together had been in June of 2014, the infamous beach trip with Erin's family. This time there was no drama. Al, Jane, Jackie, and Anthony were there with their families as well. It was a great way to spend some very quality time with Katie and Billy before Katie had to leave for college.

In the blink of an eye, summer was over, two cars were stuffed to the rooftops, and Katie was off to college. Despite the distance, I felt it was where she needed to be. A change of scenery in a brand-new state would be good for her. Even though Billy had just started his professional career, he was able to take a few days off to help his sister and me with the move.

They drove one car, while I followed close behind. It was a long trip in two short days, but in no time, we had Katie moved in. No long goodbyes, just my tearful "I will miss you and will see you soon!"

Billy and I headed north. I dropped him off in Charlotte and arrived back in Wilmington at about 1 a.m. As I neared home, I received a text from my neighbor, Matt, alerting me to the fact that he had taped something to my front door.

I am not sure that I can accurately express how I was feeling as I arrived home. It had been three long, tumultuous years and now here we were. I retrieved the envelope taped to my front door, took a seat on the couch, and sat in the quiet for a few moments. I was thankful that Billy and Katie had made it through the storm and appeared to be doing okay. I worried about the transition for Katie but also recognized that she had quickly grown up and was emotionally very strong. I opened the envelope. It contained a letter from Katie. I could manage only the first few lines before putting it down to compose myself.

Katie's letter read:

Dad,

There are not enough words in the world to explain how grateful I am for you. I am so glad last year I came and chose to live with you because I gained another best friend and even better parental figure. It's safe to say you are not in the top 1,000 Dads anymore, but you are the #1 best Dad I could ask for. You show me what it is like to be gracious, kind, loving and I pray one day I find a man that is as good as you. I am so proud of how well you have handled this divorce and how much you've grown through it. As you are reading this note, you have already dropped me off at college, drove the dreadful nine hours, and probably shed a few tears.

I am writing this just to say it's going to be okay. You have a lot of life ahead of you, and maybe one day a woman will be lucky enough to call you theirs (hopefully awhile from now because I don't need another Mom right now). As I have said before, I will never take for granted the year of fighting because it has truly made us stronger and better together. I am glad

I showed you the Christian faith, how to do a real workout, and how to cook something besides Bob Evans mac and cheese. Thank you for growing me into the woman I am today and for giving me a hell of a life. I will always be your 'little princess.' I love you forever Dad.

XO, Katie

It ended up being a very late night. I stayed up until about four-thirty in the morning reading this letter from Katie many times. I revisited all the letters, cards, and text messages that I had received from Billy and Katie in the last few years. Jane was right. I had both of my kids in my life, and that is something money could not buy!

September 5, Mr. Dependable (Al) arrived in town. Before our meeting with Zoe, we grabbed a quick lunch. As we exited the restaurant forty-five minutes later, I discovered that my car was gone. A few friendly nurses at a surgery center close to Zoe's office had had my car towed. I failed to notice the sign tucked in the corner alerting me to the fact that it was parking for patients only. Fortunately, we could walk to Zoe's office.

Al chuckled, "The book you are going to have to write continues to get better and better."

We met with Zoe for about thirty minutes and then caught an Uber to retrieve my car. A mere $165.00 later, we headed home. You can't make this shit up!

Rule 59 Motion Eve was another restless night. As was becoming customary, Al and I arrived at the courthouse early. Because Erin was not obligated to attend, I was not sure if she would be present. It was my motion after all. As Al and I exited the stairwell, there she was, a picture of health, dressed to the nines and toting a beautiful new handbag. Between her part-time job and alimony, it appeared that she was now living well above the poverty line. Southwest Florida living agreed with her. A quiet, carefree life with her mom and her dogs! I had long since realized that is now all she wanted and needed. Our kids be damned!

Calendar call came and went, and our case would not be heard! Zoe approached Al and me to inquire, "Are you available December 12?"

My gut response was, "Are you fucking shitting me?"

I immediately apologized, but it was not a big deal to her. Zoe was well aware of the long, frustrating, and disappointing journey I had already endured. The broken system was wearing on me. My head ached at the thought of waiting three more months while Erin and the attorneys continued being paid!

A small victory for me was that Erin had to bear the expense of flying into Wilmington to be in court. She would return to Florida with Hurricane Irma headed her way, both Doris and Erin caught in the eye of the storm. Privately, I referred to it as Hurricane Karma. Destruction seemed to follow Erin wherever she went!

With the delayed hearing, I had time to follow new advice from our STD expert. He had suggested it would be incredibly helpful for me to have a western blot herpes test. It is not commercially available but is the gold standard test used in clinical trials. There are other commercially available tests, but this test is even more accurate. Blood drawn by my family practitioner was sent to the University of Washington for analysis.

We got a trifecta! Yet again, I was negative for both herpes 1 & 2. I have no antibodies, Your Honor!

Fortunately, the months flew, as I continued to immerse myself in work. I made a trip to Katie's college for parents' weekend. I was relieved that she had adjusted so well and had made many friends. Billy was flourishing in his first professional role, and it felt like things were calming down. Once again, Kay and James graciously opened their home to Billy, Katie, and me for Thanksgiving. A fantastic meal with a real sense of family surrounded us.

December 12 was right around the corner. My dad's birthday was on the fourteenth, and I was praying that his spirit would shine down on me and provide me with some good luck.

I am sure my dad did his best, but higher powers had different plans. We would not even make it into the courtroom. What? Old Reliable Al made his way to town on the eleventh, and at six-thirty, as we sat at dinner, I received an e-mail from Zoe:

"Danny—Sorry to be the bearer of bad news. My judge will not let me out of my trial tomorrow, AND opposing attorney has the flu. She has asked for a continuance. Additionally, there is an emergency custody hearing [on the schedule], which means we get pushed back farther on the docket. It's like a perfect storm."

What a blessing it was to have Al there. My disappointment tank was beyond full! Al and Jane had sacrificed so much for me. I know what this had cost me, but I often wondered how much they had to spend to support their "fifth child." God bless you both!

December 12 would give way to February 28, 2018, the new date for our hearing!

We celebrated my third Christmas without a resolution to my dance with Erin. We would spend it in Orlando with Al, Jane, and their kids. In spite of the weather not being ideal, we had yet another great time. My spirits were elevated by being around their family, and I did not take for granted that I had Billy and Katie with me. They blessed me with two beautiful Christmas letters. From Billy:

Dad,

Thank you for all that you do for Katie and me. We would not be where we are and who we are today without you! You've taught us how to be strong through all the tough times and how to be good people! I hope that one day I will be half the man that you are! Sometimes, I wish we could go back to the good old days of night fishing out on the pier and getting kicked out by the cops—we were and still are bonafide badasses!

I am looking forward to many more new traditions, good

memories, and laughs! I hope you have a great Christmas this year because you deserve it. We will all have a great time together in Florida. We can go on riverboat gambling trips and shit with the door open!!

I love you Dad!

Billy

From Katie:

Dad,

Thank you for being the most selfless person I know. I am thankful for our small family and how well you have handled everything. Being away at college has made me appreciate even more all you do, and I am so thankful for that.

Every Christmas has for sure been different, but I wouldn't trade it for the world when we all get together. Thank you for never failing to make us laugh, for understanding the rough days, being a mother and father, and for being the best Dad out there. Merry Christmas! Billy and I love you.

XO, Katie

These framed letters grace the walls of my bedroom. If you did not notice it, the last line of Billy's message is from the movie *Stepbrothers*. We are big fans of the film!

Katie and Billy were not as fortunate with the love letters they received from Mom.

2/01/2018

Dear Billy and Katie,

I just want to begin my letter saying that I love you both so very much and I would never intentionally hurt either one of you. You both are my greatest gifts in life, and I am blessed that

God put you in my arms. This letter is not to speak ill of anyone, you deserve to have a happy and healthy relationship with both your father and mother.

I have been silent for two years with the hope that we could rebuild our relationship, however rebuilding a relationship on an unstable foundation will never be successful. This unstable foundation has been formed due to the false accusations of infidelity, drug use, lies and God only knows what else and I was never given the opportunity to be heard. These distorted and painful accusations against me must be extremely terrifying to hear. Right here, right now, I want to set the record straight. I have never been unfaithful, I never have misused medications or lied to you, and there are VOLUMES OF EVIDENCE proving these facts! You've never seen any of this evidence because you never had an interest in Mom's side of the story.

I found the courage to leave a volatile and abusive marriage with documented help from a women's abuse center, legal advisement and counseling, including the deacon of our church. Leaving the marriage, I did not realize the extent of the emotional turmoil that would affect both of you so deeply. Did I make mistakes while we were all in such pain? The answer is yes, and I apologized over and over again. However, it just wasn't good enough to begin rebuilding the close relationship we once shared. There is nothing worse than feeling unimportant to those people who are so important to you and that you love with all of your heart.

I am the same loving mother who [chose] to be home and raise my children, that has never changed. What has changed is how you both view me now and how you're excluding me from your lives, and you won't share the reason why. What I have learned through life lessons and counseling, is running away from difficult situations will not make them go away. You can move out of state, throw yourself into work or college, but the only way to deal with problems is head on! We are not doing that.

Just by sending this letter to both of you, I hope you realize I've come to a crossroad. I can continue down this path of exclusion and not being loved by my children, or we can make a turn together by taking steps forward to an open and honest relationship. You know I love you, and I always will be here for you when you are ready, you now know how I feel in regards to our relationship, the ball is in your court of what path we take at this crossroad. For now, I am stepping back and giving you space that you need to make your decision. You know where I live and are always welcome, you know my phone number that will always be answered, and you know you are in my heart and in my mind always. Whenever you are ready to rebuild on a solid foundation, I am here and always will be. I will answer any questions or listen to any concerns you may have, but you are the only ones who can initiate this. My life is empty without the both of you. If we do this together, the hurting will stop, and the healing will begin. I love you.

Sincerely,

Mom

Thirteen months after the judge's ruling, the day finally arrived. It was quite fitting that the two people that I started this journey with would be by my side this day. Al and Jane had come into town the day before and kept my mind occupied by making homemade ravioli. Among her other talents, Jane is one hell of a cook. They graciously brought all of the necessary ingredients and equipment all the way from Pittsburgh.

It would be my eighth visit to the same courtroom. Hallelujah! Our motion would be heard at two that afternoon.

As our hearing began, the courtroom was relatively empty. I took my seat at the table that was all too familiar. Olivia and Zoe sat alongside me. Erin's fourth attorney was the lone occupant at the plaintiff's table, since Erin chose not to make the trip from Florida.

I briefly took the stand. My message was simple. "It was my name and my character that was being slandered by the finding that 'I may not have antibodies yet.' Secondarily, it was the law. If there is proof of infidelity, then no alimony should be awarded."

Our STD expert would follow my testimony, but would be unable to discuss my February 2017 negative test or the results of my western blot test. Zoe attempted to have these addressed but could barely get a word in before an objection was raised by Erin's attorney. She argued that I could have taken the second test between July 2015 and August 15, 2016, the start of our trial, but failed to do so:

"The results of the February 6, 2017 blood test are not newly discovered evidence which was not discoverable through reasonable diligence for presentation before the hearing on August 15–18, 2016.

"Even if the test result could be construed as newly discovered evidence consistent with case law and Rule 59, there is no sufficient evidence to show plaintiff engaged in illicit sexual behavior with a third party during the marriage. Thus the result would be the same."

I had waited thirteen months, thrown more good money after bad, for less than forty-five minutes of the honorable judge's time. Consideration of our new evidence was denied by the court. Convenient that the judge would now uphold the letter of the law that my evidence could have been obtained with reasonable diligence before our trial.

The judge was plain in her position with her final statement, "Even if I were to consider this new evidence, I would only change a few of my words in the findings. It would not change the order. At trial, there was a lot of debate about whether or not the Plaintiff contracted Herpes 2 after the date of separation. Motion denied! You can appeal this if you want to!"

I was practically catatonic . . . stunned and disappointed yet again! I wanted to yell out, "Of course there was no evidence of illicit sexual behavior because she destroyed it. How could you even broach the topic of her contracting herpes after the date of separation when Erin testified that I was the only person she had been with in the last twenty-eight years?" Pardon my bitterness, but it must be a tremendous rush to be both judge and jury.

I exited the courtroom first, as I needed a few minutes alone. Al, Jane, and I briefly met with Zoe, Olivia, and our expert in a conference room to revisit a potential path forward. I truly appreciated that our expert stuck around following the conclusion of the hearing to offer some support.

Everybody echoed what Jane had already said, "You have your kids in your life, and she does not."

They were all very empathetic about the outcome, and as Zoe stated, "It was a miscarriage of justice. I am pissed." Zoe also offered, "We have time before we need to decide on an appeal. The Court of Appeals could reverse the judge's ruling (highly unlikely), affirm the decision, or send the case back down to the same judge to be heard again. If that is the case, the judge will be pissed. Among attorneys, the North Carolina Court of Appeals is flippantly referred to as the North Carolina Court of Affirmations!"

Zoe previously had advised that an appeal could take a year or two and would cost an additional $25,000 to $50,000.

I was done! I wanted off the legal merry-go-round that I had ridden for three-and-a-half years. I wanted to move on with my life. I despised the fact that Erin could further cement her victim mentality with this latest verdict. I did not like my odds of winning in the Court of Appeals. Then again, it was not about winning or losing, it was about right and wrong.

Al and Jane left the following day. I hated to see them go. Words cannot adequately express what they both mean to me. In addition to all of the love, emotional support, and advice they provided, they taught me so much. I learned how to live life and make the most of each day. They modeled what a real relationship looks like, mutually giving and taking. They embody what it means to make each other better. I am not suggesting theirs is a perfect union, but they recognize imperfections and work hard to improve on them. They have four beautiful adult children and two amazing grandchildren that love being at home and around each other every chance they get.

Disappointment, hypocrisy, and betrayal should have drowned me by now. I kept treading water. My life jacket was choosing to focus on what I had, versus what I had lost, or what had been taken away from me.

I moved beyond this quickly by recognizing that the judge's decision could have been worse. I could have been ordered to pay Erin seventeen years of alimony and attorney's fees. Strangely enough, I took solace in the fact that this was not a criminal case and my freedom did not rest in this judge's very biased hands. I was not the first male that ended up on the wrong side of her gavel. And, I won't be the last!

Throughout this journey, the Man above had a strange way of dropping people into my life when I needed it the most. The judge's recent decision coupled with adjusting to life as an empty nester hit me hard.

Then one day, a six-foot-five, 250-pound baby boy arrived at my door. Al and Jane's only son, Sammy, had moved from the Northeast to work in the Wilmington area. My door was wide open. He has been excellent company, and he too knows his way around the kitchen, having inherited Jane's passion for cooking. His culinary magic happens while strutting around the kitchen in his boxers . . . I really don't want to ask if that knack came from Al.

There will never be any way to make sense of all that happened in the last six years of our marriage. Eventually, you have to move from what was to what will be.

I am a work in progress, and therapy has dramatically helped me come to terms with all that has happened. Kasey's guidance was, "Erin had an underlying mental illness that was only made worse by her abuse of psychiatric medications."

Our marriage was bookended by science, physics, and an infectious disease expert. Our engagement occurred early as a pick-me-up for Erin, who believed she had failed a physics test. It came to a shocking end with incontrovertible DNA evidence that Erin had contracted an incurable STD that she did not get from me.

Writing this book was emotionally exhausting. In the process of doing so, it forced me to rip off the scabs to relive all the lies, deceit, mental abuse, and character assassination. I had compartmentalized so much, but all of those boxes had to be opened. No amount of therapy will ever enable me to live with or accept the fact that the woman I loved tried to kill me with arsenic.

She took full advantage of our pathetic mental health system, broke me down, and set me up to be involuntarily committed, all the while telling our kids, "Dad was in Holy Hell for depression and drug addiction. He denies using drugs, but he tested positive."

This brilliantly wicked woman was able to navigate a disconnected healthcare system, receiving treatment and medications for illnesses she did not have, the same system that allowed her to supplement her amphetamine supply in both her and our kid's names from any number of prescribers. Erin did her best to juggle me, our immediate and extended families, lawyers, friends, neighbors, and healthcare professionals. Too many balls in the air, too many spinning plates . . . something had to fall!

Thank goodness for the Third Gift *and* advanced data technology. This Gift inspired me to dig through so much detail, helping me to piece together this puzzle . . . not entirely, but enough for me to see a picture, which may have literally restored my life in many ways.

Reliving these gloomy years, I now see there was more light than darkness. The good outweighed the bad, the laughter surpassed the tears, and I am now free! I renewed old friendships, established new ones, strengthened family ties, and grew even closer to my kids. I have experienced every emotion possible, but the one that rises to the top is gratitude. I am grateful for Billy and Katie, my extended family and friends, and for all of those good people that supported us.

The Third Gift was expensive, but peace of mind and clarity are price-less. I have been blessed, having worked hard for decades in an industry I enjoy, for which I am well compensated. Yet, my retirement account has been torpedoed. A friend of mine offered a unique perspective,

"You spent tomorrow's money. Tomorrow may never come!"

So true! We are not promised another day.